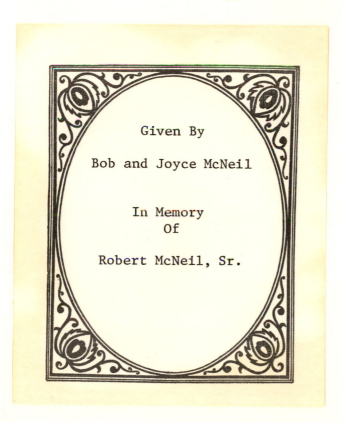

Given By

Bob and Joyce McNeil

In Memory
Of

Robert McNeil, Sr.

THE FAMILY CHRONICLE

THE FAMILY CHRONICLE

By

S. T. AKSAKOV

Translated by
M. C. BEVERLEY

Introduction by
RALPH E. MATLAW

GREENWOOD PRESS, PUBLISHERS
WESTPORT, CONNECTICUT

Library of Congress Cataloging in Publication Data

Aksakov, S. T. (Sergeĭ Timofeevich), 1791–1859.
    The family chronicle.

    Translation of: Semeĭnaĭa khronika.
    1. Aksakov, S. T. (Sergei Timofeevich), 1791–1859––
Biography––Ancestry. 2. Authors, Russian––19th
century––Biography. I. Beverley, M. C. II. Title.
PG3321.A5Z53513 1985   891.73'3 [B]   85-7977
ISBN 0-313-24835-4

Reprinted in 1985 by Greenwood Press
A division of Congressional Information Service, Inc.
88 Post Road West, Westport, Connecticut 06881

Printed in the United States of America

10 9 8 7 6 5 4 3 2 1

CONTENTS

SERGEY AKSAKOV:
THE GENIUS OF INGENUOUSNESS

Sergey Timofeevich Aksakov, who in his person in-
carnated the best in traditions and customs that may truly
be deemed "Russian" and who masterfully projected them
in his literary works is, paradoxically, too little known to
the American reader, for whom he does not sufficiently
embody the accepted notion of Russian writers and their
substance. While widely read in Russia, he is almost completely neglected by critics who apparently mistake the
ease and spontaneity of Aksakov's works for the effortless
reminiscence of an acute observer. Aksakov's success as
a writer began in the late 1840's and reached its peak in
the late 1850's with his autobiographical triptych *The
Family Chronicle, The Childhood of Grandson Bagrov*
and *Reminiscences.* At almost the same time Leo Tol-
stoy's fame was solidified by a somewhat similar trilogy,
Childhood, Boyhood and *Youth,* and Turgenev was already an established, major writer. It comes as something
of a shock, therefore, to learn that Aksakov belonged to
an entirely different and far earlier age, that his literary
career and fame came very late, and that he created these
works when he was well past sixty.

He was born in 1791 in the city of Ufa, located at the
juncture of two rivers at the foot of the Ural Mountains,
on the very edge of European Russia. His grandfather
many years before had bought an enormous tract of land
practically fronting on the Bashkir steppe, and Aksakov
spent an ailing childhood both in Ufa and on his grandfather's estate. He went to school in Kazan', several hundred miles west of Ufa, but still almost a thousand miles
from the capital, and was graduated from its newly-

founded university in 1807. After an interval spent in St. Petersburg and in Moscow, where he was an amateur of the theatre, and some time spent on the estate, he settled in Moscow in 1826, serving first as censor and then as a school director. He fathered a large family, and even though he had received a part of his inheritance quite early, life in Moscow became more and more a financial strain. His house became the center and forum of the Slavophiles, who championed the national Russian heritage in all phases of life. Again, Sergey Aksakov's views were those of an earlier generation, and his temperament was conservative but moderate. The Slavophiles of the 1840's were far less restrained. Two of Aksakov's sons became famous in their own right as leaders of the movement and as writers of secondary importance. Ivan was a poet and an outspoken critic of Russian life. Konstantine, essentially not a creative mind at all, idealized the peasant commune as a voluntary association for self-government, and in his zeal dressed in the traditional garb of old Muscovy, being taken for his pains by modern Muscovites for some visiting eastern potentate.

Aksakov retired to the country from government service in 1839, partly as a result of unpleasant experiences he had undergone for publishing two satires that dealt sharply with corruption and malpractice in government. In 1843 he bought an estate not far from Moscow, where he could enjoy the rustic setting and manorial life so important to him without being too far removed from the center of his intellectual life, which, characteristically, was associated with Moscow, the historical and traditional center of Russia, rather than with St. Petersburg, the new capital, an artificial, bureaucratic, western city. On his new estate and on his father's Ufa estate, which he inherited three years later, he wrote on fishing and hunting, on literary figures he had known, and on his family history. His eyesight began to fail in the 1840's. Increasingly he came to rely on domestic amanuenses to whom he dictated his works. He was actively in the midst of a number of literary projects when he died in 1859 at the age of sixty-eight, the beloved and acknowledged "patriarch" of Russian letters.

It is a function of Aksakov's date of birth that his first move in the literary world occurred when modern Russian was just being shaped, when the controversy between the followers of Shishkov and of Karamzin—between the champions of Slavic linguistic purity and the champions of European terms and grace and elegance in prose—was at its height, and it is a function of Aksakov's background that he was of Shishkov's party. But it was surely his youth that impelled him to devote himself to that cause so wholeheartedly and so militantly. Indeed, when he wrote his reminiscences of Shishkov in 1852, he recognized his excessive zeal and recognized, too, that Shishkov's stature was far smaller than he had thought it at the time. He acknowledged that Shishkov's enthusiasms were frequently unmerited, and that the enormous amount of literary work he was engaged in was antiquarianism or even barren pedantry. This is symbolized in the unfortunate disposition of Shishkov's papers, including the monumental dictionary, the fruit of his extensive reading in ancient documents; shortly after his death they were sold to a book dealer and have for the most part disappeared. Yet the portrait of Shishkov, whose name came to stand for entrenched opposition to all innovation and progress, is, on the whole, a sympathetic and appreciative depiction of a kindly man and a somewhat distraught scholar. Similar understanding for the foibles of elderly dignitaries and just appraisal of their achievement, coupled with an insight into his own attitudes in these early days, appears in his other reminiscences written in the 1850's: those about the great eighteenth-century poet Derzhavin, whom Aksakov met shortly before the former's death, the actor Shusherin, the blind poet Nikolev and others. His reminiscences of theatrical life between 1812 and 1830 contain material that is primarily of anecdotal and antiquarian interest, being concerned with writers, actors and stage conditions. They describe the rise and growth of the great Russian actor Mochalov, whose entire career Aksakov witnessed, and whose shortcomings and failure to live up to his capacities he lamented. During those years Aksakov also wrote on the theatre and served as a reviewer. His views on naturalness in acting, on repertoire, on the modern and the classical theatre occasionally show a genuine attempt to modernize the stage and eliminate its artificiality. According to all reports, Aksakov was an extraordinary reader and actor in his own right, but as a member of the gentry, he could only appear in amateur theatricals and recitations, distinguishing himself by the depth of his interpretations and the range of his roles. His original work and criticism during this period are at best second rate, however, and by 1830 he had almost completely stopped writing.

He was encouraged to resume his literary activity by the young Gogol', who was introduced to him in 1832, right after the former's initial success with *Evenings on a Farm near Dikanka*. Gogol' put him on the right road and helped liberate him from the constraints of the neo-classical age to which Aksakov at that point still belonged. Gogol', in whom Aksakov saw something both unique and uniquely Russian, first convinced Aksakov of the possibility of presenting material without forcing it into arbitrary and artificial literary forms, and by his own example showed the extent to which the commonplace and even the sordid might serve literary ends. Apparently under this influence Aksakov wrote *The Snowstorm* (1834), a short description of the onset of a snowstorm in the steppe that communicates the elemental beauty and force of the storm far more than it does its danger, a description that adumbrates the visual clarity and the verbal simplicity of Aksakov's later works. It was Gogol', too, who apparently encouraged Aksakov to begin *The Family Chronicle,* although that work was finished and published only many years later.

A very complex relationship developed between the

two men. Aksakov championed and almost worshiped Gogol', but the latter was probably not at all congenial to Aksakov's personality. After Gogol's death in 1852, Aksakov embarked on his reminiscences of Gogol', but did not finish them. They first appeared complete only in 1890. They still remain a central document in the study of that genius's strange and warped personality, and are also a source of an important correspondence between the two writers that reflects their profound spiritual crises. Aksakov was obviously very much involved with Gogol', so that these reminiscences are frequently as much a spiritual autobiography of Aksakov as a biography of Gogol'. They show a constant conflict between Aksakov's admiration for Gogol's genius and his disappointment in the latter's baseness and vile personality.

Since his earliest days Aksakov had been a passionate fisher and hunter. In 1847 he published his *Notes on Fishing,* which received great acclaim. Like Izaak Walton's *Compleat Angler,* it is both a practical and a literary guide to fishing, but Aksakov does not expatiate upon the pleasures of the sport, nor does he present fishing as a pastoral idyll. It contains no digressions or ruminative dialogue. Aksakov addresses himself to the reader, tackle and fish. The pleasures of the sport are communicated through the loving detail and expert analyses of angling and of fishes. The reader is constantly amazed by the remarkable observations Aksakov has made on the habits and peculiarities of various species, by the extent of Aksakov's knowledge of nature, and by the bounty of the streams he must have frequented. Aksakov even anticipates Pavlov's experiments on the conditioned reflex: in the section on carp he mentions that crumbs would be thrown to the fish and a bell rung simultaneously. After a while if only the bell were rung and no crumbs were cast, the fish would still come.

He followed this work by moving to another important realm of activity, and published the *Notes of an Orenburg Province Rifle Hunter* in 1852. Turgenev, himself a passionate hunter, who had read and heard parts of it before he wrote an ecstatic review of the published book, said that the hunter would read it with profit and pleasure, while the non-hunter would find it so interesting he would read it like a novel. Gogol', who was particularly pleased by the description of certain birds, including the gold-duck, called *gogol'* in Russian, maintained that there was more life in Aksakov's birds and fishes than in the human beings of his own fiction. Pheasant and snipe and hare and foxes, and creatures far more exotic but evidently still within the ken of hunters—animals that frequently emerge in a kind of complete portrait and occasionally even with a personality—all populate his book. In keen-ness of observation it matches Jean Henri Fabre's *Souvenirs Entomologiques,* but the dispassionate quality of its summaries precludes the fascination that Fabre's mar-velous narratives of the insect world possess for the reader.

Like its predecessor on fishing, this is a book whose descriptions of equipment and of hunting are very matter of fact, but are greatly impressive in the steady manner in which they convey the richness and variety of nature. Turgenev's own early stories utilize as narrator a hunter who is singularly unsuccessful in bagging anything except stories. The editor of the periodical where they first ap-peared provided them with the general title, *Notes of a Hunter.* In Turgenev's stories there is a certain amount of similar material, dealing with the procedures and the for-tunes of the hunt, and these are sometimes felt to be too technical to fit into the framework of the story, too much of a "hunter's note." The procedure here is reversed, and is signaled in the more technical-sounding title. Aksakov's work is, after all, a kind of guide to hunting. After deal-ing with the varieties of equipment and approaches, Aksa-kov embarks on characterizing the customs and peculiar-ities of birds and game, which he treats according to their habitat.

Here Aksakov's unique style is in full evidence, a style

entirely devoid of "literariness," a style which sounds almost conversational, not as Herzen's brilliant conversational style deals with ideas, but in the sense of a rich and supple discourse that is capable of dealing with its subject without losing its air of spontaneity and reality. It is in part, no doubt, the result of oral composition, or at least of dictation, but it is also a consciously wrought style. In any case, it is the expression of something completely grounded in the native tradition, of a purity of vocabulary unequaled in Russian. Foreign words are introduced rarely, and for the most part are only such words as have already been assimilated into the language. On rare occasions they appear when Aksakov wants to create a special effect. A key instance is the title of his masterpiece (*The Family Chronicle*), where he utilizes the Greek derivative *khronika* rather than the Russian *letopis'*, precisely to avoid the connotations of antiquity and historical authority connected with the *letopisi,* the Russian chronicles. On the other hand, Aksakov's style is equally free of archaisms and dialectical expressions.

The books on hunting and fishing are further characteristic of Aksakov's mature work in the way that nature dominates them and in the kind of detail Aksakov adduces. It has already been mentioned that Aksakov's description of a snowstorm vividly presents the physical phenomenon without attempting to communicate its effect on the peasants caught in it, without evaluating its horror or psychological effect. Similarly, in his other works nature is always depicted with an astonishing clarity and exactness, independent of man, sufficient unto itself, with life and movement and grandeur that endow it with a kind of active existence. To be sure, man moves and acts within it through ordinary necessity, for his pleasure or his livelihood, and man is dependent on nature's state. But few writers (Thoreau is a notable exception) communicate so well the total acceptance of nature, the joy in its beauties, without forgetting that man participates in it only as one of its lesser dependents.

It is part of Aksakov's conception of nature as a viable entity that accounts for his ability constantly to present natural phenomena in sharp outline and clear detail. Whatever effect nature will produce on man or reader must arise from nature itself, rather than the mood of the author or of the figure he presents in nature. It is instructive here to compare two descriptions of a similar scene by two great poets of nature, written, moreover, within several years of each other. In Turgenev's *Bezhin Meadow,* one of the stories in his *Notes of a Hunter,* the following evocative passage occurs:

> . . . about the fire a red ring of light quivered and seemed to fade away in the embrace of a background of darkness; the flame flaring up from time to time cast swift flashes of light beyond the boundary of this circle; a fine tongue of light licked the dry twigs and died away at once; long thin shadows, breaking in for an instant in their turn, danced right up to the very fires; darkness was struggling with light. Sometimes, when the fire burnt low and the circle of light shrank together, suddenly out of the encroaching darkness a horse's head was thrust in, a bay, with sinuous markings or all white, stared with intent blank eyes upon us, nipped hastily at the long grass, and drawing back again, vanished instantly. One could only hear it still munching and snorting. From the circle of light it was hard to make out what was going on in the darkness; and therefore everything close at hand seemed shut off by an almost black curtain; but farther away hills and forests were dimly visible in long blurs upon the horizon. The dark unclouded sky stood, triumphant, inconceivably immense, above us in all its mysterious majesty. One felt a sweet oppression at one's heart, breathing in that peculiar, overpowering, yet fresh fragrance— the fragrance of a summer night in Russia. Scarcely a sound was to be heard. Only at times, in the river

nearby, the sudden splash of a big fish leaping, and the faint rustle of a reed on the bank, swaying lightly as the ripples reached it. The fires alone kept up a subdued crackling.

In the Russian text we note in Turgenev's splendid, consciously poetic description a constant attempt to find epithets that will convey the particular shade of meaning that the author wishes to evoke, adjectives that seem to make the description more precise yet in reality make it only more general. The whole play of light and shadow leads to a specifically human, a philosophical, reflection: "light was struggling with darkness." The swaying reed in Turgenev's description might with some justice be taken for Pascal's "thinking reed," the single image of man's frailty and his most distinctive feature.

In the *Childhood of Grandson Bagrov* Aksakov has occasion to describe a similar scene:

> The sky sparkled with stars, the air was full of the sweet scents of the ripening steppe grasses, the stream gurgled in its course, the fire glowed and threw a bright light over our men, who sat around the fire eating hot buckwheat porridge and cheerfully chatting together; the horses, which had been loosed to get at their oats, were also lit up on one side by a streak of light. "Isn't it your bedtime, Seryosha?" my father asked.

There is no attempt here to evoke a mood, but rather to present a picture where things, even at night, have a clear and palpable shape. There are therefore few adjectives and no attempt to refine them. There is activity throughout: water gurgles, the sky sparkles, people chatter around a fire rather than talk in hushed tones, the fire throws a bright light rather than casts shadows. There is no attempt to philosophize about nature, to develop the implications of the scene except to note that it is past the young boy's bedtime. What makes Aksakov's descriptions so much more impressive in their context, particularly in the narrative framework of *The Family Chronicle* and *The Childhood of Grandson Bagrov,* is the sense of this nature existing in a pristine and inviolate state, of a freshness and immediacy of vision by and large lost to the refined sophisticate who may, like Turgenev, love nature deeply and describe it movingly, but in his own rather than in its terms.

In a primary sense, nature thus plays the leading role in Aksakov's work. Nature acts as the instructor of mankind—from it one learns about the richness and complexity of life, the limits of man's activity. The reader also gauges the characters that Aksakov introduces from their attitudes toward nature, from the degree to which they are attuned to it or are indifferent to it. As with nature, Aksakov follows a similar procedure in describing his characters: his observation is delicate, his comprehension and analysis of human beings profound, but he is content to present it to the reader without offering extensive qualification and explanation. This may well be a carry-over from his youth when he was able quickly to penetrate and comprehend literary creations, and utilize his talent for acting to project them with great skill. He had an eye for minutiae, but abstracted the essential from them.

Another trait he mentions in connection with the theatre—his remarkable memory—explains a further aspect of his work. That he was able to write of his early childhood in such detail when past sixty is made a little more credible when we read of the fantastic ease and speed with which he committed entire plays to memory, feeling it necessary to know all the parts. He might well retain, then, the formative episodes in his early life and the physical sensations and mental joy or anguish that were particularly significant. Aksakov was a sickly, highly emotional child, adored and tended by his mother to an astonishing degree. The insomniac night that begins Proust's work represents a minor difficuty in comparison to the dependence established between Aksakov and his doting mother. At one time, having just given birth, she learned that her son was ill in Kazan'. Despite the fact that the roads were impassable during the spring thaw and that the ice was about to break up on the river she had to cross, she made the harrowing trip, and did herself permanent physical damage. Fortunately, Aksakov overcame his early dependence, and even his physical ailments disappeared when he was eight.

His fame ultimately rests on his autobiographical triptych, or even more narrowly on *The Family Chronicle,* his greatest work, which finally appeared in 1856 after sections of it occasionally appeared in the preceding ten years. The leading and dominating figure of that work is Aksakov's grandfather, while the major portion of the work is devoted to the courtship and marriage of Aksakov's father and ends with the birth of Aksakov. The second volume, *The Childhood of Grandson Bagrov* (it was under the name Bagrov that Aksakov presented his forebears, in part to avoid embarrassment for those involved), appeared two years later and dealt with Aksakov's first seven years, ending with the comment: "Here grandson Bagrov's narration of his childhood stops. He maintains that subsequent events no longer deal with his childhood, but his adolescence." The third volume, *Reminiscences,* had appeared together with *The Family Chronicle,* and covers Aksakov's experiences during his secondary education and university years in Kazan'. Aksakov now already uses his own name and narrates chronologically material far less arresting than that of the other two works. Aksakov sharply distinguishes the chronicle, that is, the narration of something heard but not experienced personally from the narration that emerges out of his own experience, and he further distinguishes between the two first-person narratives as a re-creation of childhood and as mere reminiscence. He does not hesitate to interject his own remarks into the first two books, however.

INTRODUCTION

The Childhood of Grandson Bagrov best illustrates those literary virtues of Aksakov's that have been dwelt on so far: the grandeur of nature, for the most part benign, the unhurried passage of time, and the even-paced calmness, all of which emphasize the permanence and immutability of life. There is nothing in Russian literature to compare with its celebration of the manorial life. In Goncharov's masterpiece, Oblomov's dream demonstrates the total concentration on physical well-being in the bountiful lap of nature which dehumanizes the participants. But in Aksakov the awareness of nature's gifts and active participation in it bespeak a far higher level of awareness and consciousness, in fact, a morality of its own. The long book is plotless, but it is organized according to an internal principle of structure rather than according to mere temporal sequence. The added distance between Aksakov the writer and Sergey Bagrov the subject serves to increase the illusion of objectivity and to impose a larger meaning on the recital of youthful events. The book is not without development: young Bagrov increasingly learns of the conflict between human beings, of suffering and pain, of inequality and inequity, and of the kind of duplicity adults indulge in. The book, indeed, goes far beyond childhood in its range of experience and knowledge. Although *The Childhood of Grandson Bagrov* is a unique book, it still occupies a secondary place to Aksakov's masterpiece, *The Family Chronicle*.

Of all books in Russian literature, *The Family Chronicle* is the one that at first glance should appeal most to Americans. But for the fact that Stepan Bagrov faces east and our pioneers faced west, the situation is exactly comparable: the limitless expanse of the new frontier, the sense of space and freedom, the abundance of the land, the simplicity and occasional starkness of life, the necessity for self-reliance, and the moral fiber that manifests itself in the process. It is also a strange fact that these qualities are otherwise rather ignored in Russian literature. We read in the main of control and confinement in the artificial cities, rather than of the immensity of Russia and the implications of its sense of space. Similarly, there is no great American work dealing with the subject. The outstanding novel of that time, *Moby-Dick,* presents its microcosm of America contained and "federated along one keel" of the *Pequod,* relentlessly pursuing leviathans of the sea and monsters of the mind.

Aksakov conveys the special qualities of frontier life primarily through the colossal figure of his grandfather, Stepan Bagrov, who is presented in the first of the work's five sections, and dominates the rest of the work, casting his shadow over at least two generations of his family. He has frequently been likened to an Old Testament patriarch, which he resembles in his simplicity, his strong moral sense, his wisdom and understanding, the fundamental nobility of his character, his deep religious sense, and perhaps, too, in the complete arbitrariness of his actions and his terrifying rages. Finding himself constrained in Ufa in the second half of the eighteenth century, he acquired a large tract of land in the wilderness of the Bashkirian prairie and moved his entire household there. He disapproved of the methods of other colonists, who acquired land by the very simple and economical expedient of wining and dining the Bashkirian tribesmen for a number of successive days and then asking for a portion of land, which the Bashkirians would grant in enormous tracts, casually marked by natural boundaries— mountains, rivers and the like. Instead, Bagrov did an unheard-of thing: he bought approximately 50,000 acres for a sum preposterously low, yet considerable for Bagrov's reduced means. There he cultivated the rich land and contemplated the bounties of nature. He would rise daily before dawn and sit majestically and silently to contemplate the rising sun, an act that assumes a moving and profoundly religious character. His rages, too, are elemental and grandiose. His love for his family was great and constantly apparent, but members of the household would literally flee for their lives when Bagrov started to rage. The worst of these was so fearful that the family would not talk of it. It was a long time before they recovered, and a year passed before Aksakov's grandmother regrew the hair Bagrov had pulled out in his rage. Usually his rages were more short-lived: Bagrov would rise the following morning serene and peaceful, and watch the sunrise as usual.

Stepan Bagrov is presented as an elemental creature in spontaneous communion with life and nature. Aksakov's portrait is the more successful because this elemental quality is never reduced. Bagrov is inarticulate and uncultured, though fully formed morally. He is most impressive when presented physically or when Aksakov communicates the awe he inspires in others. But Bagrov cannot formulate his essence. There is a fine, moving passage near the end when Bagrov meets his son's wife and forms a strong attachment to her. Aksakov very delicately shows the expressions of this attachment in the understanding between the two, in the way Bagrov presses food on her, in Bagrov's admitting her into the sacrosanct family group despite his initial coolness. Bagrov would like to make his feelings clearer to her, but, unlike Aksakov, he cannot.

> . . . he was happy when he looked at them, but his happiness had a shade of fear, a certain disbelief in the solidity and permanence of this fine state of things. . . . He would-.have liked to tell them something, to point out something to them, to give them some useful advice; but whenever he began to speak he could not find the right words for thoughts and feelings which he could not make clear even to himself, and he went no farther than those trivial commonplaces, which nevertheless contain eternal moral verities that have been bequeathed to us by the practical wisdom of past generations and are verified by our experience. He was vexed by his inability and candidly spoke of it to the intelligent bride; how-

ever, she could not understand what was going on in the old man's mind and what was hidden in his soul.

The section that follows is the antithesis of the first. Its events are extraordinary; its central character a villain bereft not only of morality but even of any decency; its implications a reversal of the first. An officer named Kurolesov, a social charmer who courts Stepan Bagrov's cousin and incurs Bagrov's dislike, manages, after much manipulation and maneuvering on the part of the family, to marry the heiress. After some years odd rumors are heard of his behavior on one of his wife's distant estates, where he spends much time. He has established a harem there, and heads a gang which appropriates whatever it wishes, insults, maims, and occasionally kills those who oppose it, and is so powerful that even the provincial forces dare not institute proceedings. When the wife learns of this, she goes to verify matters for herself, is incarcerated by her husband, beaten and threatened in order to extort from her a power of attorney for all her property. Stepan Bagrov is alerted by a runaway peasant, arrives on the scene when the band is asleep and incapacitated after a lengthy carouse, and rescues his cousin. Shortly after his fall from power Kurolesov is murdered by two of his cronies.

It seems odd that Aksakov should have portrayed such criminal oppression and mistreatment and that he should have shown authority so helpless against such flagrant abuses. Unlike many of those writing at that time, however, Aksakov had no intention of serving a political or civic cause, and was not interested in writing of these events merely to air injustice in the Russian land (he even toned down the events which were more horrifying than he presented them). The episode has a distinct function in developing a major theme of *The Family Chronicle:* the relationship between power and character. Bagrov's violence is an expression of his elemental per-

sonality; Kurolesov's actions are petty and directed only
to personal enjoyment, and turn out to be vicious. Mere
confrontation of frontiers and wilderness does not suffice
to elicit man's nobility; it may as easily enable him to
fulfill his meanest drives. Aksakov makes a particular
point of setting the episode back in time, to give it the
specious appearance of an age less civilized than the
present. We know that such abuses were possible and
were expressed in literature (Troekurov in Pushkin's
Dubrovsky immediately comes to mind), but never yet
had so radical an instance been presented.

Kurolesov anticipates the cruel and quasi-demented
characters in Dostoevsky and elsewhere in later Russian
literature, people who find their only outlet in dissipation
of an extraordinary kind. But the reason for such behavior, the motivating force behind Kurolesov, is never
examined by Aksakov. The character merely exists. Nor
does Aksakov elaborate on the wife's reaction. She refuses to take steps against her husband, maintaining that
she still loves him. There is material here for a great
novel, but Aksakov again contents himself merely with
indicating the possibility without developing it.

Against the background of these two episodes the concluding sections deal with the courtship and marriage of
Aksakov's father. Here Aksakov finally gives full range
to his narrative talent in depicting the endless maneuvering, struggles and bitter recriminations involved in the
playing out of what would be an excellent comedy had it
not been shown from the first that the characters were
too seriously taken with their jealousies and with the
kind of strife a powerful figure like Bagrov is bound to
breed in those around him. Young Bagrov, as might almost be expected, was a kindly but weak man, given to
tears, a man of limited abilities, poorly educated. Sofya
Nicolaevna was brilliant, beautiful, willful, proud, with
an excellent education, who had been mistreated for years
by her stepmother and who then had great social success
in Ufa, where young Bagrov was serving. It is a mys-

tery why she should have considered him at all among the many suitors for her hand, unless, perhaps, he struck her as a sufficiently pliant and deferential companion. When she did accept him as a suitor, objections were raised on the part of both families, but they were finally overcome, and the couple married. Sofya Nicolaevna evidently hoped to embark on a long reclamation project to make her husband a fitting intellectual companion, but in this she was unsuccessful. Her talents were later devoted to educating her son Sergey, and she may well be responsible for rousing in him so early in life an appreciation for literature and for delicacy of observation.

Sofya Nicolaevna's visit to the estate almost immediately established a deep bond between herself and Stepan Bagrov, each recognizing the other's stature, the difference between themselves and the others in the family. Yet the power of the grandfather and Sofya Nicolaevna did not insure her acceptance in the family. Ultimately it is the husband, young Bagrov, who protects her against the machinations and innuendoes of the other women. Quite early she became dependent on him for comfort and support, and if he had little satisfaction from the frequent and violent arguments she seemed to provoke, he found consolation—at least on the estate— in winning lesser battles with the fish that populated near-by waters.

Stepan Bagrov was the only male descendant of his father, and Timofey his only son. The continuation of the line, then, was a matter of great concern to the old man. Like the cousin who married Kurolesov, Sofya Nicolaevna lost her firstborn, but she was more fortunate later. The work closes appropriately when Bagrov is informed of the birth of a grandson. The urgency of his desire and the importance of the birth to him are made manifest as he rushes to enter the name of Sergey on the family tree.

The courtship of Sofya Nicolaevna might well have served for a novel; the career of Kurolesov for a story;

INTRODUCTION

the figure of Stepan Bagrov for a sketch. Aksakov was able to mold the material he derived from family tradition in such a way that each episode far extends the range and depth of the other. His narrative constantly maintains the illusion of simplicity, of forthright statement, event of a kind of ingenuousness. In the struggle for usable forms, solved so conspicuously by Russian novelists such as Gogol', Turgenev and Dostoevsky, Aksakov may well have achieved far more than his modest role as chronicler indicates. He knew very well (and wrote to his son) that his Orenburg hunter was a "literary man who pretends to be a simple man." There is but little evidence in correspondence and in jottings, yet it suffices to indicate the conscious craftsmanship that went into the composition of *The Family Chroncle,* the shaping of its parts, the deletion and mutation of material just as valid, but artistically not appropriate.

Aksakov's work appears simple, but it is a simplicity achieved through clarity of artistic vision and mastery of style. He was able to imbue his recital of a time long past with a sense of the fullness and acceptance of life that speaks eloquently and unequivocally to the reader today. The form of the work, like other idiosyncratic masterpieces, is sufficiently unusual to obscure its originality, but not its quality. Turgenev saw that it ranks, with Herzen's *Past and Thoughts,* as a "just picture of Russian life, only seen from opposite ends and from two different points of view," that is, as a work of fact. Turgenev also saw it as a work of imagination and invention. His comment to Aksakov summarizes its achievements: "There it is, real tone and style, there you have Russian life, there is the earnest for the Russian novel of the future."

RALPH E. MATLAW

University of Illinois
February, 1961

THE FAMILY CHRONICLE

SKETCH I

STEPAN MICHAILOVITSCH BAGROV

EMIGRATION

My grandfather found his home on the family estate in the Province of Simbirsk, where his ancestors held the land in fief from the Muscovite Tsars, distasteful to him. It was not for lack of this world's good things—for forests, corn-fields, meadows, and all necessary appurtenances were his in great abundance—but because this estate, which had been the sole property of his great-grandfather, was now shared by others. Briefly, the case was as follows. Three generations of the Bagrov family in succession had had but one son and several daughters. Certain of these daughters had married, receiving serfs and estates as dowries. The latter, it is true, only represented a small part of the whole property ; but the ownership was to a certain extent mutual ; and, now, besides my grandfather, there were four other masters. My grandfather found this intolerable, for he was a straight-forward, impulsive, passionate man, and could endure no intriguing in his household. For some time past he had heard much of the Province of Ufa—of the inexhaustible wealth of its vast plains of virgin soil, of its incredible abundance of game, fish and all the fruits of the earth ; also of its simple inhabitants,[1] and how they were easily persuaded to part with whole territories for a trifling sum. To make such a bargain it was merely necessary, so the tale ran, to gather together a dozen or so of landed proprietors of the Bashkirian Districts of Kartobyn and Karmalin, and to place two or three fat wethers at their disposal, which they could kill and dress

[1] The Bashkirs, a race of Finnish stock mingled with a strong Tartar strain. They are, for the most part, Moslems ; and speak a Turkic dialect allied to Kirghiz. In 1897 they numbered 1,492,983. Those who inhabit the Steppes are pastoral nomads, whose culture dates back for a period of more than a thousand years. [Tr.]

according to their custom. The next items were a cask of brandy, some jars of the strongest Bashkirian mead, and a huge barrel of country beer—a striking proof that the Bashkirians of that day were not quite scrupulous in their observance of the laws of Mahomet—and the whole affair was in trim. Certainly, one would think, such an entertainment might well last a whole week, and possibly two. Among the Bashkirian folk it is not considered etiquette to settle business at once, but each day the would-be purchaser must say: " Well, friend, worthy man,[1] let us talk over this little affair of mine !" If the guests, after eating and drinking the live long day, are not quite gorged, and not too utterly weary to sing their monotonous ditties, to blow away at their *Tschebysgas*[2] ; and to dance—or rather to strike the absurdest attitudes while remaining standing or squatting in one spot—then the oldest of the party, clicking his tongue, shaking his head, and turning away from the petitioner with pompous mien, will exclaim " The time has not yet come—bring along another wether !" Naturally another wether is promptly produced, brandy and mead follow in due course, and the eating, drinking, singing and snoring recommence. But like everything else in the world the revels come to an end at last ; and there comes a day when the oldest landowner, looking the purchaser straight in the face, says : " Thanks, little father, heartiest thanks ! Now tell me what you want." Thereupon the purchaser with true Russian subtlety and cunning, will protest that he wants nothing at all, but as he has always heard that the Bashkiris are the best of folks, he wishes to be on friendly terms with them, and so forth. Casual remarks will follow about the boundless possessions of the Bashkirs, and of the scant reliance to be placed on leaseholders,[3] who

---

[1] A formal and polite form of address in Bashkiria. [Tr. S. R.]

[2] A native flute, from which the Bashkirians can extract a great variety of notes.

[3] These tenants, or, as they were called, permit leaseholders, were people to whom the Bashkirians let their lands for a yearly rent, or for a lump sum which covered a certain number of years. It frequently fell out, however, that when the leases were expired, the permit-tenants declined to vacate their new dwellings. Hundreds of law suits were the result which generally ended in the leaseholders being left in undisturbed possession of their very-cheaply-acquired estates. In this way enormous areas of Bashkirian lands are now in the hands of Tartars, Mescheryaks, Tschuvasches, Mordvins, and other Crown Peasants.

are ready enough to pay the ground rent for the first two or three years, and then will cease payment altogether, and refuse to quit the land, thereby forcing the Bashkirs into wearisome lawsuits, which, as often as not, are decided against the landlords. After a bit of this sort of talk which, alas, describes a state of affairs only too true, it naturally comes about that a proposal is made to relieve the good Bashkirs of some of their burdensome property ; and frequently whole districts are purchased for trifling sums, and the purchase duly legalised by a formal deed, in which it is impossible to state the exact area of the land, as it has never been measured. Usually natural features of the land serve as boundaries, for example : " From the mouth of the Konlyelg rivulet as far as the withered birch tree beside the Path of the Wolf—and from the withered birch straight along to the Parting of the Waters—and thence to the Fox Holes, and so on." Such accurate and incontestable boundaries would often enclose tracts of ten—twenty—even thirty thousand dessiatines. And for these vast properties a few hundred silver roubles were willingly accepted, not counting a hundred or so of roubles for the feast.

My grandfather was greatly interested in these tales, although he was a man of the strictest integrity, and considered it no light matter to cheat and betray the kindly Bashkirs. He reflected long on the subject, and finally concluded that, without in any way wronging the natives, it would be possible to purchase a good-sized estate in the Province of Ufa for a quite reasonable sum, and to transfer half of his serfs to this country, where, later, he and his family might set up their dwelling. This last part of the project was the most important in his estimation, as of late years he had been so worried by the endless wrangles with his kinsmen, as to the mutual control of the ancestral property, that his dearest wish was to quit the house of his forefathers, to forsake the old family nest, and in another country to seek that peaceful unmolested life, which to him—a young man no longer—had become an absolute necessity.

So, as soon as he had saved up a couple of thousand roubles, my grandfather decided on his venture. He took an affectionate leave of his wife—Arischa as he called her, when

5

he was in a good temper ; and Arina, when he felt cross. He kissed and blessed his four little daughters, but especially his newly-born baby son, the last scion, the sole hope of his ancient and noble stock. He never set great store by his daughters. " What good are girls to me ? " he was wont to grumble. " They run away from home as soon as they get a chance. To-day they are Bagrovs, to-morrow Schlygins, Malygins, Popovs, Kalpakovs . . . . My only hope is in Alexei." Thus, my grandfather, on the day of his departure ; and he crossed the Volga and set off for the Province of Ufa.

And now I had better describe my grandfather to the reader. Stepan Michailovitsch Bagrov, as he was called, was slightly below the middle height ; but his deep chest, his strikingly broad shoulders, his sinewy hands, and the massive muscular build of his limbs all bore witness to his extraordinary bodily strength. He used to relate how, in his youth, when he and his comrades used to test their strength in military sports, he could shake off a whole mass of attackers as easily as some stately oak shakes the raindrops from its leaves at the first puff of wind. His features were regular ; his eyes were large, beautiful, and darkest blue ; easily lighted up by passion, but beaming with kindness and good humour when nothing had occurred to put him out ; thick eyebrows, a well-shaped mouth—all these gave his countenance an open and noble aspect : his hair was light brown. All who knew him, trusted him : his word, his spoken promise, were more sacred and reliable than any known or unknown oath, or legal act. His innate judgment was clear and sound. It is true that he, like all his contemporaries of the Russian landed gentry, had little or no education ; he could scarcely read or write Russian, and when he first entered on his military service he had only learnt the first four rules of arithmetic and the use of the counting board, as he was wont to relate in his old age. Most probably he only remained a short time in the service, for he never rose higher than Regimental Quartermaster. However at that time the nobles had to serve long periods as privates and non-commissioned officers ; (unless indeed they had been passed through all the intermediary stages while yet in their cradles, and from Sergeants of the Guard blossomed out direct into Captains of the Line). I know very little about Stepan Michailovitsch's military life. I only recollect that he was employed in the pursuit of the Volga thieves, that he distinguished himself by his astuteness and reckless daring ; that the robbers knew him only too well, and feared him like the Devil. On leaving the Service, he spent some years on his estate of Troizkoie—also known as Bagrovo—and developed into a capital landlord. He was none of those who overlook every bit of farm labour like an overseer, and must always be on the watch when any grain is stored or sold. It was but seldom that he interfered with the management of the estate, but his suggestions were judicious and of the greatest service. Any act of injustice or fraud roused his inexorable wrath. My grandfather, according to his own light, and influenced to a certain extent by the spirit of the times, argued in this way : " It is not well to punish a peasant in such a way that his day's work is ruined, and his own comfort as well as his family's is destroyed : . . . . to withhold his wages is just as bad ; to separate him from his family, to send him to a distant estate, or to inflict hard labour upon him, is still worse, because of the evil moral consequences likely to ensue through the same separation from his relatives—to send him to prison—God forbid ! That would be such a disgrace and ignominy, that the whole community would bewail him as one dead, and the culprit would henceforth consider himself a lost and ruined man." Furthermore I must explain that my grandfather was only inexorable in the heat of passion. With his rage, his severity vanished. This trait of his character was so well known, that the offender often hid himself until the storm had passed. But as time went on the peasants were in such perfect accord with him, that he had no longer any occasion for anger.

As soon as his affairs were in good order, my grandfather wedded Arina Vasilievna Neklyudova, a young lady of impoverished, but old and noble family. And I take this opportunity to observe that ancient family descent was my grandfather's weakness. His serfs numbered a bare hundred and eighty souls—all told—but he could boast his descent, and with perfect right, from the Varangian Princes, and prized his seven-hundred-year-old nobility far beyond all riches or honours. He had relinquished all thought of marrying a wealthy and charming girl, to whom he was greatly attached, simply and solely because her great-grandfather had not been of noble family.

So much for Stepan Michailovitsch's character. And now to resume our interrupted narrative.

My grandfather crossed the Volga from the Simbirsk side, and travelled across the steppes on the left bank, past Tscheremschan, and Kandurtscha, past the Red Village—a settlement of time-expired soldiers—and gained Sergijevsk, a high-lying spot situated at the mouth of the River Surgat in the Bolschoi Sok. Sergijevsk is now a little town and has given its name to the sulphur springs which lie twelve versts distant, and which were formerly known as the Baths of Sergijevsk. The farther my grandfather penetrated into the Province of Ufa, the richer and more luxuriant grew the land. Within the circle of the Buguruslan District, near the Abdulsch Government brandy distilleries, the mountains first came into view. My grandfather stayed awhile in the District town of Buguruslan in order to ascertain details as to the land for sale ; this town rests on the flank of a lofty mountain beside the Bolschoi Kinel, of which the natives sing :

" The Kinel flows
Not deep—yet swift,
Full of green slime. . . ."

In this part very little Bashkirian land was available for purchase, A very considerable part had been given away to the Crown Peasants—after the Akayevian Revolt, and before the general Amnesty—which had formerly been owned by the Bashkirs ; part had been seized by the lease-holders ; and part had been bought by settlers from the West. From Buguruslan my grandfather made excursions in the districts of Bugulma, Birsk, and Menselinsk (the last two-named places being now included in the Circuit of Belebei). He visited the exquisite shores of the Ik and the Djoma. An enchanting land ! To the end of his days Stepan Michailovitsch loved to recall the wondrous impression made on him by the sight of the fruitful and verdant shores of these delightful streams. Nevertheless he would not permit himself to be carried away by their charms, and decided on a spot in a district where the purchase of an estate from the Bashkirs would not entail a string of inevitable quarrels and lawsuits ; where his right of possession could be made perfectly clear to these people ; and where the sum agreed upon could be handed over to the then possessor of the land. My grandfather, to whom the word lawsuit was as bad as the plague, resolved only to purchase a demesne which had already been sold to an earlier purchaser, whose legal right to the land was indisputable. In this way he hoped to avoid any future litigation. But in the long run it turned out that he had been sadly taken in, for when the youngest of his grandsons succeeded to the estate in his fortieth year, all sorts of disputes over the purchase had arisen and had to be settled. Very unwillingly my grandfather quitted the banks of the Ik and the Djoma, and wended his way back to Buguruslan, where he bought an estate from the lady of the manor, Madame Gryasevau, situated five-and-twenty versts from the town, on the banks of the deep, impetuous, brimming Buguruslan. From the town to the Crown demesne, Krasny Yar—a stretch of forty versts —the country at that time was quite uninhabited. And what wealth—what beauty this river could offer ! The water was so clear that a coin dropped to a depth of fourteen feet could be easily distinguished lying on its sandy bed. The banks were covered with luxuriant undergrowth, with here and there upstanding birches, aspens, ashes, wild cherry trees, and willows ; all entwined by wreaths of wild hops, which waved their golden tassels from the topmost twigs. And there grew long succulent grass, dotted with countless flowering shrubs, fragrant clover, scarlet gilliflowers, Turk's Cap lilies, and valerian. The Buguruslan flows through a valley. On each side rise mountains, now steep, now softly swelling, here approaching the stream, and there retreating far into the distance. In those days each slope and cliff of the heights was clothed with linden woods. On climbing the hills you entered the immeasurable, immense solitude of the steppe, where the rich black soil lay a yard deep. On the river banks, and in the surrounding marshes all manner of water fowl— ducks, snipe, and wild geese—had their nests, and filled the air with cries and screams. But high above, from the mountainous

tableland there resounded over the valley the thousand voices
of the birds of the steppes, which had their habitation in these
lofty altitudes—bustards, cranes, crested snipes, heathcocks,
and hawks. The river teemed with fish of every sort that could
exist in its icy waters ; pike, perch, carp, even salmon and
salmon-trout. On every hand forest and steppe were rich in
wild life ; in short, it was and is, even now, a blessed land.
My grandfather bought some five thousand dessiatines[1] of
land for which he paid a price, which at the time appeared in-
credibly high : half a rouble per dessiatine. Two thousand
five hundred roubles were a considerable sum in those days.
After the purchase was concluded and duly ratified, Stepan
Michailovitsch returned—well content and in high spirits—
to his anxious family in his native Province of Simbirsk ; and
set to work with all haste to make the necessary preparations
for the transport of his peasants. This was a pretty difficult
business on account of the length of the journey, for the
distance between the Troizkoie estate and the newly-acquired
property was not less than four hundred versts. It was only
in the autumn of that year that twenty labourers arrived at
Buguruslan, bringing ploughs, harrows, and seed troughs.
In certain carefully-selected spots they broke up the virgin
soil and sowed twenty dessiatines of the lightly-ploughed land
with winter seed ; they likewise prepared another twenty
dessiatines for the summer sowing ; erected a few huts, and
returned home. Towards the end of the winter another twenty
men wended their way towards the new estate, and, as spring
was awakening, they sowed the summer seed in the ready-
ploughed twenty dessiatines, enclosed the courtyard and
stables with wicker fences, built clay stoves in the huts, and
then returned to Simbirsk, for they were not amongst the
men selected for the new settlement. These latter had remained at home, preparing for the removal, and had been
engaged in disposing of superfluous cattle and grain, huts,
sheds, and implements. And at last—towards mid-June,
about Saint Peter's Day, (O.S.) the time of the hay-harvest
—the emigrants set out, escorting their heavily-laden
wagons, packed with all manner of farming gear, on top of
which were perched women, children, and old folks, sheltered

---

[1] Dessiatine—a Russian measure of land = 2-7 English acres. [Tr.]

alike from storm or sun by canopies of woven strips of bark. Above their heads poultry screamed and cackled ; and the cattle, tied at the cart tail, plodded patiently behind.

What bitter tears these poor peasants shed, as they quitted their old homes for ever—the church where they had been baptised and wedded, and the graves of their fathers and forefathers ! Of all mankind the Russian peasant is he who most abhors emigration : but in those times such an exodus towards a distant and heathenish land, where amongst much that was good, so much more evil was related—where the church was so far away that a man might die any day, unabsolved ; and where children perforce must remain for months unbaptised,the prospect was something hideous to contemplate.

My grandfather followed the serfs almost immediately. He gave the name of Snamenskoie to the newly-founded village, and vowed, in the fulness of time and when his circumstances would permit, to build a church and dedicate it to the Miraculous Apparition,[1] which festival is celebrated on the 27th November, [O.S.]. This vow was fulfilled in later years by his son. But the peasants, and, following the example of these, the neighbours all called the settlement New-Bagrovo, after my grandfather's own name, and in remembrance of the old Bagrovo. To this day the place is only known by the latter name—the other only exists in the ancient deed of purchase, and no one in the neighbourhood dreams that this beautiful estate, with its noble, white stone church and stately manor-house, is in reality called Snamenskoie.

My grandfather himself superintended the field labour untiringly—the peasants' allotments as well as his own fields. The hay was cut and carried in good time : the summer and winter corn reaped, and stored ready to be threshed. The harvest was incredible—fabulous. The peasants took heart. By November all the huts were ready for occupation, and a beautiful, little manor-house had been built. It is true that all this progress owed not a little to the friendly assistance of the neighbours, who in spite of immense distances, came to help their genial and shrewd

[1] This festival commemorates the Apparition of the Saviour to the Virgin Mary after His Resurrection and is celebrated in the Greek Church. [Tr.]

fellow-settler. They enjoyed his liberal hospitality, and went to work singing their native songs most lustily. When winter came, my grandfather returned to the Simbirsk estate, and brought away his family. During the following year it was a simple matter for him to introduce another forty men, and to accommodate them quite comfortably and economically. My grandfather's next task was to build a mill, as for lack of one it had hitherto been necessary to send the grain a distance of forty versts to be ground. So a suitable spot was chosen, where the water was not too deep, where the ground was solid, and the river bank of a good height and very firm : and there was erected on each side of the water a bank of earth and brush wood, after the fashion of a pair of hands about to clasp one another. This embankment was farther strengthened by a covering of interlaced willow boughs. All that remained to be done now, was to imprison the wildly-rushing stream in its appointed basin. The mill itself was already built on the lower bank ; with its two millstones and crushing gear complete. The water was to be conducted through great wooden pipes and might then dash against the huge mill wheels, when, checked by the dam, it had found its level, filled the wide pond, and risen above the bottom of the lock. When all was ready, and four mighty oaken posts had been driven firmly into the clayey bed of the Buguruslan, my grandfather bespoke his neighbours' help for two days, bidding them bring horses, carts, axes, pitchforks, and shovels. On the first day great masses of straw, brushwood, dung, and turf were piled on each bank of the Buguruslan, which still flowed unchecked, and undisturbed. At sunrise on the second day, nearly a hundred men assembled for the damming of the river.

Every face wore an expression of concentrated and even solemn expectancy. There had been no sleep in the village during the night. At a given signal, and at the same moment, loud cheers were raised, and from each bank great masses of brushwood and bundles of faggots were hurled into the river bed. Much of this was instantly whirled away by the current, but a considerable portion was checked and held by the stakes, and settled on the sandy bottom. Bundles of straw, weighted by stones, followed the brushwood, and after that came dung and clay ; a layer of brushwood next, more straw and dung ; and, over the whole, a heavy stratum of sods. As soon as the mass began to appear above the surface of the water, twenty nimble and hardy fellows sprang upon the rapidly-rising barrier, and set to work to stamp it firmly down. All this work was executed with such speed, such zeal, and above all, with such a terrible racket, that any passer-by— hearing the uproar, and not knowing what it was all about— might very well have been frightened out of his wits. But in these parts were no wayfarers to be terrified. Only the wild steppes and the darkling woods resounded to the excited shouts of the hundred labourers—to whose voices were added the shrill trebles of a crowd of women and children, for everyone took a hand in the great work ; and all screamed and shrieked in the greatest excitement. It was no light task to restrain the impetuous stream, which continually burst its way through the rising dam, sweeping away straw and branches, dung and sods. But victory was on the side of Man. No longer could the water escape through the stout barrier. The flood paused, as if in doubt ; and filling the whole river gorge, rose over the banks, overflowed into the meadows, and by evening lay—a wide shining lake—unconfined by bank or hedge, and dotted here and there by upstanding clumps of trees. The very next day the mill started stamping and grinding—and grinds and stamps to the present time.

THE GOVERNMENT OF ORENBURG

Oh Heavens, how beautiful must this land have been in its first wild, virgin luxuriance ! But thou art no longer the same as in those long-vanished days, nor even the same known to my childhood, ere thy verdant blossoming plains were riven by the ploughs of the gaily-dressed peasants who invaded thee from every side ! Oh, Orenburg, thou art indeed still fair and wide—full of luxuriance, and endless variety—but no longer the same ! Thy name is changed, and sounds strangely in mine ears ! Whence, in Heaven's name

comes this " burg " ? When first I learned to love thee
blessed land, thy name was Ufa.

> *Dear land ! with gifts beyond all measure*
> *By Nature's kindly hand bestrown—*
> *Henceforth thy plains' and pastures' treasure*
> *Not for the herdsman bloom alone !*
> *Scarce can I tell thy face of old . . . .*
> *From every region, every place*
> *Come eager crowds of alien race ;*
> *And, with their skilful hands and bold,*
> *They fell the forest, check the stream,*
> *Clouding its pure and azure gleam.*
>
> *Their picks on mountain sides resound,*
> *Where veins of noble metal lurk :*
> *And dazzling crystals heap the ground,*
> *Where they the seething salt springs work.*
> *With scanty labour—scanty toil*
> *The stranger for his children gains*
> *A hundred-fold the sowers' pains—*
> *So inexhaustible thy soil.*
> *Far o'er the Steppe wild creatures flee,*
> *And seek the forest's sanctuary.*

Thus wrote one of thine own sons,[1] thirty years later.
And all this has in part been fulfilled—and the rest will yet
befall thee—yet still art thou beautiful, land of enchantment !
Thy lakes—Kandry and Karatabyn—slumber deep and mur-
murous as vast pearl shells. Thy rushing rivers, rich
in fish, foam and dash through the gorges and valleys
of the terraced slopes of the Ural Mountains ; or softly
meander through the billowing steppes like strings of
sapphire beads. Marvellous are these rivers of the steppes,
with their countless, deep, lake-like pools—or when they
can only be traced by the merest thread of a streamlet. Trout
of stately size and most delicate flavour lurk in every pool of
thy impetuous welling streams—clear as crystal, and cold as
ice even in the sultriest days of summer—which gush forth
from beneath the shady trees and bushes, and ripple joyously
along. The fish vanish like flashes of light, when the unclean
hand of man disturbs the virgin current of their cool, sequestered
dwelling. Thy pastures and meadows glow with luxuriant
verdure, shimmering milky-white in spring-time with the
bloom of cherry and peach trees, and the white carpet of wild

---

[1] The Author himself. [Note by Ivan Aksakov, one of the Author's
sons.]

strawberries : and glowing red in summer with the spicy strawberries and the little cherries, which wax darker as they ripen in the autumn. Richest recompense rewards the indolent, unskilful labour of thy sons, as they rend thy rich soil with their uncouth ploughs ! Thy vast linden forests clothe themselves in their green robes, while swarms of wild bees fill their waxen cells with fragrant honey, culled from the bloom of the lime tree. Here, amid the forests where the Ufa and Bielaia have their source, dwells the Ufa marten —most highly-prized of his race. Friendly and peaceful are the wandering tribes of Bashkirs ; thine own primeval, patriarchal children. Though scantier than of yore, great herds of horses, and vast numbers of kine and sheep still are thine. . . The stern wild winter has departed, and with the first warm beams of Spring sunshine the famished Bashkirs, meagre as flies in winter, lead the remnant of their herds to feast on the earliest fresh grass already springing up on the open steppe—and wife and child accompany each man. Yet a week or two, and neither man nor beast is to be recognised. The skeleton horses are fiery, untameable steeds—each mighty stallion the jealous guardian of the feeding-ground of his mares, and intolerant of any intrusion thereon. The withered cows are stout and strong—their udders dripping with perfumed milk. But the Bashkir reckons little of the rich cows' milk—already the wholesome *Koumis*[1] is prepared, it has been fermented in the horse-hide bag, and each who will—babe or infirm elder—drink to intoxication of the life-giving beverage. The sufferings of famine-stricken winter vanish like magic ; even the wrinkled sunken features of the aged fill out, and a healthy red flush replaces the sickly pallor of their cheeks. But sad and strange are the deserted villages ! To any casual traveller in these parts, who has never seen the like before, the sight of the empty houses— silent as the grave—is terrifying. Wild and sorrowful are the scattered *Yourts*,[2] with their whitened chimneys, and gaping window frames, from which the bladders have been removed, like faces with the eyes put out. Here and there bays a

---

[1] An alcoholic drink made from fermented mares' milk. This milk is very rich in sugar. [Tr. S. R.]

[2] Bashkirian huts, which in winter have bladders fixed in the window frames instead of panes of glass. [Tr. S. R.]

chained and famished dog, at long intervals fed and tended by his master ; here wails a half-wild deserted cat, seeking a scanty living. A little farther—and nothing stirs—all human traces vanish. . . .

.   .   .   .

But how picturesque and unique are the three regions of the Province now, the steppes, the forests, and the mountains . . . above all, the mountain lands, the outposts of the Urals—so rich in metals—the gold-fields of Russia ! What a vast extent from the frontiers of the Provinces of Perm and Viatka, (where the quicksilver frequently freezes), to the little town of Guriev on the borders of the Province of Astrachan ; where tiny grapes thrive in the open air, producing a wine which cools in summer, warms in winter— a stock-in-trade for the native Cossacks. What glorious fishing in the Urals ! Unique indeed, both as regards the capture of the abundant Red Fish,[1] and their excellent flavour when caught. This singular mode of fishing is known as *Bagrenie*, and still awaits a vivid and accurate description, such as might well excite universal interest in the sport. But methinks I have already written far too much about my beloved home. We shall now see how my energetic grandather lived and worked in his new sphere.

THE NEW HOME

How good it seemed to Stepan Michailovitsch, and how often he crossed himself in the fulness of his joy, when at last he was settled on the wide plains of the Buguruslan. The increasing gaiety of his heart was only equalled by his improved health and increased strength. No favours asked, nor reproaches uttered—no quarrels, nor tears ! No Vojeikovs no Moschenskis, no Suschtschevs ![2] No thefts of wood, and no damage done to forest, field, or crops ! His sway extended—not over his own land alone, but far, far beyond it—over the wilds ! To the herdsman might he grant permission to pasture his flocks, and give the woodman

---

[1] All the larger-sized sturgeons are called Red Fish.
[2] The names of my grandfather's neighbours in Simbirsk.

leave to cut down trees—or mow the steppe for hay—just as he willed : and no man questioned his authority ! The peasants soon grew reconciled to their new home, and grew to love it. How, indeed, could they have done otherwise ? From the arid, wooded estate of Troizkoie—where the pasturage was so scanty, that each peasant's family found it hard work to maintain a single horse and cow : where the once-fruitful ground had been so tilled and cultivated from remotest times, that it was now fairly exhausted—they found themselves transferred to boundless and fertile plains, as yet untouched by plough or scythe. Here, they were in the neighbourhood of a clear and sparkling river, with a multitude of tributary streams and springs ; and near the banks of a limpid pool, where the mill stood close at hand ; while in the old days they were forced to drag their sacks of corn along a weary stretch of twenty-five versts to be ground ; and frequently had to wait a couple of days until their turn came for grinding. You will wonder why I have described Troizkoie as arid. Had my ancestors indeed been so imprudent as to set up their dwelling in a barren country ? Not so, for a different state of things existed formerly, and no reproach attaches to my forebears. Troizkoie once lay situated on the beautiful little stream of the Maina, that, three versts distant from the village, took its rise in the wonderful Mossy Lakes. Moreover, beside the village lay a narrow, but long and clear pond, deep in the centre, whose bed was of the whitest sand ; out of this pond flowed a brook, called the White Brook. Of course this was ages and ages ago. According to the tradition, the Mossy Lakes were formerly deep round basins in the depth of the forest, filled with transparent icy water and surrounded by marshy banks. At that time, so the tale goes, no one had ever dared to approach the lakes, except in winter time ; for the quaking banks would instantly swallow up the venturesome intruder who had dared invade the realm of the Water-Devil. But the Will of Man triumphed over Nature. Folks ceased to attach any credence to the old tale, which failed, as time went on, to give any proof of its miraculous power—and the Mossy Lakes grew foul through the soaking of flax, and the watering of cattle. As the surrounding forest was cut down, they became smaller and shallower. A thick layer of peaty moss grew upon their surface, whereon sprung up many sorts of grasses whose matted roots constituted a certain amount of solidity. Soon thick cushions of moss and bushes appeared, and lastly a tolerably vigorous, young pine-sapling forest. One basin is now completely overgrown, and only two huge, deep holes remain of the other, which are best avoided, for their margin—weighted with its growth of herbage bushes, and saplings—quakes and wavers like a quicksand under the traveller's footstep. As the result of the dwindling of the Mossy Lakes, the main part of the Maina rivulet has been lost, and now only makes its first appearance some versts beyond the village. The deep, clear, long pond has been metamorphosed into a stinking slough. Its sandy bed is fathom-deep with slime ; and its surface is covered with filth and refuse from the peasants' barnyards. The last trace of the White Brook has long since vanished, and soon its very name will be forgotten. . . .

Scarcely had my grandfather established himself in his new surroundings than, with his characteristic energy and perseverance, he set himself to work on agriculture, and cattle breeding. The peasants, encouraged by his example, developed into willing and skilful labourers, and soon nothing remained to be done in the building or carpentering line. The threshing-floor of New-Bagrovo occupied an area three times the size of the village itself ; and the magnificent herds of horses, cattle, and swine, and flocks of sheep bore striking witness to the wealth of the new settler. It really seemed as if Stepan Michailovitsch had set the fashion of emigration ; for a stream of folks flowed into Ufa and Orenburg. From all sides came the Steppe Mordvins, Tscheremisses, Tschuvasches, Tartars, and Meschtcheriaks : nor was there any lack of Russian emigrants, of Crown Peasants from various districts, and of more or less well-to-do owners of serfs. My grandfather soon had neighbours. His brother-in-law, Ivan Nasil-ievitsch Neklyudov, purchased a tract of land twenty versts distant from New-Bagrovo, transferred his serfs to this estate, built a wooden church, called the place Neklyudovo, and established himself there with his family—a circumstance by no means pleasing to my grandfather. For he detested all his wife's relations—the whole Neklyudovery, as he called them. A landed proprietor—Bachmetev—bought an estate still nearer at hand, only about ten versts from Bagrovo, near the source of the Sovruscha, which flows parallel with the Buguruslan in the South-East. He brought along his serfs, and called his place Bachmetevka. On the other side, on the banks of the Nasjagai (or Motschagai, as the natives now call this river) lay the demesne of Polibino, which is now the property of the Karainzins. The Nasjagai is wider and more beautiful than the Buguruslan ; deeper and more full of fish ; and aquatic birds are found in greater abundance on its shores. On the road to Polibino, eight versts from Bagrovo, and lying directly to the East, is the big Mordvin village of Noikino. Two versts farther on, a mill was built on the Bokla, a stream which flows parallel to the Buguruslan towards the South. Not far from this mill the Bokla joins the Nasjagai, which whirls its mighty current from North-East to South-West. Seventeen versts from New-Bagrovo our own Buguru-slan is drawn into the flood, which, strengthened by this new volume of water, finally unites itself with the Kinel, thereby losing its sonorous and significant name.[1]

In the end, quite a little Mordvin village grew up under the name of Kiwazkoie, only two versts away from Bagrovo, but farther towards Buguruslan. Stepan Michailovitsch at first was somewhat inclined to pull a long face at such near neighbours, who reminded him of the old days at Troizkoie. But the case was different here. These were decent, quiet folk, who never caused the slightest trouble to my grand-father in his capacity of District Inspector. In a few years my grandfather had gained the love and respect of the whole country side. He was a true benefactor to all, far and near ; old and new neighbours ; especially to the latest comers, who, as is so frequently the case with emigrants, came poor and empty-handed into a strange land ; frequently unprovided with seed, corn, and with no money to buy any. To all such my grandfather's bursting granaries lay open. "Take all you need ; and if the first harvest yields enough and to spare, you can repay me. If not—accept it as a gift in God's name." With such words as these my grandfather shared his store generously with those who lacked corn or bread. And here let me add, that, with all this, he was so clear-sighted, so

[1] Nasjagai means " Swift Pursuer ". [Tr. S. R.]

charitable, and sympathised so heartily with all in need and want ; and kept his plighted word and promise so faithfully and constantly—that he came to be a veritable oracle in those parts. And not only a friend in the day of distress was he ; but an adviser and a prudent guide to all who needed advice. Only tell him the plain truth, and his assistance might be reckoned upon. But those who had lied to him to excite his compassion, were well advised never to shew themselves on his land again. They would get nothing more, and well for them if they escaped with whole skins. Many a family quarrel was healed by him—many a lawsuit nipped in the bud. From every part of the country people sought him out for advice and arbitration : and his decision was respected, and observed to the uttermost degree. I have known grandsons and even great-grandsons of that bygone generation, who have testified their gratitude and indebtedness to the firm and just decisions of Stepan Michailovitsch, as handed down to them by their fathers and grandfathers. To many a simple, but strangely moving story have I listened, and the narrator at the end would cross himself, and pray for the repose of the soul of Stepan Michailovitsch. Small wonder then, that the peasants had a genuine affection for such a master ; but this affection was equally shared by the house servants, who frequently had to bear the brunt of his ungovernable outbursts of passion. In years to come, many an ancient servitor of my grandfather ended his days under my roof ; and often have these old men —while tears rained down their cheeks—spoken lovingly to me of their choleric, but generous and just old master.

And this noble, magnanimous, often self-restrained man —whose actual character presented an image of the loftiest human nature—was subject to fits of rage in which he was capable of most barbarous cruelty. I recollect having seen him in one of these mad fits in my earliest childhood [at a much later date than that of the foregoing narrative]. I see him now. He was angry with one of his daughters, who had lied to him, and persisted in the lie. There he stood, supported between two servants, for his legs refused their office ; I could hardly recognise him as my grandfather : he trembled in every limb, his features were distorted, and the frenzy of rage glared from his enraged eyes. " Give her to me ! " he howled in a strangled voice. (All this remains clearly in my memory; what came later has often been related to me). My grandmother threw herself at his feet, beseeching him to have pity and forbearance, but the next instant off flew her kerchief and cap, and Stepan Michailovitsch seized his corpulent and already aged better half by the hair of her head. Meanwhile, the culprit as well as all her sisters—and even her brother, with his young wife and little son—had fled into the woods behind the house; and there they remained all night: only the young daughter-in-law crept home with the child, fearing he might take cold, and slept with him in the servants' quarters. My grandfather raved and stormed about the empty house to his heart's content. At last he grew too tired to drag his poor old Arina Vasilievna about by her plaits, and fell exhausted upon his bed, where a deep sleep overpowered him, which lasted until the following morning. He awoke calm, and in a good humour, and called to his Arischa in a cheery tone. My grandmother immediately ran to him from the adjoining chamber, just as if nothing had happened the day before. " Give me some tea! Where are the children? Where are Alexei and his wife? Bring little Sergei to me! " said this erstwhile lunatic, now that he had slept off his rage; and everyone—with the exception of the daughter-in-law and her son—made their appearance with bright and serene countenances. This daughter-in-law was a woman of strong character, and no entreaties would induce her to betake herself so promptly to the madman of yesterday, and greet him civilly: and the child kept crying: " I won't go near my grandfather! I'm afraid of him! "

As she really was not very well, she pleaded indisposition, and kept her son with her in her own apartments. All held a terrified council, and awaited a fresh storm. But the man had conquered the wild beast of the previous evening. After Stepan Michailovitsch had drunk his tea, and chatted amicably with his children, he went himself to visit the young wife, who was in fact in a very shattered condition, and lay, pale and exhausted, on her bed. The old man seated himself beside her, kissed and embraced her, called her dear, beautiful little girl; caressed his little grandson, and at last left the room saying he felt lonely without his beloved daughter-in-law. Half an hour later the door of my grandfather's room was gently opened, and in walked his daughter-in-law, elegantly dressed in a gown which the old gentleman had once declared became her better than anything else in her wardrobe. My grandfather was much touched. " What's this ? " he said tenderly, " My poor, sick little daughter has got up and dressed in spite of her illness, and come to cheer up the old man ! " The mother-in-law and her daughters, who could not endure the young wife, cast down their eyes and bit their lips, while she responded gaily and respectfully to the friendly greeting of her father-in-law, and cast a glance of sly triumph at her malevolent relations. . . .

But enough of the darker side of my grandfather's character. I prefer to describe one of his cheery happy days, of which I have heard so much.

ONE OF STEPAN MICHAILOVITSCH'S GOOD DAYS

The end of June was at hand, and already the heat was intense. After a sweltering night, a cool East wind had sprung up as the dawn broke, which gradually fell as the sun's rays grew more powerful. My grandfather awoke at sunrise. It had grown too hot for him to remain asleep any longer in the narrow space within the bed hangings of homespun linen, even with the old-fashioned window opened to its fullest extent. Without the bed curtains he would have been persecuted by the irrepressible mosquitoes, and would never have had an instant's sleep. These winged musicians came in veritable swarms, thrust their long rapiers through any thin barrier, and buzzed and hummed their persistent song from night-fall to dawn. However strange it may sound to you, I must here confess that I love the shrill soprano, and even the bite, of the mosquito. It awakens memories of those glowing summers of long past days—with their wondrous, sleepless nights, echoing with the song of countless nightingales on the wooded banks of the Buguruslan : I can feel the yearning throbbing of my young heart, and that eternal, sweetest melancholy of youth, for which I would now willingly barter all my later existence. . . .

STEPAN MICHAILOVITSCH BAGROV

My grandfather was awake. With his hot hand he wiped the drops from his forehead, thrust his head through the curtains, and laughed aloud. His two body-servants, Vanka Masan and Nikanor Tanaitschenok, lay upon the floor, in grotesque abandon and snored as if for a wager. " How these sons of dogs do snore, to be sure ! " said my grandfather, and laughed again. In truth Stepan Michailovitsch was a puzzle. After such a remark, one might have expected him to administer a hearty blow with the willow staff which always stood at the head of his bed—or a good kick—or an early morning compliment in the way of a bang with a chair : but my grandfather had woken up with a laugh, and for the rest of that day was sure to be in a good humour. He got out of bed very quietly, crossed himself a couple of times, thrust his bare feet into his fox-skin slippers, and stepped out upon the balcony staircase, clad only in his homespun linen shirt— (his wife would never permit him to wear fine shirts)—where the damp morning breeze blew refreshingly. I have just remarked that Arina Vasilievna would never let her husband have any fine linen shirts, and the reader may with perfect justice retort that the characters of the two old married folks hardly bear out such a statement. All I can say is, that it was so. Here, as in every like case, the will of the woman triumphed finally over that of the man ! In spite of all my grandfather's grumbling over the coarse linen, my grand-mother took her own way, and supplied him with nothing else, until he grew quite accustomed to wearing it. Once indeed my grandfather had recourse to a last desperate expedient. He took an axe and hacked all his coarse shirts to rags, and strewed the bits on the door-sill of his room— heedless of my grandmother's lamentations, as she wildly entreated him to scold her as much as he liked, if he would only spare his own property. But even this frantic act availed him not. New and coarser shirts came to light, and the old man had to confess himself beaten. . . .

But I must crave the reader's pardon : in my wish to entertain him with the story of my grandfather's shirts I have wandered away from my history of his happy day. Without awakening anyone, he unhooked one of the felt curtains from the wall, spread it on the topmost step of the outside staircase or *flier*,[1] and seated himself, as was his wont, to await the sunrise. This awaiting the sunrise was an especial delight of my grandfather's, and his enjoyment was enhanced by the sight of his courtyard, which even in those days was well equipped with numerous buildings. It is true the court was not enclosed; and the peasants' cattle, when assembled in a herd ready for driving out to pasture, came in to forage each morning or evening, as the case might be. Sundry far-from-clean pigs were rubbing themselves against the very staircase where my grandfather was seated, grunting and gobbling away at the crawfish shells and other scraps of food which littered the foot of the steps; cows and sheep wandered up to the door, and naturally left unsightly traces of their visit behind them. But things of this sort did not disturb my grandfather's serenity in the least; on the contrary he rejoiced at the sight of so many beautiful animals, which bore witness to the prosperity of his peasantry. Soon however the resounding crack of the herdsman's whip caused these early visitors to make off with all speed. . . . The household began to bestir itself. Spiridon, the stalwart groom, known to the end of his long life as Spirka, brought out three gallant stallions, one after the other; two being roans and the other a black-brown: each of these he tied to a post, rubbed him down, and then exercised him by lounging him with a rope, while my grandfather admired their shape and size with great complacency, and already in imagination saw the splendid race of horses which he hoped they would breed for him, which indeed eventually came to pass. The old housekeeper, who preferred to sleep in the cellar, roused herself, and wended her way to the banks of the Buguruslan to perform her morning toilette, sighed and groaned according to her invariable custom, repeated her prayers, turned towards the East, and set to work scrubbing, washing and rinsing her pots and pans. Swallows darted, twittering, through the air. The meadows resounded with the rattle of the corncrake; and the song of the lark echoed high above in the clouds; in the bushes the hoarse cries of the ring-quail vied with the piping of the water hens, and the tremulous clack of the wood-

---

[1] A " flier " is an outside gallery or balcony with a staircase leading to the ground. [Tr.]

cocks in the adjacent marsh. . . . the nightingale paused in his song, and the mocking bird took up the refrain. The sun's glory streamed from the heavens . . . . smoke arose from the peasants' huts, and these azure columns wavered in the breeze like the unfurled flags of a procession of boats on a river . . . . the peasants set out for the fields. My grand-father, being minded to perform his ablutions with cold water, and to drink his tea, was obliged to disturb his two servants, who still snored peacefully in their inelegant attitudes. They sprang up in terror, but Stepan Michailovitsch's cheery voice soon reassured them : " Masan, my washing water ! Tanait-schenok, wake Aksiutka and the mistress, and make the tea ! " It was not necessary to speak twice. Off dashed the clumsy Masan headlong to the well, with the glittering copper water-jug in his hand ; while the nimbler Tanaitschenok roused the extremely ill-favoured young maid, Aksiutka ; who, hastily setting her handkerchief to rights on her head, scampered off to shake her stout old mistress out of her comfortable slumbers. In a very few minutes the whole house was astir, and every-one knew that the old master was in a good humour. A quarter of an hour later a table, covered with a white homespun linen cloth, was set out on the balcony, on which stood the steaming samovar, presided over by Aksiutka : and the old mistress Arina Vasilievna greeted her husband—not with groans and sighs, (as often was her wont in order to protect herself from his ill humour)—but cheerfully and brightly, while she asked after his health and what he had dreamt about. For his part, my grandfather spoke kindly to his Arischa as he called her. He never would kiss her hand, but frequently gave her his own to kiss, as a mark of special favour. Arina Vasilievna positively blushed with pleasure at his compliments, and even seemed to grow younger. Her unwieldiness and corpulence were not nearly so noticeable. She lost no time in bringing a stool out on the balcony and seating herself on it beside my grandfather, a thing she never would have ventured to do unless assured of his good humour. " Shall we drink our tea together, Arischa ", said Stepan Michailovitsch, " while the morning is cool ? The night was certainly terribly hot, but I slept so soundly that I cannot remember any of my dreams. And you ? " An enquiry like this was such an extraordinary piece of civility that my grandmother hastened to reply that she always slept very soundly whenever Michailovitsch had a good night : Tania,[1] however, had had a very bad night. Tania was the youngest daughter, and the old man loved her more than all the others, as is so frequently the case. He was quite concerned to hear this, and gave orders that Tatiana was not to be awakened, in order that she should get her full amount of sleep. However Tatiana had already been awakened at the same time as her sisters Alexandra and Jelisaveta, and was already up and dressed ; but no one ventured to tell her father this. Tania undressed hastily, slipped into bed again, had the shutters closed, and remained for two hours lying in the dark, although she was quite unable to sleep : my grandfather, however, imagined she was having a sound sleep to make up for that lost during the night. His only son, who at that time was nine years old, was never awakened early. The elder sisters were not long in making their appearance, and Stepan Michailovitsch, giving each his hand to kiss, called them by their pet names, Leksania and Lisynka. Both were clever girls. Alexandra joined to a subtle intellect the lively irritability of her father, without, however, possessing any of his good nature. My grandmother was an extremely weak-minded woman, who was entirely ruled by her daughters : whenever she ventured, (as she sometimes did) to deceive her husband, it was always at the instigation of these girls : and she lied so unskilfully that she, as often as not, failed to carry her point. The old fellow was perfectly aware of this, and he also knew that his daughters never missed an opportunity of lying to him. Out of indolence and indifference, or when he was in a good humour, he sometimes led them to believe that he did not see through their tricks. But, at the first explosion of rage, out flashed his relentless animosity, and he would rate them soundly. However the girls, as became true daughters of Eve, were never discouraged : the storm once past and their father's face cleared, they set to work again to carry out their artful designs, in which they generally succeeded.

After he had finished drinking his tea, and had chatted cheerily with his wife and daughters, my grandfather

[1] Pet name for Tatiana. [Tr. H. R.]

prepared to set out on the round of the estate. Masan had received orders some time back to have the horse put in, and already the old brown gelding stood at the foot of the balcony steps, harnessed to a comfortable and commodious peasant's cart. The groom Spiridon sat in front as driver, simply dressed in a blouse, bare-footed, and wearing a red woollen scarf girded round his waist, from which hung his keys and his copper comb. On a former occasion Spiridon had set out on one of these expeditions wearing no hat, and my grandfather having scolded him for this, he now wore a queer sort of cap on his head manufactured out of wide strips of linden bark woven together. My grandfather burst out laughing at the sight of this remarkable head-gear, as he drew on his own country coat of unbleached, homespun linen, and put on his cap. In case of a shower, he threw his overcoat on the seat and climbed into the cart. Spiridon likewise had brought his overcoat, which was made of common peasants' cloth, but dyed a brilliant red with madder, plant which grew in great profusion in our fields. This red dye was so popular among our peasantry that the neighbours gave the nickname of "The Reds" to the Bagrovian serfs. Fifty years after my grandfather's death I recollect hearing them called by this name. Once out in the fields, Stepan Michailovitsch was pleased with everything he saw. He looked at the blooming rye, which stood erect, the height of a man, in a solid wall. A soft wind rustled in the ears of corn, which rose and fell in gently-swelling, bluish waves—now lighter, now darker, as the sun's rays caught its undulations. Such a crop was a veritable joy for the owner's eye. My grandfather visited the fields of young oats, the spelt-wheat, and what remained standing of the summer harvest. From thence they went to the fallow land where they drove slowly over the ploughed-up ground in every direction. This was my grandfather's invariable custom, in order to test the accuracy of the ploughing. Every clod of earth, every rough patch untouched by the plough, gave the lightly-hung cart a jerk; and were my grandfather out of humour, he promptly leant out and made a hole in the ground with his staff; sent for the farm-bailiff, unless indeed the latter happened to be accompanying him, and called him over the coals, there and then. To-day everything went off splendidly. Even when the cart bumped over a few stray lumps Stepan Michailovitsch either noticed nothing, or did not choose to notice. He gave a look over his beautiful Steppe meadows and revelled in the sight of the lush, rich grass, that would be ready for the scythe in a day or two. And he also spent a considerable time in the peasants' fields, observing for himself whose corn was in good, and whose in bad condition : he tested their ploughed land ; saw everything and forgot nothing. Driving over a waste bit of land, he noticed some ripe strawberries, and, with Masan's assistance, picked quite a good basketful of splendid fruit for his Arischa. In spite of the heat, his round lasted until nearly twelve o'clock. . . . Scarcely had his cart been seen in the distance than dinner was steaming on the table, and all the family were assembled on the balcony awaiting his arrival. " Well, Arischa," he said, in high good humour, " God has indeed blessed us this year with a glorious harvest ! Great is His goodness ! And here are a few strawberries for you." My grandmother beamed with pleasure. " Half the strawberries are ripe already," he continued, " and we must begin to pick them to-morrow." And saying thus, he marched into the ante-room. The good smell of cabbage soup was wafted to him from the dining room. " Ah, dinner laid already ! " he said gaily : " this is good, indeed ! " and without going to his own room he went straight to the dining hall, and sat down at the table. I must explain that my grandfather's explicit orders were, that at whatever time he might return from the fields, dinner must be ready on the table. And woe if he returned unobserved, and the midday meal was not served. Such neglect frequently had tragical results. But on this happy day everything went smoothly : no untoward event occurred to disturb my grand sire's equanimity. A lusty fellow, Nikolka Rusan, placed himself behind the old man's chair, and whisked the flies away with a long birchen bough. My grandfather ate his steaming cabbage soup— [which a true Russian relishes even in the hottest weather]— with a wooden spoon, as he feared to burn his mouth with a silver one : next came an iced *Batvinia* ;[1] salted sturgeon, as yellow as beeswax ; shelled crawfish, and light dishes of

[1] Beetroot Soup. [Tr. H. R.]

the same sort. Home-brewed beer and iced *kvass* [1] were drunk. The meal was very merry. All talked and chattered at the same time, and laughed and joked. There were days, however, when dinner was eaten in gloomy silence, and in expectation of an explosion. . . . Somehow or other all the young people of the household had got to know that the old master was in a particularly good temper, and in they all came, pushing their way into the dining room, in the hope of getting a few stray bits from the meal. My grandfather shared every dish generously with his folk, and as there was about five times as much food on the table as he and his family could eat, there was plenty to spare. Directly after dinner he went to bed. All the flies were chased from under the bed canopy, and as soon as my grandfather lay down, the curtains were drawn all round the bed and fastened together under the mattress. And very soon loud snores announced that the master of the house was wrapped in deepest slumber. Everyone scattered in different directions ; some decided to have a rest, too. Masan and Tanaitschenok stretched themselves on the floor of the antechamber outside my grandfather's door, but not until they had devoured as much of the remains of the dinner as they could secure. Although they had both slept during the forenoon, they were quite ready for another nap. But the intense heat of the sunbeams streaming through the window panes fell full upon them, and soon woke them up again. Their uncomfortable nap had made them excessively thirsty, and feeling a great inclination to cool their parched throats with some of the ice-cold beer reserved for the " *quality*," the saucy knaves devised the following cunning plan. . . Just at the entrance to my grandfather's room his dressing gown and night-cap lay on a chair, and it was a quite simple matter to stretch one's hand through the half-opened door, and secure them. Having done so, Tanaitschenok proceeded to array himself in his master's costume, and seated himself outside on the balcony, while Masan hurried down to the cellar with the beer jug, woke up the old housekeeper—who, like all the rest of the household, was fast asleep—and imperatively demanded iced beer for

[1] A sour fermented drink, made from black bread and malt. [Tr. T. R.]

the master. As the old woman demurred, saying that it was impossible that the master should be awake so early in the afternoon, Masan begged her to step outside, which she did—and having duly observed his friend Tanaitschenok perched aloft, disguised in my grandfather's cap and bed-gown, she filled the jug with beer without farther ado, added some lumps of ice, and gave it to Masan, who ran off with his booty. The beer was shared in all brotherly love, and the night clothes carefully replaced on the chair. . . . A good hour elapsed before the master awoke. He sprang up in a yet gayer mood than in the early morning, and his first words were : " Cold beer ! " . . . . Consternation reigned ! Tanait-schenok hastened once more to the cellar-dame, who instantly guessed what had become of the first jug of beer. She said nothing, however, but refilled the vessel, and brought it herself to the balcony where, this time, the real master, crowned with his night-cap, was sitting. In a very few words she described the trick played upon her ; while Masan and Tanaitschenok, trembling with fear, threw themselves at their master's feet. And what did my grandfather ? He roared with laughter, sent for his wife and daughters, and related the servants' ruse to them amid fresh bursts of merriment. The two poor devils breathed again, but one of them was so ill-advised as to laugh too. In an instant Stepan Michailovitsch stopped laughing, and glared at him, ready to burst into a rage : but the sweet influence of the happy day was still strong enough to chase the momentary scowl from his brow, and he merely remarked in a severe tone : " This time I forgive you ; but another time . . . ." it was not necessary to finish the sentence. . . .

You may well be surprised at the servants of such a passionate—and occasionally even violent and cruel—master, daring to play such a trick. Nevertheless I have frequently observed that it is precisely the servants of the severest masters, who take the greatest liberties. The foregoing occurrence was by no means the only specimen of its kind which took place in my grandfather's house ; for that very same Vanka Masan, while sweeping out his master's room one day, took a fancy to have a nap in the beautiful white bed, promptly lay down therein, and fell asleep ! Some time later my grandfather discovered him in this posture—and only laughed. He certainly gave him a good thump with his willow staff but merely out of amusement and surprise. But many worse tricks than these of the poor servants were played on my grandfather. For instance, the case where his fourteen-year-old cousin, Praskovia Ivanovna Bagrova—an orphan heiress, an inmate of his house, and most dearly loved by him—was married during his absence to a detestable man whom he abhorred. It is true that the marriage was duly arranged by the orphan's own relatives, but it owed much to the connivance and co-operation of Arina Vasilievna and her daughters. But I will tell this story of sorrow later, and will now resume my tale of the Happy Day.

My grandfather had awakened towards five o'clock in the afternoon, and, having supped his cold beer, had a fancy to drink tea. He was of opinion that a hot drink is very refreshing in hot weather. But first he took a bath in the cool waters of the Buguruslan, which flowed directly past the house. On returning from the river, he found all the family gathered round the tea table, which had been set out on the shady side of the house. The tea urn was bubbling merrily, and Aksiutka stood ready to pour out. Hot tea was my grandfather's veritable elixir for producing perspiration, and after drinking sundry cups tempered by the thickest and richest yellow cream, he suggested that all present should drive to the mill. The proposal was hailed with delight, and my two aunts, Alexandra and Tatiana, who were expert anglers, took their tackle with them. In a very short time two large carriages made their appearance. My grandfather and grandmother seated themselves in the first, while between them sat their only son, the precious heir of their ancient and noble family. In the second carriage were my three aunts and the young servant Nikoala Rusan. The last-named was taken to collect earthworms and fasten them to the young ladies' hooks. Arrived at their destination a seat was found for my grandmother in the shadow of the mill near the lock, and there she sat, while her younger daughters fished close at hand. The eldest girl, Jelisaveta Stepanovna—partly to please her father, and partly from a real interest in the matter —went with Stepan Michailovitsch to inspect the grinding and crushing machinery. The little boy watched his sisters angle, (he himself was not permitted to fish in deep water), and then played about near his mother, who never let him out of her sight, lest he should fall into the pond. Both millstones were working : one husking wheat for the master's household, and the other grinding rye for a stranger. The stamping gear was crushing millet. My grandfather was very expert in all branches of country industry. He knew all about the working of a mill and explained every detail of the machinery to his attentive and intelligent daughter. He could instantly detect any fault in the wheels or defect in the adjustment of the millstones. He had one of the latter lowered a notch, and the result was a stream of much finer meal, which gratified the owner of the corn exceedingly. On examining the other mill-set, he guessed by the jarring noise that a pin of the driving wheel had been nearly rubbed away : he shut off the water, and the miller, Boltunenok,[1] sprang down, tested the wheel and said : " You are quite right little father Stepan Michailovitsch, one of the pins is a little worn." "Hm, a little ! " replied my grandfather, without, however, losing his temper ; " if I hadn't happened to notice it to-day, the wheel would have broken in half during the night." " Forgive me, Stepan Michailovitsch, I quite over-looked it." " Very well, I forgive you ; be quick and bring another wheel : put another pin in the old one, and take care it is neither stronger nor weaker than the others—that's the main point. . . ." A new wheel, that had previously been fitted and tested, was immediately produced, fixed in position, and well greased : the water was then gradually released, until the current ran at its full strength—all this was done under my grandfather's personal supervision—and very soon the humming millstone was grinding merrily away, with none of its former rattles and hitches. Next my grandfather and his daughter visited the stamping millhouse, where Stepan Michailovitsch took up a handful of the crushed millet, spread it out on his open palm, blew on it, and said to the Mordvin assistant, whom he recognised : " Now listen to me Neighbour Vasili ! Look here and you will see there is not a bit of uncrushed grain left. If you don't stop stamping

---

[1] Chatterbox. [Tr.]

your millet now, you will only reduce the quantity." Vasili made a test for himself, and finding that my grandfather had judged correctly, thanked him heartily, bowed or rather nodded a salute, and rushed off to stop the water wheel. From thence my grandfather and his pupil trotted off to the poultry-yard, where they found everything in the best order. Geese, ducks, fowls and turkeys were there in the greatest abundance, and all throve under the charge of the old hen-wife and her granddaughter. As a mark of especial favour my grandfather gave his hand to both women to kiss, and told them that in future, to their monthly ration of meal twenty pounds of wheaten flour for cakes should be added; and then, very well satisfied with his survey, Stepan Michail-ovitsch returned to Arina Vasilievna, and informed her that the mill was in excellent working order, his daughter was a most intelligent girl, and old Tatiana a capital henwife.

The heat had long since abated, and the approaching cool of the evening was even more noticeable at the waterside ; a long cloud of dust marked the road winding towards the village ; and more, and yet more audible the lowing and bleating of the home-going flocks and herds came on the breeze ; the sun was sinking behind the hills. Stepan Michailovitsch stood in a reverie beside the mill dam, gazing at the smooth motionless pool extended like a mirror between its level banks. Now and again a playful fish leapt high in the air, but my grandfather was no fisherman.

" It is time for us to return home, Arischa," he said at last, " the steward will be waiting for me." The younger daughters, taking advantage of his good humour, begged permission to remain a little longer at the dam, as they said the fish always bite better after sunset. They themselves would make their way home on foot, in half-an-hour, or so. My grandfather willingly agreed, and he and his wife drove home together, while Jelisaveta Stepanovna and her little brother followed in the second cart. Stepan Michailovitsch had guessed right—the steward was waiting on the doorstep, nor was he alone, but accompanied by two serfs and two women. The truth was that the steward had seen my grandfather earlier in the day, and having noted the master's wonderful good humour, had mentioned the circumstance in the hearing of the serfs. Hence certain of these, who had special petitions to make, took this favourable opportunity of approaching their master ; and all quitted the house well content. My grandfather made a gift of corn to one man, who already owed him a quantity which he could easily have repaid had he chosen to do so : to another peasant he granted permission for his son to marry without waiting until autumn,[1] and not even to wed the girl to whom he had been previously betrothed, but another woman—a soldier's widow, who had been threatened with exile from the village owing to her bad conduct : and, in addition, he gave the couple permission to live with the bride's father ; and so forth. More than this, each person present was handed a silver cup filled with strongest home-brewed brandy. In a few short words my grandfather gave the necessary orders respecting the management of the estate to the steward, and then hurried to the dining room, where supper was waiting him. Supper was very much the same sort of meal as dinner, but if possible more enjoyable, as the cool evening air had sharpened the family's appetites. When it was over, and he had wished his wife and children good-Night, Stepan Michailovitsch, as his wont was, cooled himself for half an hour on the balcony, clad only in his shirt. He had a whim to set Masan and Tanaitschenok to try their strength in a bout of fisticuffs, and he urged them on with such energy that very soon the pair were engaged in a serious scuffle and real quarrel. But my grandfather, who was already weary of the spectacle, stopped the fight, and brought the combatants to their senses with a few stern words.

The splendour of the brief summer night dwelt everywhere. The glow of the sunset shimmered unextinguished in the West, till overtaken by the first red beams of Morning. Darker and darker grew the canopy of Heaven ; clearer and clearer twinkled the stars ; louder and louder echoed the shrieks of the night-birds as they approached their haunts among the dwellings of mankind. Nearer and nearer resounded the rattle and rumble of the mill through the misty twilight. . . . My grandfather rose to his feet, gazed up towards the starry heavens, crossed himself twice ; and then, careless alike of his sultry chamber and his hot feather bed, lay down and drew the curtains close.

¹he serfs are permitted to marry. [Tr. S. R.]

SKETCH II

MICHAIL MAXIMOVITSCH KUROLESOV

I have already promised to relate the full story of Michail Maximovitsch Kurolesov and of his marriage to my grandfather's cousin—Praskovia Ivanovna Bagrova. My chronicles begin in the sixtieth year of the Eighteenth Century, consequently at an earlier date than the occurrences already related : on the other hand, the end comes very much later. And having explained this much, I hasten to fulfil my promise.

Stepan Michailovitsch was the only son of Michail Petrovitsch Bagrov ; Praskovia Ivanovna the only daughter of his uncle, Ivan Petrovitsch Bagrov. Hence my grandfather regarded her with a two-fold affection, both as the sole female shoot of the Bagrov Family, and as his only cousin. The girl lost her mother while still in infancy, and was but ten years old when her father died. The mother came of the wealthy stock of the Bakteievs, and the daughter inherited her dowry of nine hundred serfs, a large fortune, and great store of silver and jewels. To these rich possessions were added the three hundred serfs of her late father, and the orphan became a great heiress . . . and a good match ! After her father's death, she went, at first, to live with her grandmother, Madame Bakteieva ; but as time went on she visited Troizkoie more and more frequently, each time making a longer stay, until in the end Stepan Michailovitsch persuaded her to settle for good and all in his house. Stepan Michailovitsch loved his cousin as well as his own daughters and manifested his tender regard for her in his own fashion ; but Praskovia Ivanova was too young, or—to speak more justly—too childish to value her cousin's affection at its true worth ; for he never stooped to the flattery and adulation to which the girl had been accustomed in her grandmother's house. Small wonder, then, that she soon grew tired and sick of Troizkoie, and began

35

to wish herself back again in the old life with her grandmother Bakteieva. Praskovia Ivanovna was not pretty, but she had regular features, earnest, intelligent grey eyes, and the broad long, dark eyebrows which betoken a strong, and even masculine, character. She was tall, and looked fully eighteen when she was but fourteen years old. But in spite of her physical development, she was only a child in heart and mind. Her disposition was very lively and artless, and she would sing and frolic from morning to night. She had a marvellously beautiful voice, and loved romantic songs, dancing, and games. When left to herself, she would spend the whole day playing with dolls, while she beguiled her play with every possible variety of folk song, of which she knew an incredible number.

The year before she took up her abode with Stepan Michailovitsch, a young officer of some eight-and-twenty years, one Michail Maximovitsch Kurolesov, one of the native aristocracy, was spending his furlough at his home in the Government of Simbirsk. He was fairly good-looking— many indeed considered him handsome—others however affirmed, that in spite of the beauty of his features his face had something repulsive about it, and, as a child, I recollect hearing my grandmother and aunts arguing about his looks. Since his fifteenth year he had served in a regiment which enjoyed a distinguished reputation in those days, and he was already promoted major. He seldom took any leave, for with his hundred and fifty serfs and small estate, he was not able to keep up any sort of establishment. Although he had no real culture, he was very clever and adroit in conversation, and wrote in a dashing and correct style. I have several of his letters in my possession, and they prove him to have been a man of cunning and suave, withal of a firm and practical mind. I know not indeed, how he came to be related to our immortal Suvorov [1] ; but among Kurolesov's papers I find certain letters from the genial Commander-in-Chief, all of which begin as follows : " Dear Sir, and Cousin Michail Maximovitsch," and conclude in like manner. " With the expression of deepest respect for yourself, and my esteemed lady and cousin, Praskovia Ivanovna, I have the honour to remain. . . ." and so forth. Very little was known of Michail

[1] Suvorov, Alexander Vasilevisch (1729-1800) Russian field-marshal. [Tr.]

MICHAIL MAXIMOVITSCH KUROLESOV

Maximovitsch in Simbirsk ; nevertheless, " the world is full of rumour," and during his short furloughs he may have permitted himself sundry excesses, which were whispered abroad, in spite of the severity he invariably shewed towards gossiping servants. Briefly he had earned a certain reputation, which may be summed up in the following aphorism: " The Major will permit no liberties ; you must always be on your guard with him, and make no slip : he takes an interest in his soldiers and protects them to the best of his ability : but let one of them commit but the smallest fault, and he need expect no mercy : Kurolesov's word is final : as an enemy he is a match for the Devil himself —he is a fox, a madcap, a demon ! " All the same he was universally regarded as a sound man of business. Later rumours, from the same source, had it that the Major was addicted to drink, and his amours were too numerous : the latter failing however was excused by the old adage : " Such a thing brings no shame on the man " ; the former with similar excuses : " One drink is no disgrace to a man," or " He who is drunk and keeps his wits, is two steps ahead of anyone else." And they added that the Major always knew the right place and the right time for his pranks. And so it befell that Kurolesov was regarded in a charitable, and, in some quarters, even a favourable light. It is only natural to suppose that he was always careful to be amiable and polite, especially towards old and important people, so that he was welcomed everywhere. As a near neighbour and distant relative of the Bakteiev family, (through Madame Bakteieva's son-in-law, Kurmyschev), he soon found means to establish himself in her house on the most easy and familiar footing. At first he had no special design, only following his usual custom of ingratiating himself as much as possible with people of wealth and rank ; but later, noting the rich and lively young heiress, Praskovia Ivanovna, (who already looked almost a woman), he resolved to marry her and secure her fortune for himself. With a view to this end he redoubled his attentions to Praskovia's grandmother and aunt, and had soon assured himself of the support of both ladies ; while he courted the girl herself so skilfully, that she soon grew very fond of him, merely because he deferred to her in every thing, anticipated her wishes, and above all, spoilt her. Michail

Maximovitsch disclosed his love to Praskovia's relations, played the rôle of lover, and everyone believed him when he vowed his passion was wasting him away; that night and day he dreamt only of his Praskovia; and that he was crazy with love for her. He was pitied and lamented—encouraged to hope—in short he was the heart-broken lover. With such sympathetic encouragement from the relations, the rest of the comedy was an easy business. He was able to procure the girl a thousand little pleasures. He took her for drives in his carriage with his beautiful horses, he would spend hours in the swing with her, he sang her favourite folksongs with her; he made her all sorts of little presents, and sent to Moscow for beautiful playthings for her.

The consent of the cousin-guardian being absolutely necessary for the full accomplishment of his design, Michail Maximovitsch next tried his utmost to obtain the good-will of my grandfather. Under various pretexts, and amply supplied with the highest of high recommendations from Praskovia's relations, he paid several visits to Stepan Michailovitsch at his own house, but he never succeeded in gaining the old gentleman's favour in the least degree. This at first sight, may appear somewhat strange, especially as the Major possessed so many qualities in common with Stepan Michailovitsch: but over and above his sound judgment the old man possessed such a keen moral instinct for none but upright and honest people, that he could instantly detect any crooked or base traits in any man's character; he perceived evil intentions from the start, even when concealed under the most attractive exterior. The smooth speech and courteous bearing of his visitor were of no avail, and did not mislead Stepan Michailovitsch for one moment; for he instantly guessed that some sinister design underlay all this politeness. Withal, my grandfather's principles exacted a blameless course of life; and the reports of the Major's profligacy, so easily condoned by others, filled the strict old man with real aversion for Kurolesov: and although he himself in the heat of passion was capable of acts of blind fury, it horrified him to hear of people who could commit barbarities without anger and in cold blood. In consequence of these impressions, he received Michail Maximovitsch on his first visit, in the most distant manner, in spite of the latter's interesting conversation on various subjects, especially farming ; but the instant the guest turned to Praskovia Ivanovna—(who had already made her home with my grandfather)—and began treating her quite as an old friend, while the girl listened with obvious delight to his flattering remarks, my grandfather made a wry face, drew his heavy eyebrows together as was his wont when angry, and cast suspicious and unfriendly looks in Kurolesov's direction. The lady of the house and all her daughters, on the contrary, were charmed with the visitor—as he had taken good care from his first entrance into the family that they should be—he flattering them, while they were only too pleased to chat with him in the friendliest way. Unfortunately, however, the very visible signs of the approaching storm depicted upon my grandfather's countenance struck terror into their hearts, and an awkward silence ensued. In vain the guest endeavoured to start a cheery general conversation : he only elicited nervous, monosyllabic replies to his polite remarks ; and my grandfather became positively rude. Nothing remained possible for the visitor but to take his departure, although it was already late in the evening, and he had been invited, country-fashion, to spend the night. " A good-for-nothing fellow, and a scamp : and it's to be hoped he never shews his face here again ! " was Stepan Michailovitsch's verdict to his family ; who, naturally, did not venture to contradict him ; but the stately Major was very favourably discussed in the ladies' apartments—and the unsophisticated young heiress talked much, and heard much talk, of his charming manners.

After this unequivocal rebuff Michail Maximovitsch hurried back to Madame Bakteieva, and related to her the foregoing events. They knew my grandfather too well to hope that he would ever give his consent to the betrothal, after such a reception. They considered how best to appease him, but could think of nothing feasible. The bold Major proposed that the grandmother should invite the girl to stay with her, and then the wedding could take place without Stepan Michailovitsch's consent ; but Madame Bakteieva and her daughter, Madame Kurmyscheva, guessed rightly that my grandfather would never permit Praskovia to leave his house alone, so shortly after the Major's visit ; and the latter's leave was drawing near its end. Kurolesov next suggested a desperate plan : to persuade Praskovia to elope with him, to carry her off, and to marry her straightway at the nearest parish ; the relations, however, would not hear of such a scandal ; and so it came about that Michail Maximovitsch had to rejoin his regiment without having attained his object. But mysterious are the ways of Providence, nor is it in our power to comprehend how Fate willed that such evil business should be carried out successfully. Six months passed, and old Madame Bakteieva heard that Stepan Michailovitsch was preparing for a long journey. I cannot recollect whether it was to Moscow or Astrachan that he was bound, but his errand must have been one of considerable importance, as his steward accompanied him. Immediately a letter was sent to my grandfather, begging that Praskovia should be allowed to stay with her grandmother during his absence—which request received the prompt and curt reply that Praskovia was perfectly happy at Troizkoie, and anyone who wished to see her, must exert themselves to pay her a visit there. After sending this ultimatum, and after solemnly impressing upon his docile Arina Vasilievna that she must guard Praskovia as the very apple of her eye, and on no account permit her to quit Troizkoie, Stepan Michailovitsch departed on his journey.

Madame Bakteieva kept up a brisk correspondence with Praskovia and my grandfather's womenkind. So, as soon as she heard Stepan Michailovitsch was safely out of the way, she wrote and informed Michail Maximovitsch Kurolesov, adding that the old fellow would be a good while absent, and that his best plan would be to come himself and conclude the business that he had in view . . . . and that she and her daughter would meet him at Troizkoie. She and Arina Vasilievna had always been on most friendly terms, and when she learnt that the latter was very prepossessed by Kurolesov, she described how the charming young Major was dying for love of Praskovia, and sang the praises of the suitor with great warmth and energy. She added that her dearest wish was to see her darling, fatherless granddaughter married before she died ; and she felt that her beloved child would be happy with this man Kurolesov ; that she herself had not long to live, and therefore wished to hurry on the affair. On her side, Arina Vasilievna had nothing to say against the plan, but expressed great doubt whether Stepan Michailovitsch would ever give his consent ; as Michail Maximovitsch, in spite of all his perfections, in some extraordinary way had failed to please her husband. The two elder daughters of Arina Vasilievna were called to a family council, presided over by old Madame Bakteieva and her daughter, Madame Kurmyscheva—an especially ardent partisan of the Major— and it was decided to leave the entire management of the business in the hands of Praskovia's grandmother, as the girl's nearest relative—all this of course on the clear understanding that Stepan Michailovitsch's wife and daughters took no hand in the game, and were supposed to know nothing about the affair. I have already described Arina Vasilievna as a good natured and somewhat weak-minded old lady ; and as her daughters were entirely on Madame Bakteieva's side, it was quite easy to persuade her to a step which was certain to bring her husband's unbounded wrath upon her. Meanwhile the gay, heedless Praskovia was quite ignorant of her impending fate. Many allusions were made in her hearing to Michail Maximovitsch, in fact no praise was too high for that excellent man—he adored Praskovia, he loved her better than life itself—night and day he thought but of her, and she might be sure that when he next came on a visit he would bring all sorts of beautiful presents from Moscow. This sort of talk was very delightful to Praskovia Ivanovna, and she vowed that she, too, loved Michail Maximovitsch more than anyone else in the world. During Madame Bakteieva's stay at Troizkoie, a letter arrived from Kurolesov, in which he arranged to come over as soon as he could get leave. Finally the old Bakteieva and her daughter returned to their own estate, after they had persuaded Arina Vasilievna to say nothing of their visit in her letters to her husband ; and to permit Praskovia to visit her grandmother at an early date, under the pretext that the latter was dangerously ill. Praskovia Ivanovna wept and entreated permission to leave with her grandmother, especially when she heard that the Major was coming soon. But she was not allowed to leave, out of fear of Stepan Michailovitsch's anger. Kurolesov, meanwhile, had not been able to get any leave of absence as yet, and it was a good two months before he arrived on the scene. But soon after his arrival an express messenger arrived at Troizkoie, with a letter from Madame Kurmyscheva, who wrote that her mother was sick unto death, and desired to see her grand-child once more before she died ; doubtless, the letter continued, Stepan Michailovitsch would offer no objection to the girl hurrying to her grandmother's bedside to receive her dying farewell. The letter was evidently written with the intention of giving Arina Vasilievna every opportunity of exonerating herself in the eyes of Stepan Michailovitsch. True to her promise, and quite easy in her mind as to the future, Arina Vasilievna set off immediately, and conveyed Praskovia to the so-called deathbed of her grandmother, spent a week with the invalid, and returned home enchanted alike by Michail Maximovitsch's charming manners and the extremely costly presents that he had brought from Moscow for herself and her daughters. Praskovia Ivanovna was in a state of rapture ; her dearest grandmother was already better when she arrived ; and the dear kind Major was there with all sorts of lovely toys from Moscow. Not a day passed but he came to Madame Bakteieva's house, always ready to chat and joke with Praskovia— in short, he so played on the girl's affectionate and grateful heart, that, as soon as her grandmother told her he wished to make her his wife, she, mere child that she was, went wild with joy, and ran about the house telling everyone she met that she was going to marry Michail Maximovitsch—how happy they would be together— what joy to drive with him all day long with his beautiful horses ; and to swing, or sing songs, or play with dolls together—even with great big dolls, as big as babies, which could walk and curtsy. This was the sort of life anticipated by the poor little bride. The conspirators hurried on affairs, lest any rumour of what was happening should reach the cousin's ears : friends and neighbours were invited to the betrothal, the young people exchanged rings and kisses, and sat side by side in the place of honour while all present drank to their good health and happiness. At first the bride was extremely bored by all this ceremony, the endless compliments, and the long sitting-in-state ; but as she was allowed to have her new Moscow doll to sit beside her, she recovered her good humour, told the guests it was her child, and made the doll bow and curtsy her thanks for their polite congratulations. A week later the pair were married with full observance of all necessary rites, the fifteen-year-old bride being described as seventeen, a statement which her build and height fully justified. Although Arina Vasilievna and her daughters must have known that this would be the inevitable end of the plot, they heard of Praskovia's marriage with extreme terror : the scales, as it were, fell from their eyes, and they realised that neither the pretended illness of the grandmother, nor the crafty letter of Madame Kurmyscheva would save them from Stepan Michailovitsch's fury. Before the actual news of the marriage had reached Troizkoie, Arina Vasilievna had written and told her husband that she had taken Praskovia to visit her dying grandmother, that they had found the old lady somewhat better, but needing her grandchild's company in order to make a full recovery ; that she herself had returned home, not wishing to leave the girls too long by themselves—but that it would have taken force to remove Praskovia ; nevertheless she was afraid she had incurred his displeasure. Stepan Michailovitsch's reply to this letter was that Arina had behaved very stupidly, and she must set off immediately to Madame Bakteieva's house and bring Praskovia home with her. Arina Vasilievna sighed and wept over his letter, and was at her wits' end how to act in the matter. Shortly after this the young couple paid her a visit. Praskovia appeared to be perfectly happy and cheerful, though less childish and less inclined to give vent to open expressions of her happiness. The husband seemed equally happy, and withal so calm and judicious, that he quite comforted poor Arina Vasilievna by his sage counsels. He argued in his most convincing and reassuring manner that the whole of Stepan Michailovitsch's wrath would fall on the grandmother's head : that the latter, in consideration of her serious illness, had had a perfect right to anticipate Stepan Michailovitsch's consent, which would certainly have been granted in time ; that the wedding would never have taken place, had it not been that the grandmother was likely to expire any day, and leave her beloved granddaughter alone in the world—a desolate orphan—whose cousin indeed was a poor exchange for a loving grandparent. A great deal of this sort of soothing conversation took place between him and the Troizkoie ladies, accompanied by the presentation of costly gifts, which they—the ladies—accepted with the greatest pleasure, mingled with a certain amount of guilty fear. Presents were even left for Stepan Michailovitsch himself. The Major advised Arina Vasilievna not to mention anything about the marriage in her letters to her husband, but to leave the announcement to be made by the newly-married pair themselves ; and he promised that he and Praskovia Ivanovna would take the earliest opportunity of sending a long joint letter. But the fact was, he had not the slightest intention of writing to Stepan Michailovitsch : his idea was to postpone the inevitable storm as long as possible, while he made haste to establish himself firmly in his new position. Directly after his marriage he had asked for his discharge from the army, which was promptly granted. His first step was to pay visits, accompanied by his young wife, to all relations, his own as well as hers. In Simbirsk—starting with the Governor himself—he paid his respects to every person of any standing whatever. Everyone was delighted with the charming pair ; and the Major was so successful in currying favour everywhere, that very soon all the gentry of the district quite approved of the marriage. And so another few months passed.

Meanwhile Stepan Michailovitsch, who had received no letters for a long time, and whose lawsuit was still undecided, was suddenly seized with such an irresistible longing to see his home, that he set off and arrived quite unexpectedly at Troizkoie one fine morning. Arina Vasilievna trembled in every limb when she heard the awful news : The master has arrived ! Stepan Michailovitsch rushed joyfully into the house, asked if all were alive and well, clasped his Arina and his children to his heart, and then enquired : " But where is Praskovia ? " Encouraged by the loving tones of his voice, Arina Vasilievna replied with a forced laugh ; " I really do not exactly know where she is at present : probably with her grandmother. But of course you know, little father, that she

is married ! '' The astonishment and fury of my grandfather
at these words were absolutely beyond description. His rage
increased when he heard that Praskovia had married Kurolesov.
He would have attacked his wife there and then, but she and
all her daughters fell at his feet and vowed that everything
had been done without their knowledge, and that they had been
utterly deceived by Madame Bakteieva. The letter was
produced as evidence of their innocence. My grandfather's
rage was instantly directed against the old Bakteieva : he
ordered fresh horses, and after a few hours' rest set out for
her estate. It can well be imagined with what ferocity he
attacked Praskovia's old grandmother. After the first outburst the old lady adopted a haughty attitude, and set to
work in her turn to abuse my grandfather, growing more and
more heated as she proceeded. '' How dare you insult me,''
she screamed, '' do you take me for one of your serfs ? You
seem to forget that I am as good as you are, and my husband
was of much higher rank than you ! I am much more nearly
related to Praskovia than you are : I am her grandmother,
and my rights as a guardian are every bit as good as yours !
I only had her happiness in view, and I was not going to
wait for your consent, because I thought I was dying and
had no intention of leaving her at your mercy—I know you
only too well, you're a madman and a wild beast ! You knock
people about in your house. Michail Maximovitsch is a very
good match, and Praskovia was in love with him. And I should
like to know who objects to him ! Only yourself. Ask your
daughters and your wife : they can appreciate him.'' '' You
lying old harridan,'' roared my grandfather, '' you deceived
Arina, you pretended to be ill, and sold Praskovia to that
scoundrel Kurolesov, who seems to have bewitched you all ! ''
These remarks sent old Madame Bakteieva nearly beside
herself with rage, and she blurted out that Arina Vasilievna,
and her daughters too, knew everything there was to know
about the marriage, and had accepted plenty of presents
from Michail Maximovitsch. These disclosures gave a new
direction to my grandfather's anger. Threatening to separate
Praskovia from her husband on the ground of her minority,
he set off home again, calling on his way at the house of the
priest who had married the couple. He called him to account

with the utmost vehemence, but the priest calmly produced all the marriage documents, the signatures of the bride, her grandmother, and those of the witnesses, as well as Praskovia's baptismal certificate, which proved she was over seventeen years old. This was a fresh blow for my grandfather, who now lost all hope of ever being able to annul the hateful marriage, and whose fiery wrath kindled more and more against Arina Vasilievna and her daughters. I prefer not to give an exact account of what actually happened when at last he reached home. There was a frightful and horrible scene. Even thirty years later my aunts could not recall that day without a shudder. Enough that the guilty women confessed everything, that all Kurolesov's presents were sent back to Madame Bakteieva with orders to return them to the donor ; that the older daughters were ill for a very long time, that my grandmother lost most of her hair and was compelled to wear a plaster on her head for a year afterwards. The newly-married pair were advised never to shew their faces to my grandfather again, and the name of Kurolesov was forbidden to be mentioned in his house.

Meanwhile Time—that healer of soul and body, that queller of passions—flowed on its peaceful course. At the end of a year not only was Arina Vasilievna's head mended, but the feeling of resentment in Stepan Michailovitsch's heart had died away. At first, he would neither receive the Kurolesovs, nor listen to a word about them ; he refused even to read the numerous letters written to him by Praskovia Ivanovna. But towards the end of a twelvemonth, when, from every side news reached him of the perfect happiness of the young wedded pair and of the marvellous change in the character of Praskovia, who had suddenly become quiet and sensible, Stepan Michailovitsch's heart softened, and he felt a natural longing to see his beloved cousin once again. He considered rightly, that she was the least to blame of any-one connected with the affair, being but a child, and he granted her permission to visit Troizkoie, unaccompanied, however, by her husband. Naturally she hurried over to see her cousin at once. And the vast change in Praskovia Ivanovna after a year of marriage aroused my grandfather's veritable astonishment. How could it have been otherwise, indeed ! The past year had awakened a great tenderness and affection for her cousin, which she had never felt for him in bygone days ; and which, considering the circumstances of her secret marriage, was absolutely incredible. Could it be that those eyes which overflowed with tears, as he greeted her on her arrival, revealed to her what deep love was concealed under the rough exterior and surly obstinacy of this man ? Did some vague foreboding of the dark future warn her that here was the real stay and support of her life ? Did she at last comprehend that amongst all those who had flattered and caressed her in childhood, no one had loved her more truly than the cross old cousin, who had tried to wreck her happiness and who hated her darling husband ? I know not, but all were astounded at the change in the demeanour of the frivolous girl towards her cousin. She, who in former days had refused to recognise his right of guardianship or her duty towards him as his ward—(and who now had real grounds for offence, in consequence of his brutal behaviour towards her own grandmother)—met him as an affectionate sister, or even a devotedly-attached daughter, returning to an adored father. Be that as it may, this sudden sympathy, this deep affection, only ended with life itself. And how marvellous was the transformation which Praskovia's whole nature had undergone in this short time ! The thoughtless child had vanished for ever, and in her place was a serenely-cheerful, but thoughtful woman. She candidly admitted that everyone had done her cousin the greatest wrong ; but pleaded in extenuation of their deceit, her own childish ignorance, and the blind love of her grandmother, her husband, and all the other relatives, for herself. She did not press for the immediate pardon of her husband—the greatest offender of all ; she only ventured to hope—that in time, and when he saw how happy she was, and with what zeal and ardour her husband looked after all her interests—Cousin Stepan Michailovitsch would forgive Kurolesov, and ask him to come to Troizkoie. Stepan Michailovitsch was so much touched by Praskovia's humility that he could not reply. He did not keep his good little cousin, as he henceforth invariably called her, long, but sent her back home to her husband after a short stay at Troizkoie, saying her place was with the latter. On parting with her, he said : " If, at the end of another year, you and your husband are as happy together as you now are ; and if he goes on as well as he has done, then he and I will be reconciled."

And, indeed, at the year's end, during which time he had frequently met his cousin and seen how happy and contented with her lot she was, Stepan Michailovitsch wrote, and said : " Come ; and bring your husband to see me ! " The old gentleman greeted Kurolesov with the utmost friendliness, told him frankly that he had had serious objections to him at first, and vowed that if he continued to behave well to Praskovia, he should be recognised as a loved and esteemed member of the family. Michail Maximovitsch's behaviour was perfect—not so flattering and obsequious as formerly, but most attentive, polite, and respectful. It was plain that he had acquired perfect independence and self-reliance. He talked a great deal about his intention of taking over the full management and control of Praskovia's estates ; asked my grandfather for his advice ; was very quick to comprehend, and marvellously quick to utilise the latter's valuable information. He even discovered a distant relationship which he explained existed between his family and the Bagrovs' before his marriage, and addressed my grandfather as Uncle, while Arina Vasilievna was Aunt, and their children Cousins. Even before the reconciliation he had seized an opportunity of doing Stepan Michailovitsch a service. My grandfather was aware of this, and while thanking him for his kindness, bade him ask a like favour in return. In short, all passed off famously. Appearances were entirely in favour of Michail Maximovitsch, but my grandfather kept his opinion unchanged : " Yes," said he, " the man is clever, and sensible, and prudent ; but trust him I never could, and never can."

So another year passed away, in the course of which Stepan Michailovitsch emigrated to the Province of Ufa. Kurolesov's conduct during the first three years after his marriage was so orderly and discreet, or at least so circumspect, that nothing adverse came to light. Besides, he was very seldom at home, and spent the whole of his time travelling. At the same time a rumour arose and spread abroad that the young master was somewhat too severe. During the two following years

MICHAIL MAXIMOVITSCH KUROLESOV

Kurolesov effected such wonderful improvements in the entire management and direction of his wife's estates that folks were lost in wonder at his tireless activity, his love of enterprise, and his iron will. Previously to his taking them in hand, Praskovia's estates had been in a very neglected state. In many instances they were going to wreck and ruin owing to the lazy habits of the peasantry. Very little income was paid, not because there was no market for the country produce, but because some of the lands were very ill-cultivated, while in other parts the proportion of arable land was very small ; and Praskovia owned the estates in common with her grandmother Bakteieva and her aunt Kurmyscheva. Michail Maximovitsch arranged to transport the serfs to new properties, and to sell the old property very advantageously. He first purchased seven thousand dessiatines of Steppe land in the District of Stavropol, in the Province of Simbirsk (now Samara). This was most excellent land in the Black Soil Belt, and was two ells deep in rich soil ; it was situated on the banks of the rivulet Berlia, round whose springs grew but a scanty forest ; besides this, the ban-forest, called the Bears' Glen, was the only wood on the whole estate. To this part he conveyed three hundred and fifty of the serfs. In this way he established a highly productive estate, only a hundred versts from Samara ; and distant sixty and forty versts respectively from other Volga ports. It is a recognised fact that a convenient market for corn and other produce is the crowning excellence of a good estate. His next act was to journey to the Government of Ufa, where he purchased from the Baskhirs some twenty thousand dessiatines of land, also black earth, but very inferior to the Simbirsk property as it included a considerable amount of forest lands. This land lay in several plots on the banks of the river Usen, and beside the rivulets of the Siuiusch, Meleus, Karmalka, and Belebeika ; and at that time belonged, if I recollect aright to the Menselinsk Circuit : now it is included in the Belebei Circuit in the Government of Orenburg. Michail Maximovitsch sent four hundred and fifty of his people to the well-watered neighbourhood of the Siuiusch ; and fifty men were settled on the banks of the Belebieka. To the larger colony he gave the name of Paraschino, the smaller colony he called Ivanovka, the estate in the Simbirsk Government was called Kurolesovo, and thus the three properties were respectively called by the baptismal,[1] paternal, and married names of his wife. This piece of sentiment on the part of a man, whom I shall shortly have occasion to portray in such dark colours, has always filled me with astonishment. For his own residence he chose Tschurasovo, an estate which Praskovia had inherited from her mother, and which was situated only fifty versts distant from the capital of the Government. There he built what, in those days, was considered a most magnificent house, surrounded by equally splendid stables and other buildings. The fittings of the house, furniture, indoor and outdoor decorations, chandeliers and candelabra, bronzes and china and the superb silver plate, were the admiration of all who saw them. This beautiful house was situated on the slope of a gently-swelling hill, from which gushed more than twenty most abundant springs. House, wooded slope, and springs were all surrounded by extensive and luxuriant gardens full of the finest fruit trees of every variety. The household arrangements—servants, cuisine, horses and carriages—everything betokened the most refined and fastidious luxury. Visitors, both from the neighbourhood—where many landed gentry and nobles resided—and from the city, were never lacking at Tschurasovo : life there was an endless round of feasting, drinking, singing, card-playing, and chatter. Michail Maximovitsch was very particular that his Praskovia should always be richly and elegantly dressed, and, whenever he was at home, seemed solely occupied with her, and the carrying out of her slightest wish. Briefly, at the end of a few years he had attained such a footing in society, that good folks admired, while bad folks envied, him. Nor did Michail Maximovitsch neglect his religious duties, and in place of the shabby old wooden church, in two years arose a stately stone-built edifice, decorated in exquisite taste, and even possessing a quite passable choir, chosen from amongst the servants, and trained under the master's guidance. Four years after her marriage, a little daughter was born to the happy and contented Praskovia, and a year later came a little son. But the children did not live long : the girl died before she was a year old, and the boy

[1] Parascha is a diminutive of Praskovia. [Tr. H. R.]

when he was scarcely three. Praskovia Ivanovna was most tenderly attached to the little boy, and his loss affected her most deeply. For a whole year she took no interest in anything; her once-blooming health faded and vanished; and she never had another child.

All this time the consequence and dignity of Michail Maximovitsch increased in the country with every day, and every hour. The poor and obscure nobility had certainly a good deal to endure from his arrogant and despotic demeanour; and by this class of neighbours he was more feared than loved : but the upper ranks of nobles were by no means displeased with his methods of reminding the lower ranks of their inferior position. Each year Michail Maximovitsch's absences from home had grown longer and more frequent, especially since the unhappy year when Praskovia Ivanovna refused to be comforted for the loss of her son. It would seem that the tears and lamentations of his wife had been wearisome to him ; and that the deserted house—for Praskovia Ivanovna would receive no company—had bored him. Be that as it may, there soon came a time when even the glittering company assembled at Tschurasovo ceased to charm him.

Strange rumours meanwhile arose, which grew and spread in all directions : it was whispered that the Major was not merely severe, as had been reported of him in his earlier days, but he had begun to treat his retainers with cruelty : that he went so frequently to his estates in Ufa in order that he might give himself up to unrestrained drunkenness and vice of every possible description : that he had gathered together an unholy company who practised abominations under his directions : that the worst thing about him was the unutterable cruelties that he inflicted on his serfs when he was intoxicated ; and that already two men had died under torture. It was also said that all the higher officials in both of the districts where his new estates were situated, were entirely on his side : he having bribed some and persuaded others to become his boon companions, while he instilled terror into everyone : the lower officials and the lesser nobility trembled before him, for he was wont, if anyone displeased him, to lay hold of him in broad daylight, carry him off, throw him into a cellar, where he was nearly perished with cold and hunger, and not infrequently flogged with a frightful whip called a *Cat*.[1]

Not only were these rumours true, but they only gave hints of the truth, the facts being far worse than the timid peasants dared relate. The bloodthirsty nature of Kurolesov had developed to such a pitch under the influence of spirituous liquor that humanity shuddered at it. It was a hideous combination of a tiger's instinct and human intellect.

Finally rumours became certainty, and no one in Praskovia's neighbourhood had any more doubts as to the fearful truth. Whenever Michail Maximovitsch visited Tschurasovo for a rest between his criminal periods, his manner of old times was quite unchanged—always friendly and respectful towards his equals, and polite and affectionate with his wife, who was now consoled for the loss of her children, and was once more surrounded by a cheerful circle of friends. Although Michail Maximovitsch was careful never to lay a finger upon a soul in Tschurasovo, where all punishment was administered by the steward, yet everyone in the house trembled at the sound of his voice. Likewise, in the manner of any relatives or intimate friends who had any intercourse with him, an unmistakeable aversion could be detected. But of all this Praskovia Ivanovna saw nothing, or if she did, she attributed it to some other cause—the universal esteem and the involuntary respect, which her husband's wonderful abilities, self-won wealth, and energetic will, excited in all hearts. Kind folks, who loved Praskovia Ivanovna, rejoiced at her ignorance of the real truth, for she was both gay and serene, and they wished to prolong her happiness as long as possible. It is true that many a female to-day, and many a woman of small social importance, would have only been too delighted to take an opportunity of revenging herself upon the insolent Major—with his high and mighty manners towards his inferiors—by unmasking his real character. But over and above the actual fear inspired by the Major himself, another formidable obstacle stood in the way of such exposure. This

---

[1] This Cat was Michail Maximovitsch's favourite instrument of torture. It was a scourge of seven leathern lashes, each knotted at the end. After Kurolesov's death it was kept for many years in a lumber room at Paraschino. When the estate came into the possession of Stepan Michailovitsch's son, the Cat was burnt.

was the attitude taken by Praskovia Ivanovna herself, who would not tolerate the slightest criticism of her husband. She was too acute not to notice any sly attempt to introduce the subject into the conversation ; and without waiting to hear any more, would bring her dark brows close together, remarking in her severest tone, that anyone who had a word to say against her husband should never enter her home again. Naturally, after such an outspoken warning, no one dare utter another word. Her own personal attendants—an old and favourite servant of her father and her own faithful nurse—of whom she made great favourites—(without however making them her confidants, as was customary among ladies of rank in those times)—were quite unable to speak frankly to her. Both these old people had only too much reason to wish their mistress to know the real character of her husband, as they had near relations in the master's service, who had plenty to suffer from his unrestrained outbreaks of fury. Finally, however, they decided to tell their mistress everything, and chose a moment when she was alone to speak to her. But scarcely had the name of Michail Maximovitsch been uttered, when the once easy-going Praskovia Ivanovna flew into a rage : she threatened her old nurse with banishment for life to Paraschino, if she ever dared to mention the master's name again. By such acts she closed every avenue to the truth and sealed the lips of those who had so much to disclose. Praskovia Ivanovna loved her husband and trusted him implicitly. She knew only too well how ready folks are to interfere with others' concerns : how eager to fish in troubled waters : and once and for all, she made a firm resolution and fixed principle, never to permit her husband's behaviour to be discussed in her presence. A most praiseworthy principle, indispensable to the maintenance of family concord ! But even to this excellent precept exceptions must sometimes be made, of which the present case is an example. Had Praskovia's strong will—backed up by the circumstance that all the property was hers by right—been brought to bear as a check upon her husband, he might have been persuaded to give up his greed of wealth and power—his unbridled and furious passions would not have had free rein—and like many another, he might have lived a reasonable and happy life.

Another year passed—Michail Maximovitsch gave himsel.
up, unchecked, to his furious instincts, which, increasing and
developing, urged him on to commit fouler abominations,
which went unpunished. I prefer not to describe the details
of the horrible life he led when living on his distant estates,
especially at Paraschino and the little District town : the story
is too loathsome to repeat. I shall therefore confine myself
to mentioning only what is necessary to give the reader
an idea of this atrocious man. In the year following his
marriage he devoted himself in the most energetic and even
disinterested way to the numerous duties connected with the
administration of his wife's estates. His ability, prudence,
and industry were beyond praise. He undertook the arduous,
wearisome, and complicated task of conveying great numbers
of peasants to distant parts ; and his indefatigable and skilful
management was exerted solely for the benefit and well-being
of the serfs. For this end he spared neither money nor pains,
and saw that everyone was duly and fully furnished with
everything needful. He thus provided against any risk of want
or distress. He himself superintended the departure from the
old homestead, accompanied the expedition a great part of
the journey, then went on in advance to be ready to receive
the emigrants on their arrival at their carefully-selected and
comfortable new dwelling-places. True enough that he was
severe, if not cruel, towards offenders. But against this
severity might be set his justice to, and fair treatment of,
good workers ; and he knew when to keep his eyes closed.
From time to time, it is true, he would break out, and spend
a couple of riotous days in some little town ; but he could
throw off the effects of his drunkenness as easily as a goose
shakes water off her feathers, and after such an interlude
would only return with renewed zest to his interrupted labours.

At first this overwhelming mass of duties occupied his
mind and hindered him from giving himself up to his ruinous
habit of drinking, which aroused all his unnatural instincts.
Hard work saved him for a time. But no sooner were the new
estates of Paraschino and Kurolesovo in working order, and
all the houses, huts, and farm buildings ready for occupation,
than he had too much time and too little occupation, and gave
himself up wholly to drinking with his boon companions.

MICHAIL MAXIMOVITSCH KUROLESOV

His innate cruelty developed into a mad lust for torture and bloodshed. Encouraged by the terror and submissiveness of all around him, he rapidly lost all sense of humanity, and revelled in unrestrained acts of violence and brigandage. From among his servants and serfs he collected a body-guard of a couple of dozen infamous rascals, and organised these worthy instruments of his will into a veritable robber band. As these followers observed that their master was permitted to do exactly as he liked and that his maddest tricks went unpunished, they naturally grew to regard him as almighty ; and, themselves drunkards and ruffians, were only too ready and willing to carry out his most outrageous commands. Had anyone offended Michail Maximovitsch in word or deed, even in such a small matter as failing to arrive at the appointed hour for a drinking-bout, it needed but a sign, and the trusty retainers set off in all haste, seized the delinquent—wherever he might happen to be, either openly or secretly—and dragged him before their master, who ordered him to be chained, knocked about, as often as not soundly flogged, and then locked up in the cellar. Michail Maximovitsch was a great lover of a fine horse ; and he also admired fine furniture and pictures. When he took a fancy to anything he saw in a neighbour's or any stranger's house, he invariably offered the owner something of his own in exchange. Should the owner decline the proposal, Michail Maximovitsch, if he happened to be in a good humour, would then offer to buy the coveted possession. If this were also refused, he simply remarked he would have the article for nothing. And he would shortly make his appearance surrounded by his brigand retainers, and take the object by force. Complaints in a court of justice were of no avail, for the police were perfectly aware that any official who dared to take the step of following up a complaint by a visit of enquiry, would soon make a close acquaintance with the Cat. The end of all these affairs was that Kurolesov was left in undisturbed possession of his ill-gotten goods, while the unlucky owner as often as not would be nearly beaten to death in his own house, in the presence of his family, who would beseech mercy in vain. Even worse acts of violence were committed, likewise with impunity. After a time Michail Maximovitsch made attempts to conciliate his victims ; he either gave them money, or forced them by threats to promise not to bring any farther claim against him ; and thus the stolen property became legally his. When carousing with his friends, he was fond of boasting that the little portrait in the gold frame, hanging there on the wall, had been taken by him from such-and-such a gentleman ; the writing table with gilt-bronze mounts from another ; the silver cup out of which he was drinking from a third ; and it was not an uncommon thing that the men named were actually sitting at the table, either pretending to hear nothing, or stifling their anger and joining in the general laughter which followed these confessions. Michail Maximovitsch had nerves of iron, and could drink an amazing quantity of brandy without losing his wits. Drunkenness never stupified him, it excited him and aroused a demoniac activity in his disordered brain and deranged organisation. When he was fully primed with drink, his greatest delight was to have horses harnessed to every available vehicle in the place, fill these with his guests and servants, and then, amid the tinkling of the horses' bells and the wild songs and shrieks of the whole company, to dash at full gallop over the neighbouring plains and through the villages. A good supply of brandy was always taken on these excursions, and it was one of his jokes to invite anyone he met, irrespective of age or sex, to drink with him. Should the wayfarer refuse the favour, he or she got a thrashing. The offenders were tied to trees, posts, or fences, regardless of rain or cold. I refrain from relating other and more revolting stories. . . . In such a frame of mind as this he galloped one day through a village. As he dashed past a threshing-floor, where a peasant and his family were busy threshing, he noticed a woman of singular beauty. " Halt ! " shouted Michail Maximovitsch to his servants. "What do you say to this woman, Petruschka ? " " The deuce ! " cried Petruschka, " she is far too good-looking ! " " Will you marry her ? " " How can I marry another man's wife ? " retorted Petruschka, laughing. " You'll soon see how, Hey, children ! Seize her, and pack her into my carriage ! " Away they flew to the next parish and in spite of the poor woman's protestations that she already had a husband and two children, she was then and there married to Petruschka. No one dared report this crime to any magistrate, and it was only in later years, when the property came into the hands of the younger Bagrov, that the woman and her husband and children were restored to the real owner ; her first husband was long since dead. Bagrov returned a great deal of stolen property to the original owners, but a large portion was never claimed by anyone and mouldered away in lumber rooms. I suspect the reader will find it difficult to believe that the commission of such open crimes was possible in Russia, and only eighty years ago ; but there is no doubt as to the accuracy of my tale.

But however infamous this unbridled debauchery and boundless tyranny were, something still more horrible developed in Michail Maximovitsch's disposition—an ever-increasing instinct of cruelty and lust of blood. To torture men became an obsession with him. When he had no victim to flog, he grew peevish, restless, even ill ; hence his visits to Tschurasovo became shorter and less frequent. But once back at his beloved Paraschino, and he hastened to make up for lost time. Examination and regulation of all domestic affairs furnished him with rich opportunities to inflict punishment ; for the slightest irregularity was dealt with in the most barbarous manner ; and where is the household where some small fault or act of neglect cannot be found, if it is only sought ? In a general way, the whole weight of his tyranny fell almost exclusively on the house servants. It was very rarely, and then only under exceptional circumstance, that he would permit a peasant to be flogged ; and in consequence the stewards and overseers had as much to suffer at his hands as the household. He spared no one, and every one in his personal service had been at least once, and not infrequently several times, beaten nearly to death. It is a fact that Michail Maximovitsch would never order anyone to be flogged when he himself was in a furious passion and screaming with rage, as frequently happened : when he wished to practice his barbarity on anyone, he would address him in a calm, almost gentle, tone, after this manner : " Now, my dear friend, Grigori Kusmitsch, I am very sorry indeed to have to do it, but we have a little business to settle between us." With words such as these, he would turn to his head-groom,

Kovliaga, who, God knows why, was the person most frequently entrusted with the execution of his vile practices. " Let the pussy-cat scratch him ! " he would say, smiling at the other servants, and then would begin a long torture for the unfortunate which Michail Maximovitsch would witness, as he sat comfortably drinking his tea mixed with brandy, smoking his pipe, and cracking jokes about the sufferer, as long as the latter was conscious. Credible witnesses have assured me that the sole means of restoring life to the miserable victims was by wrapping the freshly-stripped skins of slaughtered sheep round their bleeding bodies. After gloating his full on the tortured man, Michail Maximovitsch would be sated with the spectacle, and would say : " Enough ; carry him off ! " and for the rest of the day, and sometimes even for several days, would be especially cheerful and even amiable. But just to finish off the characteristics of this monster, I will add one of his precepts that he was wont to impress upon his boon companions : " I object to sticks and knouts," he often remarked, " you can so easily kill a man with them before anyone has had time to enjoy anything. That's why I prefer my kitten, she makes folks smart and is not dangerous." I have not told the tenth part of what I know of this man's doings, but I think I have told more than enough. I must not forget, however, to observe that a singular freak of human nature was manifested in Michail Maximovitsch, who, throughout all his paroxysms of savagery and tyranny, was busily occupied with the building of his fine stone church at Paraschino. At the time reached in my narrative, the outside fabric of the church was already completed, while the whole of his own dwelling house was crowded with carpenters, wood-carvers, gilders, painters, etc., etc., who were busy with the beautiful inside decorations.

Praskovia Ivanovna had now been married about fourteen years, and if she noticed anything strange in her husband's manner, who very, very seldom came to see her now, she was still very far from knowing, or even suspecting, his true character. She led her usual quiet and happy life. In the summer she tended her luxuriant gardens and her beautiful gushing springs, which she would never suffer to be enclosed, and which she herself would dredge and clear from all obstructions. In winter she was greatly in request among her hosts of friends, and she had grown passionately fond of card-playing. Suddenly a letter arrived from a relative of her husband, an old lady for whom she entertained a great regard. The letter contained a full and detailed account of all Michail Maximovitsch's outrageous doings ; and, in conclusion, the writer explained that she considered it nothing short of a crime to leave the mistress of a thousand souls in ignorance of the condition of her retainers—crushed as they were beneath the tyranny of her own husband—when it was a simple matter for her to rescue them by depriving the madman of all authority. The blood of the innocent victims cried to Heaven, she wrote, and her own personal servant, Ivan Anufriev was lying at death's door, in consequence of Kurolesov's ill-treatment. As for Praskovia Ivanovna, she need have no fear about acting ; she was under the protection of the Governor and her own good friends, and Michail Maximovitsch would never dare to come to Tschurasovo. The letter had the effect of a thunderbolt on Praskovia Ivanovna. She has often told me that, for a few minutes after reading it, she remained as if unconscious. But her extraordinary strength of character and her firm trust in God came to her aid ; her agony of soul was conquered, and she resolved on a plan of action over which many a bold man would have hesitated. She ordered the horses to be put in her calash, giving an urgent errand to the Government capital as a pretext, and set straightway out for Paraschino—accompanied only by one man-servant, and a maid. The journey was long, more than four hundred versts, and she had plenty of time to reflect on the danger of the step she was taking. But as Praskovia Ivanovna was wont to relate in after days, she made no plans, and came to no decision on the way. She wished to see, with her own eyes, how her husband really spent his time when on his estates. The frightful letter of the old lady had not entirely convinced her of his guilt, as the writer lived at a great distance, and possibly might have been misled by exaggerated reports. She had not liked to question her old nurse at Tschurasovo. The idea of personal danger never even entered her mind ; her husband had always been so uniformly kind and loving towards her, that it appeared to her quite a simple matter to persuade Michail Maximovitsch to return to Tschurasovo with her. She arrived—as she had intended to arrive—at Paraschino late in the evening, left her carriage at the boundary fence, and went very softly, accompanied only by her two servants, through all the outbuildings to the back door of the wing of the house, where she saw lights and from whence issued a confused medley of songs, shouts and laughter. Her hand never trembled as she opened the door. The scene which presented itself to her gaze lacked nothing to prove the manner of life led by her husband. Even tipsier than usual, he sat drinking with his already drunken guests. Clad in a red silk shirt, his face a mask of coarse sensuality, he grasped a glass of punch in one hand, while his left arm encircled the waist of a beautiful woman who was seated in his lap. Before him sang and danced the whole household of half-intoxicated servants. Praskovia Ivanovna took everything in with a glance—almost fainting she tottered back, shut the door behind her, and left the house. Outside, on the steps, she met one of her husband's servants, an elderly—and fortunately sober—man. He recognised his mistress and exclaimed : " Little mother, Praskovia Ivanovna, is it you ? " Here Praskovia Ivanovna made signs to him to keep silence, until they reached the middle of the court-yard, when she spoke to him in very severe tones : " So this is the way you all spend your time here ! Your merry life shall soon come to an end ! " The man threw himself at her feet, and weeping, exclaimed : " Little mother, do you really believe we have merry lives here ? God Himself has sent you ! " Praskovia Ivanovna again ordered him to be quiet, and to shew her where Ivan Anufriev, whom she heard was still alive, was lying ill. She was conducted to the covered cattle-sheds, and there, in a hut near the cows' stalls, she found the dying Anufriev. He was so exhausted that he was unable to speak a word. But his brother Alexei, a poor youth who had been unmercifully flogged on the preceding day, crawled slowly and painfully from his pallet of straw, knelt down, and told the dreadful stories of his brother, himself, and many others.[1]

[1] Ivan Anufriev did not die, but lived to be fifty years old, his brother however never recovered from the effects of the ill-treatment, and died a year later.

MICHAIL MAXIMOVITSCH KUROLESOV

Praskovia's heart was like to break with pity and horror ; her conscience reproached her bitterly, and she resolved to make a speedy end to Michail Maximovitsch's cruel reign— a simple matter, as she then thought. She gave strict orders that the master should not be informed of her arrival ; and, as she heard that in the unfinished part of the great house there was a quite habitable room, where Michail Maximovitsch was accustomed to despatch business and regulate his accounts, she resolved to spend the rest of the night there, intending to talk to her husband in the morning, when he should be sober. But the report of her arrival had already got abroad. One of the most sinister of Michail Maximovitsch's companions whispered a word in his master's ear. In an instant Kurolesov's intoxication vanished : he recognised his danger. Although he knew but little of his wife's masculine character, having so far done nothing to bring it into play, still he had a suspicion of her real strength of mind. He dismissed his drunken crew, two pails of cold water were dashed over his head, and, refreshed in mind and body, he dressed himself decently and tried to ascertain whether his wife was asleep or not. Already he had resolved on his plan of action. He was quite convinced, and rightly too, that someone had informed Praskovia Ivanovna of his conduct ; and not being quite satisfied as to the truth of the tale, she had come to see the state of things for herself. He knew that she had been a witness of the midnight revels ; but what he did *not* know was that she had seen Ivan Anufriev and spoken to Alexei. In spite of the nocturnal Saturnalia, he still hoped to make his peace with her. He prepared to play the part of the repentant sinner with great pathos, to appeal to his wife's affection, and to get her out of Paraschino as quickly as possible.

Meanwhile the morning dawned and the sun rose. Michail Maximovitsch went softly to Praskovia Ivanovna's room, opened the door cautiously, and saw from the condition of the bed, hastily prepared for her overnight, that it had never been occupied. He gazed into the interior of the chamber. Praskovia Ivanovna knelt weeping and praying to the cross on the spire of the newly-built church, which could be seen glittering against the sky from the open window, as there was no ikon suspended in the room. After a pause, Kurolesov addressed his wife quite gaily, and said : " My dearest, you have prayed quite long enough ! Now what put it into your head to pay me this delightful visit ? " Praskovia Ivanovna rose to her feet, and without losing any of her composure refused her husband's embrace, while in cold and severe tones she told him that she knew everything and had seen Ivan Anufriev. Relentlessly she expressed her utter abhorrence of the bloodthirsty wretch, and told him that henceforth he was no husband of hers. She informed him that he must instantly deliver up the power of attorney for the administration of all her estates, and leave Paraschino ; should he ever venture to shew himself in her presence again, or even be seen upon any of her land, she would inform the Government of his misdeeds and have him sent to penal servitude in Siberia. Michail Maximovitsch was not prepared for this sort of talk. He fairly foamed with rage. " How dare you speak to me like this ! " he bellowed. " Very good, my little pigeon ! Then I can speak to you in a different tone. You shall never leave Paraschino until you have given me a deed-of-purchase of the whole of your estates. If you do not agree to this, you may go and starve in the cellar." And without more ado, he seized a stick which stood in a corner, threw his Praskovia violently on the floor, and beat her until she lost consciousness. Then, calling some of his trusty servants, he bade them carry the mistress down to the vault, fastened the door with a massive padlock, and put the key in his pocket. All the household were summoned to his presence, and in the most stern and threatening tones he enquired who had conducted Praskovia Ivanovna to the cattle-sheds. But that guilty person had long since absconded, and Praskovia's coachman and manservant had fled with him ; only the servant maid could not make up her mind to abandon her mistress. Michail Maximovitsch did not hurt the girl, but, giving her some instructions as to how to persuade her lady to listen to reason, he himself locked her up in the cellar with Praskovia. And what did the monster then ? He recommenced his orgies with the most unbounded zest. But in vain he swallowed his brandy, in vain his besotted crew of servants danced and sang around him. . . . Michail

Maximovitsch grew gloomy and uneasy. Still this gloom in no way discouraged him from pursuing his purpose in the most indefatigable way. He had a legal deed-of-purchase of the estates of Paraschino and Kurolesovo drawn up in the name of one of his worthy friends, and duly executed in the neighbouring district town. As an act of grace, Tschurasovo was left in Praskovia's possession. Twice a day he visited his wife in the cellar and tried to persuade her to sign the deed. He entreated her to pardon him for his violence, which was the act of a moment of rage ; promised never to come near her if she would only consent ; and assured her that in the event of his death all should be left to her. But Praskovia Ivanovna, aching from his blows, exhausted by hunger, and ravaged by fever, would not give up her rights. So passed five days. Heaven alone knows how it all might have ended.

All this time Stepan Michailovitsch was living tranquilly in his New Bagrovo, about a hundred and twenty versts distant from Paraschino. I have already said that he had long since been perfectly reconciled to Michail Maximovitsch and, although he had no special liking for the man, still on the whole he was quite satisfied with his behaviour. On his side, Kurolesov always treated my grandfather and his whole family with the greatest respect and politeness. Since the establishment of Paraschino, and his own residence on that estate, he had paid a yearly visit to Bagrovo, on which occasions he was exceedingly pleasant and amiable ; consulted Stepan Michailovitsch, as one experienced in all matters concerned with settlements and emigration ; took notes of all he heard, for which he expressed extreme gratitude ; and knew, too, how to profit by the information. Twice he had invited Stepan Michailovitsch to visit him at Paraschino, in order to see for himself how his advice had been followed. My grandfather was quite enchanted by the perfection of the new estate, and, on his last visit, after examining all the fields and buildings, had exclaimed : " Well, friend Michail, you are young, but already a master farmer : you have nothing more to·learn from me ! " And, in truth, Kurolesov's management of the estate left nothing to be desired. As may well be imagined, he parted from his old guest with every conceivable expression of regard and respect. After a few years, however,

63

unfavourable reports of Kurolesov began to be whispered in Bagrovo. At first these rumours were never mentioned in my grandfather's hearing, as he would never tolerate any slander or scandal : all the same, the rumours grew and increased. Stepan Michailovitsch's family got to hear about Kurolesov's behaviour, and one fine day Arina Vasilievna resolved to enlighten her husband as to the sort of debauched life led by Michail Maximovitsch. The old man refused to believe the report, and said that if anyone chose to pay heed to gossip he might expect to hear the vilest tales about his neighbours. " I am only too well aware," he added, " of the sort of folks the Bakteievian peasants are—a pack of lazy neer-do-weels and sluggards ; even my brother's own serfs were ruined by those women. Small wonder that they find regular work burdensome ! Perhaps Michail has changed everything a little too suddenly, but the fellows ought to be accustomed to the new management by now. And if he does take a drop too much now and then, after slaving himself nearly to death, it's no very great crime for a man, especially if it doesn't lead him to neglect his work. What you have told me would be disgusting enough, if it were true, but it is nothing but a pack of lies ; and I cannot understand how you and your daughters can listen to such servants' tittle tattle ! " After this withering reply no one ventured to refer to the subject again. Eventually, however, certain peasants who had formerly belonged to the Bagrov family, who from time to time came to visit their relations at New-Bagrovo, brought the most frightful tales of their master's cruelty. Arina Vasilievna thereupon tackled her husband a second time, and entreated him to interview the parish magistrate of Paraschino, a former Bagrov peasant himself, and a man whose integrity and veracity were beyond all question. This man was on a visit to New-Bagrovo, and my grandfather consented to see him. After hearing the magistrate's tale of horror, which fairly made his hair stand on end, my grandfather was completely at a loss how to act. It was very rarely indeed that he heard from Praskovia Ivanovna, and when he had news she seemed to be perfectly happy and peaceful. Evidently she suspected nothing of her husband's conduct. He himself, in earlier days, had advised her never to permit anyone to criticise her husband's behaviour in her presence ; and he now perceived that his counsel had been only too well observed. Moreover he reflected that if she were informed of the actual state of affairs, she could do nothing to help, and the knowledge would only cause her useless pain. Under the circumstances he preferred to let her remain in ignorance. He always had the utmost objection to interfering in anyone's business, and in the case of Kurolesov he considered it quite unnecessary. " May he break his neck, or be called up for a criminal enquiry,—and serve him right, too. Only God Himself can cure the fellow. He treats his peasants decently, and if he knocks the house-servants about, they are a lot of idle vagabonds who deserve what they get. I am not going to be mixed up with any disgusting tales." With this resolve my grandfather let the matter rest. He contented himself by not replying to Kurolesov's letters and by ceasing to hold any communication with him. The latter understood perfectly what was meant by this and left the old gentleman alone. The correspondence between Stepan Michailovitsch and Praskovia Ivanovna, however, grew more frequent and more affectionate than ever.

Such was the state of affairs when suddenly the three fugitives from Paraschino made their appearance at New-Bagrovo. The day following their escape had been spent in the impenetrable, marshy forests which lay around the great threshing-ground of Paraschino. During the night they had received secret visits from peasants on the estate, who had told them all that had happened to their mistress ; and they had hurried direct to Stepan Michailovitsch, as Praskovia Ivanovna's natural protector. One may well imagine the state of Stepan Michailovitsch's mind when he heard of the happenings at Paraschino. He loved his cousin as dearly, if not indeed more dearly, than his own daughters. Praskovia cruelly used by her ruthless husband, Praskovia starving in a damp dungeon—perhaps already dead—the awful picture stood so clearly before his eyes that the old man sprang to his feet almost beside himself with agony, and, rushing through the courtyard and into the village, summoned his serfs and servants together. All crowded round him : the labourers quitted the fields : all—sharing the sorrow and anxiety of their beloved master—cried with one voice that they would accompany him and rescue Praskovia Ivanovna. In less than two hours three great wagons, to which my grandfather's own fiery stallions were harnessed, were dashing on their way to Paraschino. They carried twelve of the sturdiest young men among the peasantry and servants, as well as the refugees from Paraschino, who were armed with muskets, swords, pikes, and pitch-forks. Towards evening two similar wagons set out, drawn by the pick of the peasants' horses, and each containing ten men similarly equipped, ready to help Stepan Michailovitsch in case of need. On the evening of the following day the first expedition halted only seven versts distant from Paraschino ; the weary horses were baited, and, in the first twilight of the summer dawn, the carts clattered into the wide courtyard of the mansion, and drew up before the door of the vault, close to the neighbouring building occupied by Kurolesov. Stepan Michailovitsch sprang to the door, and knocked loudly. From within a feeble voice said : " Who is there ? " My grandfather recognised the voice of his cousin, and weeping for joy at finding her still living, crossed himself and shouted : " God be praised ! It is I—your cousin—Stepan Michailovitsch. You have nothing to fear now ! " He instantly gave the servants orders to find Praskovia's calash and harness the horses, and six armed men were told off to guard the approach to the cellar, while he himself, with the assistance of the rest, broke in the door with axes and crowbars. This was but the work of a moment. Stepan Michailovitsch took Praskovia Ivanovna in his arms, laid her in the cart between himself and her faithful maid, and went tranquilly away with his armed retinue. The sun had just risen, and its glittering rays illuminated the golden cross on the church spire. It was but six days ago that Praskovia Ivanovna had prayed to that cross : now she prayed to it once more, and with tears of gratitude for her wonderful deliverance. Five versts beyond Paraschino they were overtaken by the calash, and Stepan Michailovitsch and his cousin continued their journey in it to Bagrovo.

And how could all this come about you will ask ? Had no one witnessed their arrival ? Where were Michail Maximoovitsch and his trusty band ? Had he seen and heard nothing or was he absent ? No ! Many there heard the uproar, and witnessed the rescue of Praskovia. Michail Maximovitsch was at home, knew perfectly well what was happening, and had not dared to cross the threshold of his own house.

The facts were as follows. The servants had spent the greater part of the night drinking with their master, and it was impossible to awaken a great number of them. Kurolesov's favourite servant, who never drank spirits, and who, consequently, was perfectly sober, had great difficulty in rousing his drunken master. Trembling with fear, he informed him of the arrival of Stepan Michailovitsch, and of the row of guns levelled at the house. " Where are our men ? " enquired Michail Maximovitsch. " Some of them are asleep, and the rest have hidden themselves," replied the servant, but he lied, for at that moment a drunken crew gathered at the door of the room. Michail Maximovitsch regained his senses somewhat, and shrieked : " May the Devil fly away with you ! Shut all the doors, and observe what happens through the window !" In a minute or two the servant exclaimed : " They have battered the door down. . . . Now they are carrying off the mistress. . . . They are going ! " " Be off to bed ! " retorted Michail Maximovitsch, covered himself up with the quilt, and went to sleep or pretended to do so.

Ah yes, there is a moral power in good which overcomes the might of evil. Michail Maximovitsch recognised the steady and intrepid courage of Stepan Michailovitsch : he felt that he had only wrong on his side, and, in spite of his desperate and bold character, he dare not attempt to snatch his victim from her deliverer.

With what loving and anxious care was the poor suffering little cousin brought home by Stepan Michailovitsch ! His love and pity for Praskovia were redoubled. He refrained from asking her any questions on the journey home, and, when Bagrovo was reached, he forbade his family to weary her by any sort of conversation. Her marvellous constitution, however, and equally marvellous strength of character together sufficed to restore her to her wonted good health by the end of a fortnight. This being the case, Stepan Michailovitsch determined to ask for a full account of what had happened to her, it being absolutely necessary that he should know the truth about the whole affair, as he was not one to attach importance to any but authentic histories. Praskovia Ivanovna told him all, reserving nothing ; but at the same time entreated him not to let her relatives know anything about the affair, and also expressed a wish that the subject should be allowed to drop. Knowing the irascible nature of her cousin as she did, she begged him not to take any revenge on Michail Maximovitsch, telling him candidly that she had reconsidered her former decision, and had resolved not to expose her husband and thereby bring dishonour upon a name which was her own as long as life lasted. She added that she regretted the words spoken to her husband on their first meeting, and was determined not to lay any charge against him : all the same she recognised it as her bounden duty to release her retainers as soon as possible from his merciless tyranny, and therefore intended to withdraw all authority from Kurolesov, and appoint her cousin as sole administrator of her estates. She begged Stepan Michailovitsch to write a letter at once to Michail Maximovitsch, reclaiming the power-of-attorney given to the latter : in the event of the request being refused, she would then give orders to have it legally annulled. She expressed the wish that the letter should spare her husband's pride as much as possible ; but in order to give it full weight and significance, she desired to put her own signature to it. And here I must add that she could only write very bad Russian. Stepan Michailovitsch was so devoted to her that he restrained his just anger, and carried out all her wishes faithfully. Only in one matter did he refuse to oblige her, the control of her property. " I dislike meddling in other folks' business," said he, " and I don't wish your relatives to be able to say that I make a good thing out of your thousand serfs. Your affairs are bound to be mismanaged now, but you are rich enough not to make a trouble of it. On my own account, though, I will write and tell your rascal of a husband that I am taking over the manage-ment of the estates, just to give him the fright he deserves. As for anything else that you ask ; I am only too pleased to do it for you." As the result of this conference he strictly forbade any of his family to ask Praskovia any questions. The letter to Michail Maximovitsch was duly written by my grandfather ;

MICHAIL MAXIMOVITSCH KUROLESOV

Praskovia Ivanovna added a few words, and a messenger took it to Paraschino. But while all these consultations and decisions and letter-writing were in process of happening, the Paraschino matter had been closed, once and for all. At the end of four days, the messenger returned with the news that God had willed that Michail Maximovitsch should die a sudden death, and that he was already in his grave. On hearing these tidings Stepan Michailovitsch involuntarily crossed himself, and exclaimed : " Thank God ! " His wife and daughters, who, in spite of their previous partiality for Michail Maximovitsch now as cordially detested him, also praised Heaven for this deliverance. Not so Praskovia. Judging of her feelings in the matter by their own, everyone hastened to tell her the news, which they expected her to receive with great joy. But their astonishment was great for the news was like a thunderbolt : she fell into a state of the deepest despondency, and became ill again. Once more her strong constitution got the better of her malady, but she continued melancholy and depressed. For many weeks she wept incessantly, and she wasted away to such an extent that her cousin was filled with anxious forebodings. No one could comprehend such grief and such bitter tears shed for a man who was of the veriest dregs of humanity, and who had forfeited all claim to her affection by his inhuman treatment of her. This may help to explain the mystery.

Some ten years after the foregoing events, my mother— (who was a great favourite of Praskovia Ivanovna, and who had been listening with the deepest interest to an account of the tragedy, of which Praskovia Ivanovna spoke but seldom and then only to her most intimate friends)—said : " Tell me, dearest Aunt, why did you grieve so over the death of Michail Maximovitsch ? In your place I should have commended his soul to the mercy of God, and have been rejoiced to be rid of him." " Stupid child ! " replied Praskovia Ivanovna, " I had loved him for fourteen long years : such a love is not destroyed in a month. And what concerns me most is the welfare of his soul : he died with no time for repentance."

Six weeks after the death of Kurolesov, Praskovia Ivanovna regained somewhat of her ordinary composure. She went, accompanied by her cousin and the whole family, to

Paraschino to repeat the customary prayers for the dead. It astonished everyone that, on reaching Paraschino, and even during the sorrowful ceremony, Praskovia Ivanovna never shed a tear—an effort which taxed her shattered mind and enfeebled frame to the utmost degree. In deference to her wishes the party only remained a few hours at Paraschino, and she herself never entered the wing of the house occupied by her late husband, in which he died.

It is not difficult to guess how Kurolesov's sudden death was brought about. After Praskovia's rescue, every soul on the estate was firmly convinced that the master's reign would soon come to an end. All were extremely anxious that the old master of Bagrovo, their mistress' second father, would turn her good-for-nothing husband out of the estate. No one had the slightest doubt that the ill-used and insulted young mistress would hesitate a moment in setting the law in motion against the criminal. Each day they momentarily expected Stepan Michailovitsch and the officers of justice to make their appearance ; but one week followed another, and no one came. Michail Maximovitsch drank and raved as usual, flogged everyone who approached him—(even his quiet sober-living servant, who had awakened him and warned him of Praskovia's deliverance)—because he had been thus left in the lurch. He boasted that his wife had settled all her property legally upon him. The cup of human endurance was overflowing : the future promised no hope, and so it came about that two scoundrels of his bodyguard—and, be it noted, amongst those persons who had the least to dread from his cruelty—carried out a frightful plan : they poisoned him with arsenic, which they mixed with the kvass which he was accustomed to drink during the night. They put such a quantity of poison into the decanter, that Kurolesov only lived two hours after drinking from it. The criminals had no accomplices, and the awful event filled everyone with indescribable terror. Each one suspected the other, but for a long time the real culprits remained undiscovered. Six months later, one of these fell ill, and, when near death, confessed his crime. His fellow-murderer, although the dying man had not disclosed his name, fled, and disappeared leaving no trace.

There is not the slightest doubt that this sudden death of

Kurolesov would have been followed by a strict judicial enquiry, had it not happened that a short time previously he had removed a young secretary, bearing the same name as his own, from Tschurasovo, and established him in the counting house at Paraschino. This young man acted with remarkable promptitude and prudence, and succeeded in hushing up the affair. As one result of his good offices he was eventually appointed administrator of the whole of Praskovia Ivanovna's estates, and—as Michailuschka—he became known and respected far and near in the Governments of Orenburg and Simbirsk. This worthy and indefatigable steward amassed a considerable fortune, and for a long time led a most temperate life ; he received his freedom after Praskovia Ivanovna's death ; but the loss of his beloved wife drove him to drink—he wasted all his savings and died in poverty. One of his sons, however, had a brilliant career in Government service, and, if I recollect aright, was raised to the rank of a noble.

I cannot deny that even forty years afterwards, when Stepan Michailovitsch's grandson succeeded to the estate of Paraschino, he found the memory of Michail Maximovitsch still held in affection by the peasantry. His barbarity, which, after all, had been principally practised upon the household staff, was quite forgotten. On the other hand, the unerring sagacity with which he could pick out the guilty from the innocent—the good from the bad labourers, his disinterested efforts to improve the condition of the serfs, and his readiness to help anyone in genuine need, were recollected, and extolled. The old men would smile as they told the following story of him : It seems Kurolesov was accustomed to say : " Rob and betray me as much as you like, so long as I know nothing about it : but if I catch you—don't complain ! "

After her return to Bagrovo, Praskovia Ivanovna gradually recovered her health, consoled by the fervent affection of her cousin and the kindly care of the whole family, who expected to see a great change in her. This however was not the case, her former good health was restored, her broken heart was healed, and at the end of a year she decided to return to Tschurasovo. Stepan Michailovitsch was grieved to part with his cousin. He felt himself especially responsible for her well-being, and he had grown accustomed to her constant companionship : never once in his life had he really been angry with her. Notwithstanding this, he in no way sought to persuade her to remain, but rather urged her to take her departure. " What sort of a life is this for you, my dear cousin ? " he was wont to ask. " Life here is very dull ; we don't mind it, because we have never been used to any other. But you are still young ; " (she was thirty years old), " you are rich, and accustomed to a very different style of living. Go back to Tschurasovo, and to your fine house and gardens and fountains. There are plenty of rich friends there who are fond of you and will help you to be happy. Who knows but you may make a happy marriage yet. At any rate you must not lose your chances here."

Praskovia Ivanovna postponed her departure from day to day, finding it difficult to part from the cousin who had rescued her from a terrible fate, and who had been her kind friend from her earliest childhood. But at last the day was fixed. The preceding day she had risen very early and gone to Stepan Michailovitsch who was sitting on the balcony, sunk in melancholy meditation. She embraced him, weeping, and said : " Cousin, I know how much you love me, and I love and honour you as my own father. God, who reads all hearts, knows my gratitude. But I wish everyone to know it, and so I beg of you to let me settle the estates which my mother left me on you. My father's estates, in any case, will go to your boy Alexei. All my relations on my mother's side are rich ; and you know there is no just reason why I should leave my property to them. I shall never marry again. I want the Bagrov family to be rich. Now, consent, dear cousin, if you wish me to be happy, and easy in my mind ! " And with these words she sank down at his feet, covering his hands with kisses. " Listen to me, cousin," replied Stepan Michailovitsch in a stern tone, " you know little of me, or you would never propose that I should accept another's property, or deprive your legitimate heirs of their own. No one shall ever tell that tale of Stepan Bagrov. Take heed that you never mention the subject to me again, or I shall be angry with you, for the first time in my life ! "

On the following day Praskovia Ivanovna set out on her journey to Tschurasovo, where she began a new and independent life.

SKETCH III

THE MARRIAGE OF THE YOUNGER
BAGROV

Many years had passed, much had happened : famine and pestilence, and the terrible rebellion of Pugatschev.[1] His wild bands had ravaged Orenburg. My grandfather fled with his family, first to Samara, then down the Volga to Saratov, and even as far as Astrachan. But gradually all these evils had passed away, peace was restored, and all was forgotten. Children had become youths ; youths—men ; and men—grey-beards. And among these last was Stepan Michailovitsch. He could not fail to notice it, but could still hardly believe it was so. Not seldom he would remark : " Yes, indeed, much has floated away with the waters of spring," and spoke as calmly as if referring to anyone but himself. In truth my grandfather was a changed man. Where were now his heroic strength, his activity and tireless energy ? He himself sometimes admitted his amazement at the change, but still continued his old mode of life, ate and drank to his heart's content, dressed himself without any regard to the weather ; and often had to suffer for his recklessness, too. His keen, sparkling eyes grew dimmer and dimmer, and his mighty voice weaker. He seldom fell into a passion now ; and seldom indeed was he happy and cheerful. He had married off his elder daughters : the eldest, Madame Vierigina, was dead, leaving a little three-year-old daughter. The second, Madame Koptjascheva, had lost her first husband and was married again to a Monsieur Nagatkin. The proud and intellectual Jelisaveta had become the wife of General Erlykin—and it must be admitted that the General was poor, old, and always in a state of intoxication. Alexandra had married one Ivan

---

[1] Pugatschev, Jemeljan : (1726-75). The Cossack who pretended to be the Czar, Peter III. [Tr.]

AKSAKOV'S FAMILY CHRONICLE

Petrovitsch Karataiev, a young man of rank and wealth, but a Bashkir of Bashkirs, and passionately devoted to the life and habits of that race. The youngest daughter, Tania, was still at home. The only son was already twenty-seven years old, a bonnie red-cheeked fellow. His father often remarked that he only needed a petticoat and bodice to be as fine a young lady as any of his sisters. In spite of the bitter tears and lamentations of his wife, Stepan Michailovitsch had permitted his son—when sixteen years old—to enter military service, where he remained for three years. Through Kurolesov's influence he was appointed orderly to Suvorov for a whole year. But Suvorov quitted Orenburg, and a German general (Treublut, if I mistake not) permitted the poor and quite innocent young man—in spite of his noble birth too—to be most unmercifully flogged. My grandmother nearly died with grief, and my grandfather quite failed to appreciate this kind of joke. He made Alexei ask for his discharge at once, and procured him a post in the Supreme High Court, which he filled very efficiently for many years, eventually becoming a State Agent.

And here I cannot help mentioning a very singular fact. The majority of Germans—(and other foreigners for the matter of that)—who enter Russian State Service are characterized by their extreme severity and predilection for flogging. This same German, who behaved so inhumanly towards young Bagrov, although himself a strict Lutheran, exacted the minutest observance of the rites of the Greek Church from the regiment. This was actually the occasion of the aforesaid dismal episode in our family chronicles. It being the eve of some insignificant festival, the German general had commanded vespers to be read in the regimental church in the presence of himself and the other officers. The windows of the church stood wide open, as the heat of the summer's day was excessive. Suddenly, from the main street of Ufa, resounded the merry strains of a Russian folksong: the general rushed to a window. Three young non-commissioned officers came down the street, one of whom was singing. The general had all three instantly arrested and ordered three hundred strokes to be administered to each man. My unlucky father, who was not the songster, and had only accompanied the other sergeants, tried to explain that he was a noble, on which the General, with a diabolical grin, retorted that it was a nobleman's duty to pay especial deference to the worship of God. And then and there he had the punishment carried out in his presence in a room adjoining the church, warning my father not to cry out and disturb the congregation next door. My father was carried half-dead to the infirmary, where his uniform had to be cut away from his body, which was swollen from the flogging. It was fully two months before the wounds on his back and shoulders were healed. You may picture the agony of his mother who was devotedly attached to him. My grandfather brought a complaint against the General, which was ignored; but as soon as his son was able to leave hospital, his discharge, which he had solicited, was at once granted, and he entered the service of the State as an official of the Fourteenth Class. At the time of our story the whole affair was forgotten, after a lapse of some eight years.

Alexei Stepanovitsch fulfilled his government work very tranquilly in Ufa, which lay two hundred and forty versts from Bagrovo. Twice a year he paid a visit to his parents. Life for him contained no adventures, either at home or abroad. Quiet, diffident, and unassuming, friendly with all, he lived as solitary as a field-flower, when suddenly the placid stream of the young country squire's life was ruffled.

In the town of Ufa, the Vice-Regent, Councillor Nikolai Feodorovitsch Subin, a learned and upright, but weak and vacillating, man, had his permanent residence. He was a widower with three children, a twelve-year-old daughter Sonitschka[1] and two younger boys. The father loved his Sonitschka dearly, which was not surprising, as the little girl was remarkably pretty and clever, and, in spite of her extreme youth, a faithful friend and skilful manager of all household affairs. Nevertheless, some six months after the death of his first beloved wife, Nikolai Feodorovitsch was so completely consoled that he fell in love with the daughter of a neighbouring squire—Petrov Alexander Rytschkov, the well-known writer of Orenburg—and married her shortly afterwards. The young wife, Alexandra Petrovna, a beautiful,

---

[1] Diminutive of Sofia. [Tr. S. R.]

intelligent, and imperious woman, held the weak-minded widower entirely under her sway, and developed an intense hatred for her young, but already beautiful, step-daughter. The condition of things came to this pass, that the character of Alexandra Petrovna manifested all the worst and most hateful qualities usually attributed to jealous step-mothers, and she determined to oust Sonitschka from her place in her father's affections. This was no easy matter, and the child offered such a stout resistance that she excited the step-mother's wrath to the very highest degree, so that she swore that the thirteen-year-old girl—the idol of her father and indeed of the whole city—should live in the servants' apartments, be dressed in cotton clothes, and perform the most menial tasks for her own unborn children. This threat she fulfilled literally : at the end of two or three years Sonitschka was living with the maid servants, was the worst dressed amongst them, and was set single-handed to clean and scrub the nursery in which already two new baby sisters were installed. And what of the tender father ? For whole months at a stretch he never set eyes on his daughter ; and if he chanced to encounter her—dressed like a beggar—he turned away and slunk off sighing to hide his tears. And so it is with many an old widower who takes to himself a young wife. I do not know what means Alexandra Petrovna employed to gain her evil ends, so I remain mute on this subject : neither do I care to reveal all the persecution and ill-treatment which the poor motherless girl, naturally of a proud. sensitive, spirited, and intractable disposition, had to endure. The severest punishment was meted out to her, she was not even spared blows, and frequently was chastised when she had done nothing amiss. At last the unfortunate child resolved to commit suicide, and was only prevented from carrying out her intention by a miracle. It came about in this way. The poor girl, having made up her mind to put an end to her unendurable existence, entered her wretched attic up in the roof to pray for the last time before a picture of Our Lady of Smolensk with which her dying mother had blessed her. She fell on her knees before the sacred ikon, and, weeping bitterly, bowed her head upon the dirty floor. Thus prostrated, she lost consciousness for some moments. When she recovered her senses and rose to her feet, to her amazement a light shone upon her. Before the picture of the Mother of God the taper, which she had extinguished the day before, was alight. She cried out with terror, but, quickly recovering herself, recognised the hand of God in this miracle. From that moment a hitherto unknown strength and peace took possession of her soul and body, and she made a steadfast resolve to endure all, suffer all, and live. Henceforth the orphan suffered the persecutions of her step-mother with the most unshaken fortitude, although the latter did her utmost to insult and irritate her victim. She performed every task imposed upon her and bore every wrong with incredible calm. No abuse, no degrading punishment could wring a tear from her—far less produce the nervous attacks and fainting fits to which she had formerly been subject ; and to her former title of " Vile creature " another epithet was added, whereby she became : " Vile, stubborn creature." But the patience of God was exhausted at last, and the bolt fell. The beautiful Alexandra Petrovna bore a son and died ten days after his birth. The day before her death, knowing her end to be approaching, she made what haste she could to free her conscience from its heavy load. Sonitschka was awakened in the middle of the night and bidden to her step-mother's bedside. There, in the presence of several witnesses, Alexandra Petrovna acknowledged her guilt, entreated her step-daughter's forgiveness, and made her swear before God that she would never forsake her children. The step-child forgave her, promised not to desert the children, and gave her solemn word thereon. Alexandra Petrovna then confessed to her husband that all the evil tales that she had told him about his daughter's conduct were lies and calumnies.

And what changes were wrought in the house by this death! Nikolai Feodorovitsch had a stroke, which he survived some years, but only as a bed-ridden invalid. The disgraced, degraded, ragged step-daughter, so long the scorn and derision of a base crew of menials, (especially those who had the ear of their late mistress), suddenly became absolute mistress of the house. Everything was entrusted to her by her sick father. The reconciliation between the guilty father and his innocent child was touching, but very painful to witness. The sting of remorse gave the sick old man no rest or peace : he lay sobbing day and night, and could only stammer " No, Sonitschka, you can never forgive me ! " To all and every one of his friends and acquaintances in the city he made a solemn confession of his conduct towards his daughter ; and Sofia Nikolaievna became the object of universal respect and admiration. Early matured through the sufferings which she had endured, the seventeen-year-old maiden filled the parts of woman, mother, house-keeper, and even that of an official. The helpless condition of her father compelled her to receive all the magistrates, officials, and similar residents in the city ; and to transact all his state business for him. She wrote all his business letters, superintended everything, and soon was the sole director of the Court of Chancery. Meanwhile she tended her father with the most affectionate care, and watched like a mother over her three brothers and two little sisters. She succeeded in procuring instruction for the two elder boys, one of whom was now twelve, the other ten years old. She placed them under the care of a Frenchman, M. Villemé, whom chance had brought to the city, and under a fairly well-educated Little Russian, V—ski, who had been exiled to Ufa on account of some intrigue against the Government. She herself profited by these opportunities to study with her brothers, and made admirable progress. At the end of six months she sent her brothers to A. F. Anitschkov in Moscow, whose acquaintance she had made through one of his cousins who lived in Ufa, and with whom she carried on a brisk correspondence, although they had never met. At that time Anitschkov was living with the celebrated N. I. Novikov. The two friends were so enchanted by the delightful letters of the unknown girl in Bashkiria that they sent her every work of any literary value which was published in Russia, and this literature contributed not a little to the farther development of her intellect. Anitschkov, especially, was her ardent admirer, and was only too rejoiced to be able to carry out her wishes, by taking charge of her two brothers and using his influence for their admission into the University School for the nobility. The boys were diligent pupils. Unfortunately their studies were soon interrupted, as each had been nominated for entry into the Guards' Regiment at the time of his birth.

MARRIAGE OF THE YOUNGER BAGROV

Every cultured and intellectual person brought by chance or otherwise to the city was presented to Sofia, fell under her spell, and never forgot her. Most of these acquaintances later became her faithful friends, and continued friends until death. Among these I will only mention those whom it was my privilege to know : W. W. Romanovski, A. I. Avenarius, P. I. Tschitschagov, D. B. Mertwy, and W. I. Itschanski. In addition to all these, any learned or casual travellers who visited the new and ravishing District of Ufa never failed to make Sofia Nikolaievna's acquaintance, and to leave written tributes of their admiration and regard. In truth the position of this quite young girl was a highly enviable one, and placed her, as it were, upon a glittering pedestal. But this pedestal supported a glorious figure. In especial I recall a poem written by one Count Manteuffel, who sent her a copy of Buchan's *Domestic Medecine*,[1] an early translation of the English work into Russian, which had created a great sensation. The five quarto volumes became Sofia Nikolaievna's favourite reading, and she discovered many remedies which relieved her father's sufferings. In his dedicatory poem Count Manteuffel compared the beautiful girl alike to Venus and to Minerva.

In spite of his invalid condition, Nikolai Feodorovitsch retained his post for some years longer. Twice a year he gave a great ball. He himself was not able to appear in the presence of ladies, but received the gentlemen, lying on a couch in his study. The young mistress received the whole society of the city and district. The old father insisted that Sonitschka should occasionally attend the balls given by the local notabilities. In order to please him Sofia Nikolaievna consented to appear for a short time at these balls. Charmingly dressed, the admired of everyone who saw her, she would dance a polonaise, a minuet, a country dance or an écossaise, and would vanish like a meteor. All who had a right to love her adored Sofia Nikolaievna with a devout and hopeless adoration, for it was considered an impossibility to touch the heart of the beautiful girl.

And the son of old Stepan Michailovitsch fell in love with this bewitching creature. He was not able to appreciate

[1] Domestic Medicine or The Family Physician, first published at Edinburgh in 1769, written by Dr. William Buchan (1729-1805). [Tr.]

every side of her lofty character; but her lovely person and kind and charming disposition were more than enough to enchant the young man, and make the spell complete. The very first time that he saw Sofia Nikolaievna in church, his soft heart was won. As soon as he heard that the beautiful maiden received all the officials who came to visit her father, Alexei Stepanovitsch (it is high time we give him his full name), he began to be a constant visitor at the receptions held by the Vice-regent on all great festivals, which he attended in his capacity as an official of the Supreme Court. On each of these visits he saw Sofia Nikolaievna, and fell still more violently in love with her. The visits were so frequent and lasted so long, (although the young man scarcely ever ventured to open his mouth) that they could not fail to be remarked; and the young mistress of the house was the first to guess their meaning. Sighs and glances, glowing cheeks and embarrassed silences are invariably the eloquent signs of love. Everyone is inclined to laugh at love. It was ever thus, and the whole town made merry at Alexei Stepanovitsch's expense, while he, bashful and shamefaced as a country girl, could find no reply to their jokes and sly allusions, and only blushed as red as a poppy.

To everyone's amazement however Sofia Nikolaievna, hitherto so cold and distant toward all her adorers, treated the shy lover with condescending kindness. I cannot say whether she was moved to compassion for the poor youth whose passion occasioned such merriment to others, or whether she realised that such a love as his was no passing fancy, but a life-long affection. Be that as it may, the proud beauty not only received Alexei Stepanovitsch with great friendliness, but frequently talked to him, and seemed to find nothing laughable either in his bashful, incoherent replies or in his stammering speech. But I recollect that Sofia Nikolaievna was invariably haughty and unapproachable in her manner with the arrogant and self-satisfied, and kind and affable with the timid and humble.

Matters continued in this state for some time, and then, all of a sudden, a bold thought crossed Alexei Stepanovitsch's impassioned brain—the thought of marriage. He himself was positively terrified at the audacity of the idea. What was he in comparison with Sofia Nikolaievna—the person of greatest consequence in the city—the most beautiful and cleverest maiden in the whole world ? Thinking thus, he gave up the idea in despair. But soon the thought revived, aroused by the friendly attitude of the lady herself, by her kind—and as it seemed to him—even encouraging glances and still more by his own love, which grew warmer and warmer. At length, what had begun as a sweet dream became a necessary condition of life itself. An old lady of rank, Madame Alakaieva, who was living in Ufa in those days, shewed him the greatest sympathy and kindness. She was a distant relative of his own and a friend of the Subin family. He began by paying her frequent visits and complimenting her to the best of his ability, and ended by telling her his love and heart's desire. Madame Alakaieva had been aware of his love for long enough, as everyone in the town was talking about it ; but his proposal to marry Sofia Nikolaievna astonished her extremely. "She would never dream of accepting you," said the old lady, shaking her head. " She is far too clever, and cultured, and proud for you. She has had numbers of lovers, but no one has dared to propose to her. I can't say but you are good-looking, and very well-born too. You have a little money and will be rich in time—no one can deny all this. But you are only a country squire, with no polish, no education, and utterly shy and awkward in society." All this was exactly what Alexei Stepanovitsch knew himself, but his love overruled his reason. Day and night a secret voice whispered in his ear that, in spite of all obstacles, Sofia would be his. Although Madame Alakaieva considered the young man's suit a hopeless one, she yielded to his entreaties to go herself to Sofia Nikolaievna, and without saying anything about the proposal to find out what her real feelings were towards her timid admirer. She set off immediately to the Subins' house, while poor Alexei Stepanovitsch anxiously awaited her return. The old lady was absent a considerable time, and the lover was so distracted by anxiety and melancholy that he burst into a flood of weeping, and at last, worn out by his emotion, fell asleep, leaning against the window. But at last the old lady returned home, woke him up, and said, smiling : " Well, Alexei Stepanovitsch, you were not

quite so mistaken, after all. I introduced you into our conversation, and began disparaging you ; but Sofia Nikolaievna at once stood up for you, said that you were a good-hearted, modest, pious young man, who honoured and obeyed your parents, that God's blessing was on such men, and that they were worth any number of impudent fops put together."
Alexei Stepanovitsch was nearly beside himself with joy and scarcely knew what he was doing or saying. When he was somewhat calmer, Madame Alakaieva, speaking with great seriousness, said : "If you have not changed your mind about this marriage, take my advice. Return home at once, tell your parents everything, and ask their consent and their blessing, so that the good old folks will raise no objection to the match. When you have obtained their consent, I will see what I can do to help you farther. Now, don't be in too great a hurry ! Try and coax your sisters first : your mother will never cross your wishes. Of course the principal thing is to get your father's consent. I know him very well ; he is stubborn, but he will listen to reason. Talk to him when he is in a good temper ! " Alexei Stepanovitsch was not a little surprised at his old friend's wary advice, and promptly retorted that there could be no question of his parents' delight at the prospect of his marriage to Sofia Nikolaievna, as there could be no possible objection to her. " A great many objections," replied the wise old lady, " She has next to no fortune, and her grandfather was a simple corporal in a regiment of Ural Cossacks." But this plain speaking had not the slightest effect upon Alexei Stepanovitsch.

Madame Alakaievna, nevertheless, had spoken only too truly, but her warning came too late. A week later Alexei Stepanovitsch asked for leave-of-absence, made his adieux to Sofia Nikolaievna, who very kindly wished him a successful journey, and expressed a wish that he would find all at home well and delighted to welcome him. Encouraged by these friendly words, the young man set out, his heart beating high with hope. The old people were overjoyed to see him, but did not seem exactly surprised at his unexpected arrival, and looked at him somewhat enquiringly. His sisters, who lived in the neighbourhood, were advised of his arrival by their mother, and at once hurried to see him, and overwhelmed him with caresses, laughing immoderately without any reason. Alexei Stepanovitsch was especially fond of his youngest sister, and she was the first to whom he confided his secret. Tatiana Stepanovna, an enthusiastic, warm-hearted girl, listened most sympathetically to her brother's confession of his love, and then explained the enigmatic behaviour of the others. The whole family knew all about his love affair, and quite disapproved of it. This is what had happened. A short time before Alexei Stepanovitsch's arrival, Ivan Petrovitsch Karataiev had been in Ufa, and had brought home this bit of town-gossip to his wife. Alexandra Stepanovna (we know her amiable disposition) was infuriated. She had always been the principal person at home, and all, save her father, deferred to her. She bribed one of Alexei Stepanovitsch's servants to act as a spy and to keep her *au courant* with the minutest details of her brother's daily life and his love affair. She even went to the length of looking up a godmother of her own, who lived in Ufa, and of employing her services as another spy; and this worthy woman had sent her a long letter, composed with the assistance of a former lawyer's clerk and crammed with every scrap of petty tittle-tattle which could be raked up in the town and culled from the servants of the Subin household. Information was specially sought from the late step-mother's servants, and it is easy to imagine the colours in which Sofia Nikolaievna was painted by these gentry.

We know that in the good old times—(and perhaps even now-a-days)—sisters have never liked the idea of their brothers marrying, and have been especially annoyed if an only brother proposed bringing home a young bride, who, in the natural course of events, would become the absolute mistress of the house. Human nature is a mass of secret egoism. Almost involuntarily all of us fall under its sway, and no one amongst us is free from it. Good and worthy folks often impute other and noble motives to such selfish passions, and in this way unintentionally deceive both themselves and others. In harsh, rough natures egoism is more easily detected. This was the case with Stepan Michailovitsch's family. Choose whom the brother might, his marriage was bound to be an offence to everyone. " Our brother will turn against us, and cease to care for us ; his young wife will drive us all away, and we shall no longer be welcome in our father's house ! " This would have been the cry of Alexei Stepanovna's sisters, even had the proposed sister-in-law been their equal. But anything worse than Sofia Nikolaievna was absolutely impossible. Alexandra Stepanovna sent an urgent invitation to Jelisaveta to accompany her to Bagrovo, in order that their mother and their other sisters should be duly influenced by all the numerous and necessary embellishments which they bestowed upon their brother's choice. All believed Alexandra Stepanovna implicitly ; and the family's general opinion of Sofia Nikolaievna was somewhat as follows : First, this Subinia (as Alexei Stepanovitsch's mother and sisters were wont to call her at their secret conferences) was of base origin. Her grandfather was a Cossack of the Urals, called Sub, and her mother (one Vera Ivanovna Kandalinzova) came of a tradesman's family. It would be a shame and a scandal for an old and noble family to make an alliance with such a nobody. Secondly, the Subinia was poor. In the event of her father dying or losing his post, she and her brothers and sisters would have nothing, and her future husband would have the burden and responsibility of supporting these last. Thirdly, the Subinia was a vain, showy doll, accustomed to domineer over a whole town, who would be certain to despise any country-bred relations, in spite of all their old nobility and high birth. Fourthly, the Subinia was a witch, who attracted men by means of potions and spells ; she had enchanted their poor brother, because she had heard he was likely to inherit a fortune ; and she wished to marry into a noble family. In short, Alexandra Stepanovna employed her poisonous tongue to such good purpose, that her whole following—mother and sisters alike—were fully convinced that Sofia Nikolaievna would be a most undesirable and dangerous sister-in-law. It was quite certain that she would succeed in bewitching Stepan Michailovitsch, and then everything would be lost ; so her marriage with their brother must be prevented at any cost. It was certain that the first thing to be done was to create a bad impression of Sofia in their father's mind. How was this to be managed ? In spite of their ferocious dispositions, none of the sisters had the courage to tackle the old gentleman. They knew he would guess their real design and would not believe a word they said. They had already shewn their annoyance at the idea of Alexei getting married, when various matches had been suggested for him in the past. At last they hit upon the following plan. Arina Vasilievna had a niece, Flena Ivanovna Lupenevskaia ; a stupid, gossiping woman, very much addicted to drink. She was persuaded to come on a visit to Bagrovo, and instructed, amongst other things, to begin chattering about Alexei Stepanovitsch and his lady-love, and, naturally, to tell all sorts of scandalous stories about Sofia Nikolaievna. Alexandra Stepanovna took Flena Ivanovna in hand, and drilled her thoroughly as to what she was to say, and how to say it. At last, when she was considered perfect in her rôle, Flena Ivanovna made her appearance in Bagrovo one fine day, at dinner time, When dinner was over, all, both hosts and guests, retired to bed for three hours. After this refreshment all reassembled for tea. The old man was in a good humour, and himself gave the visitor her chance of performing her appointed part. " Now, my fat Flena," said he, " tell us all the news from Ufa," (her sister had recently been staying in that town with her husband). . . . " Your folks have already brought home three cart loads of gossip, and you can finish off with a fourth load of lies." " Ah, dear Uncle," cried Flena, " you are always making fun of me. I have lots of news to tell, without having any need to tell lies." And she began an endless string of stories, both true and false, which I forbear to inflict upon the reader. My grandfather appeared to believe nothing she said ; he amused himself by perplexing and puzzling the narrator, and causing her to lose the thread of her extraordinary stories ; and behaved in such a comical way that the whole family nearly burst with laughter. The thick-headed Flena, who had fortified herself with a good dram of schnapps after her nap, at last lost all patience and replied with some exasperation : " Why do you do nothing but laugh at me, Uncle, and pretend not to believe what I say ? Wait a bit, and hear a piece of news I have kept for the last, which you will have to believe, and which won't make you laugh." The ladies exchanged sly smiles, and my grandfather laughed louder. " Out with it ! " he said gaily, " I shall certainly not believe it, but I promise not to laugh at it. I am already sick of your balderdash ! " " Oh, Uncle, Uncle," interrupted Flena Ivanovna, " you don't know what has happened to our dear cousin Alexei Stepanovitsch. He is quite ill with love. The witch of Ufa has enchanted him—the daughter of the governor there—the voivoda, or vice-regent, or whatever he's called, I'm sure I don't know which. They say she is so beautiful that she can bewitch anyone she chooses, old or young : they all run after her like dogs after a bitch. And my good cousin is so infatuated with her that he neither eats, nor drinks, nor sleeps. He sits beside her the whole day long, staring at her, and sighing. And at night he keeps guard under her window, with his gun and sword, to preserve her from harm ; and they say the Subinia is quite fond of him. He's a handsome man and of good family. She knows how to value his advantages, and she means to marry him, too And small wonder if she does. She has no money, her father is of very low birth, only the son of an Ural Cossack, Fedka Sub. Although he has an important post and is of high rank now, he has saved nothing. He has squandered everything in balls and feasts, and in dressing up his darling daughter. And the old fellow hasn't long to live, in fact he's already half dead ; and he's lots of children —having had two wives—six of them ! You'll have them all hanging round your neck, Uncle, when Cousin Alexei marries the girl ; her smart clothes are the only dowry she can bring. They say that no one would recognise Alexei Stepanovitsch now, he looks so miserable. The servants can't help crying when they look at him ; but they daren't tell you anything about him. And I assure you, Uncle, that every word I say is true. Ask the servants, and they'll tell you exactly the same." At this point Arina Vasilievna burst into tears, and the daughters all pulled very long faces. My grandfather was a little taken aback, but quickly recovered his composure, and replied with a sarcastic smile : " Well, amongst so many lies there may be a grain of truth. I have often heard tell of Mademoiselle Subina's beauty and learning ; and that explains her witchcraft[1] and enchantments. It is not surprising

[1] My grandfather in general was no believer in magic. A magician once tried to deceive him by telling him he could bewitch guns so that no one could fire them. My grandfather handed over his own gun to be

if Alexei has been smitten by her. But she has not the faintest intention of marrying him. She will look out for a better educated and cleverer husband. Alexei is not fit for her, and now the matter must drop. We will have no more of this chatter. Let us drink our tea in peace." After such a snub as this Flena Ivanovna did not venture to repeat any more gossip from Ufa, and in the evening took her departure. After supper, when Arina Vasilievna and her daughters were about to set off to bed in silence, Stepan Michailovitsch stopped them, and said : " Now Arischa, what are you thinking about ? That fool Flena has told plenty of lies, of course, but I cannot help thinking there is some truth in the story. For some time back the tone of Alexei's letters has changed. We must look thoroughly into the matter. The best thing will be to send for Alexei, and find out the whole truth from him." Upon this, Alexandra Stepanovitsch begged permission to send an express messenger to a relative of her husband in Ufa, a very upright honourable person, so she said, who would send them full information within a week. The old man agreed not to summon his son until some enquiries had been made, and Alexandra Stepanovna set off immediately for her estate of Karataievka, which was about thirty versts away from Bagrovo. At the end of a week she returned to her parents, bringing the letter which her godmother had written some time previously, and which has already been described. The letter was shewn and read to Stepan Michailovitsch, and although he had a very low opinion of women's judgment and opinion in general, still there were various points in the letter which struck him as true, and he was influenced by it to a considerable extent. He said, in very decided tones, that he would never consent to Alexei's marrying Mademoiselle Subinia, as she was not of aristocratic birth. " Write and tell Alexei to come here at once ! " were his final orders ; and after the expiration of a few days (which had by no means been wasted by the mother and sisters, who spent all their time suggesting all sorts of disasters as the probable result of

experimented upon, and then calmly fired it, after the enchanter had secretly withdrawn the charge. The latter was very much upset, but recovered himself, and solemnly declared that my grandfather was also one of the " Elect," which was implicitly believed by every one, with the exception of Stepan Michailovitsch himself.

Alexei's objectionable love affair) the young man made his appearance before the letter ever reached him. . . . .

When Alexei Stepanovitsch had heard his sister's story, he was frightfully upset and perplexed. By nature weak both in will and character, reared in fear of his father and with feelings of boundless and awe-stricken respect for the whole family, he was hopelessly at a loss how to act. At last he summoned up sufficient courage to speak to his mother. Arina Vasilievna—(who adored her son, yet always regarded him as if he were still a child, and now considered that her beloved little one desired a dangerous plaything)—replied to Alexei's avowal of his passion in the tone that a mother would speak to her child who wished to play with a red-hot poker. When he burst into bitter tears, she attempted to console him in the way one would console a child who had been deprived of a toy. When he tried to contradict and confute the calumnies and lies which had been heaped upon Sofia Nikolaievna's character, his mother would not listen to him and paid no regard to what he said. Two days passed in this way. The young man's heart was fain to break. Every hour his love and longing for Sofia Nikolaievna increased; but in spite of this he could not make up his mind to speak to his father; and it was the latter who introduced the subject of Sofia.

Early one beautiful morning Alexei Stepanovitsch, pale and haggard after a sleepless night, joined his father as usual in the outside gallery of the house. The old man was in good spirits and bade his son a cheerful Good Morning, but a glance at the latter's disturbed countenance shewed him what was wringing the youth's heart. He gave him his hand to kiss, and spoke to him seriously but not unkindly : " Listen to me, Alexei, I know what is troubling you, and see perfectly well that this silly idea is firmly fixed in your head. Now tell me everything—how the matter stands—and hide nothing from me ! " Although Alexei Stepanovitsch had never been on intimate terms with his father, whom he feared more than loved, on this occasion his love gave him courage to speak. He threw himself at his father's feet, and told him his simple love story without concealing anything. Stepan Michailovitsch listened to his son with great patience and attention. One of his daughters approached him to say Good Morning, but he made such an expressive gesture with his stick, that neither she nor anyone else—not even Aksinia with the tea kettle—dare come near until he summoned them himself. Poor Alexei's story was very vague, confused, and far from clear. But Stepan Michailovitsch's clear mind grasped the whole matter. Unfortunately the matter was not at all to his liking, and displeased him very much indeed. He had very little sympathy with impassioned love ; and his masculine dignity was contemptuous of this amorousness on the part of his son, whose attitude he considered humiliating, and not worthy of a man : at the same time he realised that Sofia Nikolaievna was not in the slightest degree to blame, and that all he had been told about her was merely lies circulated by slanderers, and the invention of his own family. After considering a while in silence, he remarked in a firm but kind tone, and with no appearance of anger : '' Listen, Alexei ! You are just of the age when a pretty girl pleases a man best. I have nothing to say against that ; but you shouldn't make such a fool of yourself over anyone. I don't blame Sofia Nikolaievna one little bit ; I consider her a most honourable young woman, but she is neither fit for you, nor for our home. To begin with she belongs to a *parvenu* family, and you to the ancient nobility. Secondly, she is city-bred, a clever accomplished girl, who, since her step-mother's death, has been accustomed to rule over a house and live in very grand style, although she has no fortune whatever. We, as you know, lead the lives of simple country gentlefolks. And you must likewise recollect that you have a very weak character, and she is a great deal too clever for you. It's a poor state of things when the wife has more sense than the husband, for she soon begins to order him about. And you are so hoplessly in love with her, that she could do as she liked with you from the start. Now listen, and obey my commands as your father : Put this love out of your mind ! For my own part I believe, and don't hesitate to say, that Sofia Nikolaievna would never consent to marry you. Like desires like. We will find you a nice, quiet, country-bred girl of your own rank, with a good fortune of her own. Then you can resign your post and lead a pleasant life. We are not wealthy folks ; we have enough, but nothing to spare. As for the Kurolesov inheritance, about which so much fuss is made, there is nothing to reckon on in that quarter. The chances are that Praskovia Ivanovna may very well marry and have children, for she is not an old woman. And now let the matter drop, Alexei ! Shake off your folly, as the goose shakes off water, and don't let me hear any more about Sofia Nikolaievna ! " Speaking thus, Stepan Michailovitsch held out his hand condescendingly to his son, who kissed it with his wonted respect. The old gentleman then ordered tea to be served and the rest of the family to be summoned. During breakfast he was very affable and kind with everyone, but the hapless Alexei Stepanovitsch remained sunk in the deepest melancholy. No furious outbreak of rage on his father's part would have reduced him to such a state of despair. Stepan Michailovitsch's rage passed quickly, and was followed by pardon and forgiveness. But in this case he had spoken in a tone of calm resolve which deprived his son of all hope. Alexei Stepanovitsch's countenance was so troubled, that his mother, observing it, enquired if he were not feeling very well. The sisters had instantly noted his agitation, but were too sly to make any open allusion to it ; and their father could gather nothing from their attitude. He scowled at his wife, and growled between his teeth : " Leave him alone ! " So Alexei Stepanovitsch was left to himself, and the day passed in its usual way.

Alexei had been terribly upset by his father's decision, and his heart was almost broken. Sleep and appetite alike forsook him, he lost all interest in life, and his health suffered. His mother could hardly look at him without weeping, and even his sisters began to feel very uneasy. Each day his mother tried to find out from him what his father had really said, but in vain. To every enquiry, he had but the one reply : " My father refuses his consent ; I am a ruined man ; I shall never get over it." And by the end of a week he was actually in such a weak condition that he lay unconscious. No fever could be detected, and yet he was delirious day and night. No one could understand the exact nature of his malady, it was purely a nervous fever. No doctor was available in the whole district. The whole family were distracted by anxiety. They plied him with home remedies, but the patient's condition grew daily worse, and at last his debility was so

great, that his death was hourly expected. Arina Vasilievna
and his sisters wept and tore their hair. Stepan Michailovitsch
never shed a tear. Dry-eyed, he sat from morning to night
in his son's sick room, and perhaps felt the deepest grief of
all. He knew too well the cause of the young man's sickness.
But youth triumphed, and at the end of six weeks Alexei
Stepanovitsch recovered. He woke up one day—a little
child, and very, very slowly life flowed back into its former
channel. The full recovery took two months. He seemed
to have totally forgotten the past. Everything, whether
out-of-doors or in the house was to him a delightful surprise ;
and at last his health was fully restored : he was sounder and
sturdier than ever before, and the bright colour returned which
had faded from his cheeks for a whole year. He fished, went
quail-shooting, slept soundly, enjoyed his food, and appeared
perfectly happy and free from care. His parents could
hardly control their joy at his restoration to good health
and were persuaded that the illness had banished all former
wishes and desires from his undeveloped organisation. This
no doubt would have been the case, had the young man been
withdrawn from Government Service, kept another year in
the country, and married to a pretty, young girl. But the old
people, being quite reassured by the actual condition of their
son, sent him back to Ufa at the end of another six months,
to his former post—and his fate was finally decided. His
former passion blazed forth with new and unbounded ardour.
I know not whether his love revived suddenly or gradually :
all I know is, that he went very seldom to the Subins' house at
first, then more frequently, and, finally, as often as he possibly
could. I also know that his protectress, Madame Alakaieva,
constantly went to visit Sofia Nikolaievna, and by dint of
cunning enquiries, convinced herself and her diffident young
relative that the proud and beautiful girl was not entirely
indifferent to the latter.

And some months after Alexei Stepanovitsch's departure
his parents received a letter from him, in which he vowed
in a quite unwontedly firm, though affectionate and respectful
manner, that he loved Sofia Nikolaievna better than life itself,
and could not live without her. He had reason to believe that
she would accept him, and he besought his parents' blessing

and permission to make her a proposal of marriage. The old folks had never expected anything of the sort, and were in a state of utter bewilderment. Stepan Michailovitsch drew his eyebrows together and spoke never a word. Everyone was silent. He waved his hand, and they all vanished. My grandfather sat alone, and traced figures with his stick on the floor of his chamber ! He realised that the case was serious, and that no fever would ever cure his son of this love, again. Under the influence of his own sincere and benevolent disposition he was quite inclined to give his consent, if he could get Arina Vasilievna to agree with him on this point.

" Well, Arischa," he said next morning, when no one was present but themselves, " what do you say about all this ? If we don't give our permission, we shall never see our Alexei again. Either he will die of grief, or go to the wars, or turn monk—and the family of Bagrov will become extinct." Arina Vasilievna, who had been drilled by her daughters, appeared not to share her husband's apprehensions, and replied stiffly : " Just as you like, Stepan Michailovitsch. Your will is mine. But in future don't look for any respect from your children, if they can set their will against yours in this way." The clumsy trick was successful, the old man's obstinacy was revived, and he determined not to give way. He dictated a letter to his son, in which he expressed his surprise at the old question being renewed, and reaffirmed what he had already said by word of mouth. Briefly, the letter contained a decided refusal to consider the matter any farther.

Two, three weeks passed, without any reply coming from Alexei Stepanovitsch. . . .

On a dreary day in autumn my grandfather sat on the bed in his room, wearing his beloved dressing gown, made of fine camlet, over his pleated shirt, and with his bare feet thrust in his old slippers. Beside him sat Arina Vasilievna at her spinning wheel, spinning goats' wool. Carefully and skilfully she drew out the fine even thread, destined to be woven by the house-maidens into finest cloth ; which in turn was to be made into a warm, light, and comfortable winter coat for her son. Tatiana sat beside the window, reading a book. Jelisaveta Stepanovna, who had come over on a visit, was sitting on the bed beside her father telling him unwelcome family news—her husband had been called up for military service ; she had next to nothing for the housekeeping ; and was in want of this and that and everything. The old man listened in sorrowful silence, his hands lying on his knees, and his already grey head sunk on his breast. Suddenly the door of the ante-room was flung open, and Ivan Malysch, a slim, good-looking youth clad in travelling dress, tripped into the chamber and gave his master a letter which he had just brought from the post town, some five-and-twenty versts distant. It was easy to see that the letter had been long and eagerly awaited, for everyone was in a state of excitement. "From Alexei ?" asked the old man with eager anxiety. "Yes, from my brother," replied Tatiana, who had sprung forward to the messenger, taken the letter from him, and read the address. "Well, done, Malysch ! You have earned a cup of brandy ! Now go and get something to eat, and then rest yourself !" The door of the high press was unlocked, and the young lady filled a silver cup from the long-necked, gaily-coloured brandy flask, which she handed to Malysch. He crossed himself, drank, took a deep breath, bowed low, and quitted the room. "Now read it, Tania !" said my grandfather to his reader and amanuensis, who had resumed her seat by the window. My grandmother left her wheel, and my grandfather his bed : all crowded round Tatiana Stepanovna, who had broken the seal, but had not ventured to give a hasty preliminary glance through the contents. After a short pause, she began to read slowly and distinctly, but in a low tone. After the usual greeting then in vogue : " Most gracious and high-born father and most gracious lady mother," Alexei Stepanovitsch wrote almost as follows : " To my last letter of entreaty to you, my dear parents, I had the unhappiness of receiving an unfavourable reply. I cannot act in opposition to your will, and I submit myself to it. Nevertheless I cannot bear the burden of my existence without my adored Sofia Nikolaievna any longer, and in a very short time a bullet will end the life of your most miserable son."[1]

The effect of this letter was stunning. My aunts broke into

[1] I know this letter almost by heart, most probably it is still in existence among the papers of one or other of my brothers. It is pretty evident that a great part of its composition was borrowed from the romances of the period, which were great favourites with Alexei Stepanovitsch.

loud lamentations ; my grandmother, who had never expected to hear anything of this sort, grew pale, wrung her hands and sank unconscious to the ground—(our grandmothers were able to faint, too). Stepan Michailovitsch remained motionless ; he made a wry mouth, as if he were about to burst out in a rage, and his head began to shake just a little . . . . it never ceased shaking until his death. After the first terrified moment, the daughters hastened to aid in the restoration of their mother to consciousness. Scarcely indeed had she recovered from her swoon than Arina Vasilievna threw herself at her husband's feet, uttering cries as though she lamented the dead. The daughters all followed her example. Arina Vasilievna, regardless of my grandfather's unpromising mien, and quite forgetting that it was entirely due to her influence that the marriage had not taken place, pleaded anxiously with him in loud and agonised tones : " Little father Stepan Michailovitsch ! Do not drive your own son to desperation ! He is your only boy ! Let Alexei marry the girl ! " The old man remained in his former attitude without moving. At last he spoke in an unsteady tone : " Stop this howling ! Alexei deserves a thrashing. Now we will let the matter rest until morning ! Night brings counsel. Be off and order dinner to be served ! " Eating always had a soothing effect upon my grandfather when circumstances of an upsetting or perplexing nature occurred. At first, Arina Vasilievna would pay no attention to his command, and continued shrieking : " Mercy, Mercy ! " But when Stepan Michailovitsch bellowed :" Get you gone ! " in a tone which resembled the roar of an approaching storm, she and her daughters hurried off as fast as possible. Until dinner time no one dared set foot in my grandfather's room. It is difficult to guess what thoughts passed through his mind, and what caused the triumph of fatherly affection over that will of iron ; but it is certain that the battle was fought and won by the time that Masan went to his door to tell him dinner was served. He came quietly into the dining room, and his wife and daughters, who awaited his arrival standing each beside her chair, failed to detect the slightest trace of anger on his somewhat pale face. He was more composed and cheerful than he had been earlier in the day, and ate with a good appetite. Arina Vasilievna had been warned to refrain from making any remarks, or asking any questions ; and to stop sighing and groaning. It was in vain she tried to read the thoughts of her husband—in vain did her small, brown fat-encircled eyes seek his in anxious enquiry. The clear, deep, dark-blue eyes of Stepan Michailovitsch vouchsafed no reply. After dinner he went to sleep as usual, and awoke in still better spirits. But of his son and his son's letter he spoke never a word, and the family came to the clear conclusion that he was quite easy in his mind, and had no intention of acting with severity. When Arina Vasilievna bade him Good-night after supper, she ventured to say : " Won't you talk to me a little about Alexei ? " " I have already told you that night brings counsel," replied my grandfather with a smile, " Sleep in peace ! "

And next day he gave practical proof that the night had brought good and salutary counsel. He rose at four o'clock. Masan had already lighted the fire in his bed-chamber. The first words which Stepan Michailovitsch uttered were : " Tanaitschenok, you must carry a letter immediately to Alexei Stepanovitsch at Ufa. Get ready at once, and let no one know where you are going ! Put the brown colt in the shafts and take the piebald as led-horse. Take two osmins of oats and a loaf of bread with you. The steward Peter will give you two roublesworth of copper for the expenses of the journey. Everything must be ready by the time I have written the letter." No sooner said than done : my grand-father's commands were always obeyed without question or delay. He then unlocked the oaken press which served him as escritoire, collected pen, ink, and a sheet of paper, and wrote —not without difficulty—for it was now many years since he had done more than sign his name—in his clumsy, anti-quated handwriting : " Dear Son Alexei ! I and your mother, Arina Vasilievna, give you our permission to marry Sofia Nikolaievna Subina, if so be it is the will of God, and herewith send you our parental blessing. Your father, Stepan Bagrov."

Half an hour later, and still long before daybreak, Tanait-schenok had ascended the long mountain slope which skirted the magnificent threshing-floor, and was hastening at a brisk

trot in the direction of Ufa. At five o'clock Stepan Michailovitsch gave orders to the maid-servant Aksiutka—who
had developed from a young and ugly girl into an old and still
uglier woman—to bring the samovar, but not to awaken
anyone. All the same the old mistress *was* awakened, and
was secretly informed in a whisper that Tanaitschenok had
already been gone an hour, carrying a letter from the master,
but no one knew where he was taking it. Arina Vasilievna
did not dare to present herself before her husband. She
remained about an hour in her room, and at last made her
appearance when the old gentleman had finished his tea and
was chatting and joking with Aksiutka. " Who woke you
up ? " asked Stepan Michailovitsch gaily, as he reached out
his hand to her. " Have you slept badly ? " " No one
awoke me," replied Arina Vasilievna, kissing his hand with
great respect, " I woke up of myself. I slept soundly all
through the night : I hoped you would be kind to our poor
boy, Alexei."

My grandfather looked sharply at her, but could gather
nothing from her face, which wore its ordinary expression.
" If that's the case," said he, " I have a pleasant surprise for
you. I have just sent an express messenger to Ufa with a
letter for Alexei, telling him that we consent to his marriage
with Sofia Nikolaievna." In spite of the fact that Arina
Vasilievna, terrified by the suicidal threat of her son, had
urgently entreated her husband to give permission for the
marriage to take place, the news caused her more astonishment
than joy. She would indeed have been heartily glad to hear
it, but she had the fear of her daughters before her eyes.
Already she knew Jelisaveta's opinion of Alexei's letter, and
could guess what Alexandra Stepanovna would have to say
about it. As a consequence of this, Arina Vasilievna received
the news with which Stepan Michailovitsch thought to over-
joy her, in such a cold and constrained manner that the old
man was quite hurt. Neither did Jelisaveta Stepanovna
shew any sign of satisfaction ; she played the part of a sub
missive and obedient daughter. Tatiana alone (who firmly
believed that her brother's letter was meant in all seriousness)
was honestly delighted. From the first moment of hearing
the letter, Jelisaveta had had no fears for her brother's life.

She wept and prayed because her mother and younger sisters did so, and she did not wish to draw attention to herself by acting differently to the others. She wrote at once to Alexandra Stepanovna, who came in all haste to Bagrovo, furious at the turn of events, and convinced that their brother's letter was only one of Sofia Nikolaievna's ingenious and humbugging schemes. Assisted by Jelisaveta, she very soon persuaded her mother, and even Tatiana, into believing the same ; but the matter was now concluded and it was hopeless to make objections. Stepan Michailovitsch excepted, it never occurred to any member of the family that Sofia Nikolaievna might possibly refuse her suitor.

And now we must quit Bagrovo, and see what was happening in Ufa.

It is difficult to say whether Alexei Stepanovitsch actually would have carried out his resolution to shoot himself in the event of his parents remaining inexorable ; or whether, influenced by reading some silly romance, he had availed himself of the idea in the hope of forcing his father to revoke his decision. When I take into consideration the various characteristics developed later by Alexei Stepanovitsch, neither one nor the other idea appears probable. My opinion is, that the young man was not lying when he threatened to shoot himself if permission to wed Sofia Nikolaievna was refused ; but he had not actually made up his mind to the deed, though such a solution of a difficulty is more frequently the act of weak and fanciful than of vehement and energetic natures. In any case, the idea of suicide was borrowed from some romance, because such an act was utterly at variance with his character and the influences amid which he had been born and bred. Be this as it may, Alexei Stepanovitsch was in such an agitated state of mind after sending his letter that he was seized with an ague. He had refrained from telling his old friend Madame Alakaieva about this last desperate measure ; but she soon noticed, on her daily visit, that in addition to the ague and the love trouble, the young man had something on his mind which gave him no rest, night or day. One day she sat beside him, knitting a stocking, and relating any bit of gossip that she thought might amuse him and divert his mind from his hopeless love affair. Alexei

Stepanovitsch was lying on the sofa, his hands clasped under his head, gazing out of the window. Suddenly he turned as white as chalk : a carriage with a pair of horses turned into the courtyard from the street, and he recognised the horses and Tanaitschenok. " From my father ! From Bagrovo ! " he exclaimed, as he sprang up and rushed into the ante-room. Madame Alakaieva seized him by the arm, and with the aid of the hall-servant prevented him dashing out-of-doors, as the weather was cold and damp. While this was happening, Tanaitschenok hurried into the house and gave him the letter. With trembling hands Alexei Stepanovitsch broke the seal, read the few lines ; his eyes filled with tears, and he sank on his knees before the sacred ikon.[1] At first Madame Alakaieva was quite at a loss what to think of his strange behaviour, but Alexei Stepanovitsch handed her the letter, and having read it, she threw herself—wild with joy—on the neck of the young man, who was nearly swooning with delight. Now, for the first time, he confessed to her the contents of his last letter to his parents. Madame Alakaieva shook her head at him. Tanaitschenok was called and minutely questioned as to how and why and when he had been sent on his errand, and the two friends were quite convinced that Stepan Michailovitsch had acted solely on his own initiative in the matter, without the concurrence and, most probably, against the wishes of his family. After the first transports of Alexei Stepanovitsch's rapture and the first bewilderment of Madame Alakaieva were somewhat calmed, and when, not daring to trust the evidence of their eyes, they had re-read the letter—(for they knew the stubborn character of Stepan Michailovitsch, and distrusted the evil influence of his family)—a long confabulation was held about the next step to be taken in the great affair. So long as the consent of Stepan Michailovitsch was still in the balance, it had seemed as if no difficulties were to be overcome in the case of Sofia Nikolaievna ; but now a sudden doubt arose in Madame Alakaieva's mind, even while taking into consideration all the favourable symptoms, as to whether she had not represented the matter in too promising a light to her young favourite. With her wonted prudence she at

---

[1] In Russia a holy picture or ikon is suspended on the walls of every room in a house. [Tr. S. R.]

once set to work to check his high hopes, and warned him that if he let himself be too dazzled by his success with his parents, it might be still harder for him to bear a sudden and possible shattering of his beautiful dream. She hinted at the lack of foundation for such premature rejoicing so very plainly that Alexei Stepanovitsch began to feel quite anxious. But Madame Alakaieva by no means faltered in her efforts on his behalf, and went next day to see Sofia Nikolaievna in order to propose the marriage to her. Quite briefly and simply, and without exaggerating a single point, she spoke of Alexei's devoted and passionate love, which probably was no secret to Sofia Nikolaievna herself any more than to anyone in the whole city. With all the partiality of a relation she dwelt on the amiable character, the good nature, and the remarkable modesty of the young man. She gave a minute and complete account of the present and future condition of his personal fortune, spoke quite candidly of his family, not omitting to mention in this connection that the previous day Alexei Stepanovitsch had received a letter from his parents, giving their permission and blessing to his request for the hand of the universally admired and beloved Sofia Nikolaievna. The lover himself, added the old lady, what with impatience and suspense while awaiting his parents consent, and what with his unutterable love, had fallen into a fever, but had not been able to withstand the desire to hear his fate decided ; and so she, as his relative, had come to ask Sofia Nikolaievna whether she would grant permission for Alexei Stepanovitsch to make a formal proposal for her hand to Nikolai Feodoro-vitsch. Sofia Nikolaievna, who had already long been accustomed to think and act for herself, replied without the slightest embarrassment, and still less of the affectation and airs which the young ladies of that period assumed in like circumstances : " I am grateful to Alexei Stepanovitsch for the honour he has done me, and grateful to you, respected Maria Pavlovna, for your friendly interest. For some time past I have been aware of Alexei Stepanovitsch's inclination for myself, and have thought it quite probable that he wished to make me a proposal of marriage ; without deciding for my own part whether I could give him a definite reply. Alexei Stepanovitsch's last visit to his home, his sudden and—as you yourself explained to me—dangerous and long illness while away, and the change in his manner when he returned to Ufa, all made it quite clear to me, that his parents had no desire for me to become their daughter-in-law. I confess that I was astonished at this attitude. I should have thought a refusal on the part of my own father much more likely. As time went on, I noticed that Alexei Stepanovitsch's old affection for me was reviving, and now I hear that he has obtained the consent of his parents. You see for yourself, respected Maria Pavlovna, that events have taken a critical turn. To marry into a hostile family is too risky an undertaking for my taste. My father would never refuse his consent to my marrying the man of my choice, but in this case I should be compelled to practise deceit. For if he guessed that any country nobleman whatever had been forced to beg and entreat his parents' permission to marry me, he would never permit me to degrade myself by entering a family where I was not welcome. And I am not in love with Alexei Stepanovitsch. I have the utmost esteem for his fine character and his constancy, and I believe he is capable of making the woman of his choice happy. And so you must permit me to consider the matter farther. And above all I must see Alexei Stepanovitsch himself, before saying anything to my invalid father, who must not be unnecessarily agitated. Will you ask your nephew to come and see us, as soon as he is sufficiently recovered?"

Madame Alakaieva reported this answer in full to young Bagrov, who considered it distinctly unfavourable to his hopes; but his old friend consoled him by saying that she herself, on the contrary, considered it very friendly.

For a long time after she had bidden Maria Pavlovna a friendly adieu, Sofia Nikolaievna sat alone in her salon, sunk in deep thought. Her bright, sparkling eyes were troubled; sorrowful thoughts filled her mind and were reflected in her charming and expressive countenance. Every word she had spoken to Madame Alakaeva was strictly true; and the question as to whether or not she should wed Alexei Stepanovitsch remained unanswered. At last the long-expected proposal of marriage had been made, and the answer—so pregnant with fate for a girl—must be decided upon. Her extraordinarily clear and lucid mind, as yet untouched by passion, foresaw all events in their true light. The future promised nothing but sorrow and trouble. Her father lay upon his death-bed, for the family physician had already warned her that he would not live much over a year. The old man's property consisted merely of two insignificant estates, Subovka and Kasimovka, comprising only a retinue of forty serfs : in ready money Nikolai Feodorovitsch had only saved about ten thousand roubles destined for his Sonitschka's dowry. To see his darling child married had been his dearest and most fervent wish ; but . . . . (and occasionally such curious cases occur) . . . so far the universally adored Sofia Nikolaievna had never had a suitor, by which I mean that no one had ever made a formal request for her hand. In the event of her father's death, the six children of his two marriages would have to be supported somehow : two trustees would have to be appointed ; in fact the three children of Alexandra Petrovna, who had inherited some fifty serfs, were to be sent to their grandmother, whose son had already promised to act as trustee. Sofia Nikolaievna's brothers by the same mother were already temporarily provided for in the Moscow University School for the nobility ; and it seemed as if she were likely to be left alone in the world, without even the support of some distant relative. She would be without a roof to cover her. Poverty, want, dependence upon strangers, are a dreary lot for anyone. But for a girl who had occupied such a high social position and had lived in such luxury, proud by disposition and accustomed to unbounded admiration and flattery, a girl too who had already experienced the painful burden of dependence and had only just tasted the sweets of ease and power, the outlook was indeed intolerable. And here was a young, honourable, modest, charming, and well-born man offering her his hand and his heart—an only son, whose father possessed an estate of nearly two hundred serfs, who had the expectation of a splendid property from his aunt, who loved and worshipped her : surely there was no cause for hesitation here. On the other hand the disparity in their mentality was too great. No one in the town would ever have dreamt of such a thing as Sofia Nikolaievna marrying Alexei Stepanovitsch. She clearly recognised the correctness of public opinion and could not but agree with it. Herself a marvel of beauty and intelligence, he pink and white as any lass (a circumstance quite annoying to her in itself) but a simple, and generally accepted rather stupid country squire : she versatile and witty—he shy and lumpish : she a cultured and, considered in the light of those days, quite a learned maiden, well-read, and interested in all the questions of the day—he an utterly uneducated man, who had read nothing in his life but a couple of inferior novels and a number of Russian songs, who found no interest in anything but catching quails with a decoy and flying falcons. She, sparkling, entertaining, and enchanting in society—he unable to utter even a few words, shy, awkward, ridiculous, covered with confusion and hiding in corners so as not to come in contact with the carpet knights of the locality (although in reality he had a great deal more sense than many of these); she the possessor of a proud, lofty unbending will—he weak, without a will of his own, and influenced by any and everyone. Was he indeed a man capable of protecting his wife at home and abroad ? Such comparisons and doubts crowded the thoughts of the young girl. Twilight had long since fallen, and still she sat alone in the salon. At length she was overwhelmed by such an intense melancholy, such an utter feeling of helplessness and absence of all guidance, everything in life seemed so gloomy and unpromising, that she felt an urgent necessity to fortify herself by prayer. She sought her own chamber, and, before the picture of Our Lady of Smolensk, which once before had miraculously endowed her with courage to bear the burden of her life, sank on her knees and prayed long, weeping bitterly.

Even while she prayed she felt new strength in her soul, combined with a will and capacity for making her choice ; although as yet she did not know what the choice would be. Revived by this feeling, she rose and went down stairs to give a look to her sick father as he lay asleep ; then returned to her chamber, lay down on her bed, and slept peacefully. She awoke next morning calm and collected ; and after short reflection she decided to carry out her intention of holding an interview with her lover, and letting the impression made on her by him at this interview decide her choice.

MARRIAGE OF THE YOUNGER BAGROV

Alexei Stepanovitsch, who awaited her decision in a state of the most feverish suspense, sent for his doctor, and begged him to cure him as fast as he could. This the good man promised to do, and for once in his life kept his word. At the end of a week's time, Alexei Stepanovitsch —wasted, pale, and weak—was seated in Sofia Nikolaievna's drawing room. The lamentable appearance of the youth, who until recently had been so full of health and strength, excited her deep compassion, and she softened down a good deal of what she had to say to him. The substance of what she told him was precisely the same as that she had told old Madame Alakaieva; but she now added for the first time that she would never leave her father while he lived, and that she had no wish to live in the country, but preferred to live in a Government town, and especially in Ufa, where she had so many friends, people of culture and position, whose society she desired for herself and her husband. In conclusion, she expressed a wish that her husband should remain in Government service and make an esteemed and honourable—if not a brilliant— position for himself. In addition to agreeing to all the usual rights and claims of a betrothed wife, Alexei Stepanovitsch humbly added that any wish of Sofia Nikolaievna would be a command, and that his sole happiness would lie in the fulfilment of her desires. And, marvellous to relate, this speech—so utterly unworthy of any man—a certain sign that a husband's love could not be relied upon and that his wife would have but a poor prospect of future happiness— met with the entire approval of a girl of the type of Sofia Nikolaievna ! However unwillingly, we are fain to confess that the love of power, which had its root deep in her being, had so waxed and increased since her stepmother's death that Sofia Nikolaievna, without even being aware of it, was strongly influenced thereby in her selection of Alexei Stepanovitsch as a husband. She desired to read the letter for herself, in which his parents consented to his making his offer of marriage. The young man had the letter in his pocket and instantly handed it to her. Sofia Nikolaievna read it through, and was convinced that her suspicion of an earlier refusal on the part of the family was only too well-founded. The young man was incapable of telling a lie, and was so deeply in love that a kind look from his adored charmer was enough to extract anything from him that she wished to hear ; and as Sofia Nikolaievna ordered him to be quite candid with her, he told her everything, in no way concealing anything unfavourable ; and, as it turned out, this candour served him in good stead in his wooing. The thought that she might transform and remodel this amiable, modest, and innocent youth according to her own mind sprang suddenly into the alert but feminine brain of Sofia Nikolaievna. In the most enchanting colours her imagination portrayed the gradual awakening and development of the yet dormant mind of this child of nature, who was lacking neither in intellect nor feeling—these qualities being as yet unawakened—whose spiritual being would melt with gratitude and love to her as its awakener. This thought took possession of the young girl's enthusiastic fancy, and she dismissed her sick lover very sweetly, promising to speak to her father and send a reply by Madame Alakaieva. Alexei Stepanovitsch was lost in bliss, according to the fashion of those days. In the evening Sofia Nikolaievna again sought counsel in prayer. She prayed long, earnestly, and with fervour. Tired out, she slept, and during the night had a dream, which she, as anyone may readily believe, considered to be a sanction of her choice. I cannot recollect the exact tenour of this remarkable dream, but I do most clearly recall that it might much more justly have been explained in quite an opposite sense. The next morning Sofia Nikolaievna informed her practically dying father of Alexei Stepanovitsch's proposal of marriage. Although the old man had no actual acquaintance with his daughter's suitor, still he had a decided notion that the latter was an utterly insignificant person. In spite of his earnest desire to see his Sonitschka settled before he died, this wooer . . . the first his daughter had ever had, be it observed . . . was utterly distasteful to him. However Sofia Nikolaievna hastened to explain to him with her usual dexterity and persuasiveness that this match was by no means to be despised. She repeated everything in favour of the marriage that we have already heard, and especially assured her father that she would never leave him, but would live with him after she was married. She dwelt so earnestly upon her desolate condition, when God should choose to make

her an orphan, that her father exclaimed with tears in his eyes :
" My dearest and best of little daughters ! Just act as you
think best ! I agree to all. Bring your future husband to
see me at once ! I wish to know more about him. I give my
full and unqualified consent to his bringing me his parents'
written proposal of marriage."

Sofia Nikolaievna thereupon promptly wrote to Madame
Alakaieva to request her to give the young man her father's
invitation, fixing the day and hour.

Alexei Stepanovitsch, who meanwhile was sunk in visions
of bliss and was revelling in the sweetest hopes, was utterly
disconcerted at receiving an invitation to wait on Nikolai
Feodorovitsch at a certain hour, as he had imagined his
future father-in-law far too weak and ill to be able to take
part in an interview. Nikolai Feodorovitsch who, in the absence of the Vice-Roy was the first person and held the highest
authority in the whole Province of Ufa ! Nikolai Feodorovitsch ! whom, hitherto, he had never approached without
experiencing the most respectful awe, now filled him with
terrified dismay. " What will he say to my presumptuous
proposal ? I, an obscure official of the fourteenth class, to
dare to think of marrying his daughter ! ' Why have you
presumed to think of my daughter ! ' he may say to me."
' Is she the bride for the likes of you ? To the guardhouse with
him ! Let him appear before the tribunal ' ! " However silly
and idiotic such thoughts may seem, it is a fact that they
passed through the youth's distracted mind, as he frequently
related himself in later days. At last he grew more composed,
and encouraged by Madame Alakaieva's exhortations, he put
on his uniform, [which hung on his shrunken form as if suspended from a clothes peg], and took himself off to the Vice-
regent. With his three-cornered hat tucked under his arm,
his shaking hand trying to keep his refractory sword in the
right position, scarce able to breathe for nervousness, he was
ushered into the chamber of the once brilliant and witty
Nikolai Feodorovitsch—now a broken, and dying old man.
Alexei Stepanovitsch made a low bow and remained standing
near the door. This sort of entry made a bad impression on
the invalid. " Please come here, Monsieur Bagrov," he said,
" and sit down at my bedside ! I am very weak, and cannot

speak loudly." Alexei Stepanovitsch advanced, and after making several more bows seated himself in an armchair beside the bed. " You are asking my daughter's hand in marriage," continued the old man. Up sprang Bagrov, made another bow, and replied that this was so and that he had dared to hope for such happiness. I could indeed repeat the whole conversation, word for word, as Alexei Stepanovitsch was fond of telling the story in later days ; but it recapitulated all that the reader already knows, and I fear to weary him. The substance of it all was, that Nikolai Feodorovitsch questioned the young man as to his family and fortune, and as to his future intention with regard to the Government service, and where he intended to live. He told him that Sofia Nikolaievna, beyond a dowry of ten thousand roubles, would only inherit two families of serfs and three thousand roubles in ready money under his first marriage settlement. Finally he observed that Alexei Stepanovitsch, as an obedient son, had certainly not omitted to obtain his parents' consent before making his proposal : it was customary however for the bridegroom's parents to write personally to the father of the bride, and until this had been done no definite reply could be made. Alexei Stepanovitsch kept everlastingly jumping up, bowing, and sitting down again : he agreed to everything, and duly promised to write to his father and mother on the following day. At the end of half-an-hour the old gentleman said he was tired, which was true indeed, and dismissed the young man in a very curt way. Scarcely had the latter taken his departure than Sofia Nikolaievna tripped into her father's room. She found him lying with closed eyes, his face expressing exhaustion and weariness of spirit. Hearing his daughter's step, he opened his eyes, looked at her enquiringly, pressed his hands to his breast, and said : " Sonitschka, is it possible that you wish to marry a man like that ? " Sofia Nikolaievna had quite anticipated the effect of the interview and was prepared for the worst. " I have already told you, dear father," she replied in a gentle but resolute tone, " that at first sight you would take Alexei Stepanovitsch to be a stupid sort of man. He has no conversation, and is shy and constrained in company. But I have had much opportunity of seeing him alone and talking to him, and I assure you that he is not in the least stupid ; in fact he is much cleverer than many of those who make fun of him. I do beg of you to let him come and see you now and then, for I am persuaded you will end up by agreeing with me." The old man looked long and earnestly in his daughter's face, as if to discover the secret workings of her mind, sighed deeply, and consented to invite the young man to pay him another visit shortly, in order to get better acquainted with him.

Alexei Stepanovitsch wrote an affectionate and dutiful letter to his parents, which he despatched by the earliest post. He thanked them for enabling him to continue living, and entreated them earnestly to write immediately to Nikolai Feodorovitsch soliciting the hand of his daughter for their son : he added that this formality was customary, and that Subin declined to give his consent to the marriage until he had received the letter. The carrying-out of this simple request placed the old couple in a pretty dilemma : they were no hands at letter-writing : they had not the faintest notion of what they were expected to say, and at the same time were exceedingly perturbed at the thought of laying themselves open to the criticism of their future connection, who was such a distinguished and learned man. It took them a whole week to compose and write the letter, but at last, and with infinite toil and labour, it was finished and sent to Alexei Stepanovitsch. It was very awkwardly expressed, and lacked utterly the usual compliments and expressions of friendly regard.

While Alexei Stepanovitsch was awaiting the reply to his own letter, he received two invitations to visit Nikolai Feodorovitsch. The second visit somewhat lessened the bad impression made by the first. Sofia Nikolaievna was present at the third, tripping casually into her father's room as if quite unaware of her suitor's presence there, and professing that she had returned quite unexpectedly from paying visits. Her advent changed everything : she contrived to bring out Alexei Stepanovitsch at his best, knowing exactly how to turn the conversation so that the natural good sense, honesty, moral worth, and true-heartedness of the young man were shewn to the best advantage. Nikolai Feodorovitsch was unaffectedly delighted, treated Alexei with marked courtesy and kindness, and invited him to come and see him as often as possible. When Alexei had gone, the old man embraced his Sonitschka with tears, and fondly caressing her, told her she was a fairy who could bring the hidden treasures of a man's soul to light, although so deeply sunken that no one had even suspected their existence. Sofia Nikolaievna herself was very much pleased, for she had scarcely dared to hope that her future husband would shew himself in such an advantageous light.

At last the long-expected letter, with the formal proposal of marriage on the part of Alexei Stepanovitsch's parents, arrived, and the young man handed it himself to Nikolai Feodorovitsch. But alas, even the magic presence and aid of Sofia Nikolaievna were powerless to aid in this case : the bridegroom again grew displeasing to his future father-in-law, who was highly incensed by the letter itself. The next day he had a long talk with his daughter, and placed plainly before her the disadvantages of such a union—where the man was so greatly his wife's inferior in intellect, culture, and character. He added that her lover's family did not like her, and probably would hate her, which was invariably the attitude of rough, towards educated people : he warned her against placing any blind trust in the promises of her plighted bridegroom, saying that such promises were seldom fulfilled after marriage ; and that even with all the good will in the world, a man of Alexei Stepanovitsch's type was incapable of carrying them out. But Sofia Nikolaievna was quite able to reply to all these well-founded objections with her usual tact and dexterity ; and knew how to set forth the advantages of a marriage with such an amiable, honourable, and worthy man—(even if he *were* rather bashful and uneducated)—in such a convincing way, that at last Nikolai Feodorovitsch was quite carried away by her sanguine hopes and gave his final consent to the marriage. Sofia Nikolaievna embraced her father affectionately, kissed his emaciated hands, and fetching the holy picture, knelt down at his bedside, and received his blessing with many tears. " Father," cried the happy girl, enthusiastically, " with the help of God I hope to make a new man of Alexei Stepanovitsch before a year is over. Reading good books, intercourse with cultured people, constant companionship with me, will supply all that is lacking in him owing to his neglected education : his shyness will disappear, and he will be able to make a good figure in society." " God grant it may be so ! " replied the old man. " Send for the priest, and you and I will pray together for your future happiness."

The evening of that same day, the bridegroom, Madame Alakaievna, and several intimate friends of the Subin family were invited to the house of Nikolai Feodorovitsch, who gave the bridegroom his formal consent. No words can paint the happiness of the young man ! In her extremest old age Sofia Nikolaievna never forgot her husband's rapture during that moment. Alexei Stepanovitsch threw himself at Nikolai Feodorovitsch's feet, kissed his hands, wept, sobbed like a child, and nearly fainted—so overwhelmed was he by the happiness, which up to the very last moment had seemed so utterly unattainable. The bride herself was deeply affected by this fervent outpouring of such ardent and boundless love.

Two days later it was decided to announce the formal betrothal, and the whole city was invited. The event caused no little surprise, for no one in the town had ever really believed the report that Sofia Nikolaievna Subina was going to marry Alexei Stepanovitsch. Now they had to believe it, and assembled in full force at the appointed time to offer their congratulations. The bridegroom beamed with joy, and was utterly unconscious of the irony conveyed in the compliments of the well-wishers, and of their sarcastic smiles and glances ; but Sofia Nikolaievna saw, marked, heard, and understood everything, although people were very careful not to betray themselves in her presence. From the outset she had been perfectly aware how her choice would be criticised by the company present ; but still she could not fail to be stung by these signs of disapprobation, though no one could ever have suspected it. She was very gay ; charming with everyone, especially with her betrothed husband ; and seemed perfectly happy in her choice. The bridal pair were duly summoned to Nikolai Feodorovitsch's room, where the rings were exchanged in the presence of a few witnesses. The old father could not restrain his tears while the priest recited the prayers.

At the conclusion of the ceremony, he was kissed by the young couple, pressed each to his heart, and, looking earnestly in Alexei Stepanovitsch's face, said : " Never cease loving her as you love her now ! God has given you such a treasure. . . ." he could say no more. The newly-plighted couple returned to the expectant company, escorted by the witnesses to the betrothal. All the men embraced the bridegroom, and kissed the bride's hand ; while all the ladies embraced the bride, and gave their hand to the bridegroom to kiss. When all this bustle and fuss was over, the betrothed couple were seated side by side on a sofa, kissed each other, and received all the congratulations over again, which the guests, each holding a glass of wine, hastened to offer them. S. I. Anitschkov presented the men, and Madame Alakaieva the ladies. Alexei Stepanovitsch, who had never drunk anything stronger than water in his whole life, was persuaded to accept a glass of wine in honour of the great occasion, which instantly took effect upon his brain, already overwrought by sickness and emotion. He grew exceedingly lively ; laughed, cried, and became quite confidential, to the extreme delight of the visitors and equal distress of his bride. The company waxed livelier, as they drank one cheery glass after another : and a splendid breakfast was served. This was greatly enjoyed ; more wine was drunk ; and everyone separated in the highest spirits. The poor bridegroom had a bad headache, and Madame Alakaieva saw him safely home.

Nikolai Feodorovitsch grew worse, and wished to hurry on the wedding ; but as on the other hand he desired the dower to include the customary magnificent jewels, the event had to be postponed for a couple of months. The maternal diamonds and pearls were sent to Moscow to be re-set according to the latest fashion : silver plate, millinery, and various presents were likewise ordered to be sent from that city, but the bulk of the trousseau, the hangings of the state bed, and the beautiful pelisse of black fox fur—(these pelts even then cost five hundred roubles apiece, and cannot be bought now for less than five thousand roubles)—were all made in Kazan. Table linen and finest Holland linen were provided in the greatest abundance. The ten thousand roubles which had been set aside for the dower were considered a large sum in those days. Much had been accumulated beforehand, having been purchased as favourable conditions arose ; and when one reads the inventory of the dower, one cannot fail to be astonished alike at the luxury and the cheap cost of living at the end of the eighteenth century.

The first business after the betrothal ceremony was to write all the necessary complimentary letters to the relatives of both bride and bridegroom. Sofia Nikolaievna, who possessed a marvellous gift for letter-writing, sent such a charming and affectionate epistle to her future parents-in law, that Stepan Michailovitsch, although unable to express himself well in a letter, was able to fully appreciate it. After listening with great delight while Tania read it aloud, he took it from his daughter, remarked on the beauty and distinctness of the writing, read the letter through twice, and said : " A clever girl, and a good-hearted one, too ! " The whole family were silent with vexation, with the exception of Alexandra Stepanovna, who, unable to control her spite, replied with a sour face : " All that sort of stuff is her book-learning, Father ; honey in the mouth and gall in the heart." The old man turned on her in a rage, and said in a threatening tone : " What authority have you for saying that ? Take care that I hear no more of these hints, and that you stop influencing the others with your black tongue ! " This rebuke made them all quiet as mice, and they hated Sofia Nikolaievna all the more, while Stepan Michailovitsch, on whom the delightful letter had made a deep impression, himself seized a pen, and in defiance of all polite formalties, wrote as follows :

" My dear, my sensible, clever daughter-in-law ! As you shew such affection and respect for us old folks, without even having seen us, we feel the greatest affection for you. And when we meet, with God's will we shall all love each other still more dearly. We shall treat you as our own daughter, and rejoice in the happiness of our Alexei ! "

Sofia Nikolaievna was quite able to value this old man's simple letter at its true worth. In actual truth, she already loved him from what she had heard of him. The bride had no relatives to whom it was necessary that Alexei Stepanovitsch should write. She desired however that her betrothed should send a letter to her friend, the guardian of her two brothers,

A. F. Anitschkov ; and naturally the betrothed was only too ready to fulfil her wish. As she suspected that Alexei Stepanovitsch did not possess any especial talent for letter-writing, she hinted that she would like to see the composition before it was sent off. Heavens ! What she was forced to read ! Alexei Stepanovitsch had heard so much talk of the great erudition of Anitschkov that he thought it behoved him to write a really creditable letter to such a great man ; and, consequently, had borrowed such wonderful phrases from this or that novel, that under any other circumstances Sofia Nikolaievna would have laughed heartily at his effort. As it was, she turned scarlet with shame, and wept. At first she was at a loss how to extricate herself from an awkward position ; but, after a little thought, she decided to write a letter to Anitschkov herself, which she set her bridegroom to copy, after she had explained to the latter that, owing to his never having been accustomed to correspond with unknown people, he had written a letter which might have offended Anitschkov. As she spoke thus, she felt deeply ashamed for her future husband, her voice trembled, and she felt humiliated at having to give him instructions. However, the bridegroom himself was quite charmed with the suggestion. He read the letter, found it splendid, was lost in admiration of the authoress's skill, and covered her hands with kisses. But this first step towards the control of and power over her future husband, which she had so much desired, was a hard one.

As he knew that his parents had but little money and were compelled to exercise economy, Alexei Stepanovitsch wrote to them asking for a very small sum ; but he persuaded Madame Alakaieva to follow up his request with another letter, dwelling on the modesty of his demand and the urgent necessity of a reasonable amount of money to meet the expenses of the wedding. He himself only asked for eight hundred roubles. Madame Alakaieva however demanded fifteen hundred. The old people replied that they had not so much money, and sent him their last three hundred roubles, adding that if he really was in want of more, he must borrow the other five hundred roubles of somebody or other. At the same time they explained that it was their intention to send him four horses, a coachman, a postillion, a coach, and a good stock of provisions. They made no reply to Madame Alakaiva's letter, as they were very much annoyed at her unreasonable demand. There was nothing more to be done with them. Alexei Stepanovitsch thanked them for their kindness, and borrowed five hundred roubles. As this was not near enough, Madame Alakaieva lent him another five hundred, without the knowledge of his parents.

Now the bridegroom's visits waxed more frequent and yet longer, and his conversations with his bride took an easier and less constrained turn. Now for the first time did Sofia Nikolaievna realise the boredom that awaited her, as she grew to understand her husband thoroughly ! It is true that she had not erred in crediting him with natural good sense, a good heart, and inviolable honesty ; but in all other matters he betrayed such a narrow intellectual outlook, such petty interests, and such a mixture of self-will and self-conceit, that, not infrequently, her strong will and high courage were subdued ; not infrequently she hesitated as to carrying out her intention of marrying him, would wrench the betrothal ring from her finger and laying it before the picture of the Mother of God, would entreat counsel and help from Heaven with bitter tears. As we already know, this was her invariable custom when any difficulty arose in her life. After prayer on these occasions, Sofia Nikolaievna would rise from her knees, strengthened and comforted ; and, recognising this consolation as coming from God, would slip the ring on her finger, and go cheerfully off to the salon and her expectant lover ! Meanwhile her sick father grew worse and yet weaker every day. His daughter comforted him by telling him that she was continually discovering new and lovable qualities in her bridegroom, and that she was firmly convinced she would be happy with him. Long-continued sickness had clouded the acute mind of Nikolai Feodorovitsch. Not only did he implicitly believe in the sincerity of his child, but himself ended by firmly believing in her future happiness. " Thank God," he often exclaimed, " now I can die in peace." The wedding-day drew near. The trousseau and gifts were all prepared. The bridegroom—or rather Madame Alakaieva in whose hands he had placed everything—had provided everything necessary on his side. That worthy dame until now had had no conception of Alexei Stepanovitsch's utter lack of knowledge of the most ordinary rules of society. Without her guidance, he would have committed blunders which would have driven his bride to desperation. For example, he proposed sending her a dress as a birthday gift that at best would only have been suitable for a servant-girl. He quite seriously contemplated setting off to his wedding in an ancient, ancestral vehicle, which would have sent the whole town into fits of laughter ; and so on. It is true these matters were not of intrinsic importance ; but it would have been perfectly intolerable to Sofia Nikolaievna to have her husband the laughing stock of the Ufa gentry. Of course Alexei Stepanovitsch was deterred from carrying out his absurd intentions through the good offices of Madame Alakaieva, or say rather by the bride herself, for she was consulted in everything by the old lady. Sofia Nikolaievna hastened to inform the young man that he must send her nothing on her birthday, as she objected to receiving birthday presents. For the wedding she had a new English coach bought, which Mursachanov, an Ufa land owner, had recently brought from Petersburg, where, in the course of one month, he had squandered and gambled away his whole fortune. For this coach three hundred and fifty roubles were paid in assignats. This money was drawn by Sofia Nikolaievna from her own cash, and the coach was sent to the bridegroom as a gift from her father, but with a warning not to disturb the invalid by expressing any thanks. Other difficulties were settled in like manner. Alexei Stepanovitsch and the bride wrote a joint letter to the old Bagrovs, in which they pressed them—both in their own name and that of Nikolai Feodorovitsch—to attend the wedding. But the old pair, accustomed to the easy and unconstrained life of country folk, declined the invitation. Town life and town company alike inspired them with terror. The daughters had no wish to go, either, but Stepan Michailovitsch overruled them and decided that Alexandra and Jelisaveta must be present at the wedding. Erlykin was absent on State Service in Orenburg, but Ivan Karataiev accompanied his wife to Ufa. The arrival of these unexpected and uninvited guests caused no end of unpleasantness to Sofia Nikolaievna. Her future sisters-in-law, sly and crafty women by nature and evilly-disposed towards her, each behaved in a cold, repellent and, frequently, downright uncivil manner. Sofia Nikolaievna was only too well aware how little friendship she had to expect from her husband's sisters ; nevertheless she considered it her duty to receive them with all kindness and affection. But she was forced to the conclusion that all her efforts to please were wasted, and that her amiable behaviour only served to make her enemies more contemptuous. In self-defence she was compelled to adopt a tone of cold politeness, which was no protection from those venomous shafts and insolent allusions, which cannot fail to be understood, and which it is impossible to resent without laying oneself open to farther slights. This cowardly habit of insulting anyone by hints and allusions, which to-day—thanks to our improved education—is relegated to its original circle of petty tradesfolk, servant girls, and lackeys, was only too common in those days amongst the country nobility, owing to their intimate association with their servants. And am I right in saying it has disappeared ? Rather, does it not exist in a still greater measure in our circles, although concealed by a mask of wit and refinement ?

It was but in the nature of things that the bridegroom's sisters—the shabby scarecrows, as they were called—detested the townsfolk of Ufa. Whatever Ivan Petrovitsch Karataiev, (who, faithful to his Bashkirian habits, did nothing but drink bitter schnapps for his health's sake from morning to night), thought about it all, one thing is certain : that on taking leave of Sofia Nikolaievna after seeing her for the first time, he kissed her hand thrice, and exclaimed with all the enthusiasm of a true-born Bashkir : "The deuce ! what a fine lass our Alexei has caught !" Poor Sofia Nikolaievna shed many a tear over the hostile attitude of her future sisters-in-law and over the rough good nature of her Bashkirian brother-in-law. The worst of it all was that Alexei Stepanovitsch appeared to notice nothing wrong, and seemed quite satisfied with his sisters' behaviour towards Sofia Nikolaievna, a circumstance which augured plenty of sorrow and trouble for the future. The two malicious serpents utilised every moment of their visit to instil their poison into the candid mind of their brother, in whose house they were staying ; and they acted with such prudence and cunning, that Alexei Stepanovitsch never suspected their tricks. A thousand sly allusions to the bride's proud disposition, to her poverty, which she concealed under silk and gold, to his own utter subordination to her will, were continually dinned into his ears. Many of these he neither understood nor heeded ; but many reached their mark, led him astray, and caused him great uneasiness of mind. And all these wily machinations, and frequently even open attacks, were disguised by the mask of love and sympathy : " You are growing very thin, little brother," Jelisaveta Stepanovna would say to him, " that's the result of eternally running about. Sofia Nikol-aievna's errands leave you no peace. You have only just come, tired and hungry, from Golubinaia Street,[1] and off you rush to your bride without even sparing the time to eat something. You don't know how miserable you make us. . ." and then hypocritical tears, or, at the least, blinking and much play of an old pocket handkerchief, would end up her sinister hints. " No," would scream Alexandra Stepanovna, breaking vehemently into the conversation, " I cannot contain myself any longer. I know very well that you will be cross with us, little brother : perhaps you'll even cease to love us. God's will be done ! But *I will* speak the truth once and for all ; you have quite changed towards us ; you are ashamed of your sisters ; you neglect us ; you think only of your Sofia Nikolaievna : your one thought is how not to vex her. You are nothing but her slave, her serf ! And what about that old witch of an Alakaieva, who orders you about just as she pleases : ' Go there ! Buy this ! Enquire for So-and-So ! ' And then she will tell you to look sharp, and takes upon herself to reprove you ! As for us, she reckons us as nought, it never occurs to her to ask our advice about anything ! " Alexei Stepanovitsch had not a word to utter in reply to this long tirade. He only told his sisters that he loved them, and should always love them ; but he must now go and see Sofia Nikolaievna. And with that he took his hat, and made off with all haste. " Now run," shrieked the spiteful Alexandra Stepanovitsch after him, " run as fast as you can, so as not to keep her waiting ; or she will be cross with you and won't let you kiss her hand ! " Scenes like

[1] An outlying street in Ufa.

this were continually taking place, and could not fail to have some effect on Alexei. It did not take Sofia Nikolaievna long to detect a change in her betrothed's manner towards her after the arrival of his sisters. He seemed embarrassed, kept his appointments with her less punctually, and visited her less frequently. Sofia Nikolaievna knew the meaning of this change very well. And old Madame Alakaieva, who was now on very friendly and intimate terms with her, knew all that went on in Alexei Stepanovitsch's house, and was continually bringing her news. Sofia Nikolaievna's disposition was hasty and passionate ; and she would not hesitate to sound a matter to its depths when needful. She decided very wisely that it was not advisable to let the sisters have time to implant their poison still more deeply in the bridegroom's mind, and that the latter's eyes must be opened and his love and constancy for herself put to the proof. If the proof should turn out unsatisfactorily, it would be better to part before marriage than to unite herself to a man with no will of his own, who, as she herself expressed it, " would prove neither a shade from the sun, nor a shelter from the rain." Thereupon she asked her bridegroom to come and see her early one morning ; shut herself up with him in the salon ; gave orders that no one was to be admitted ; and addressed the young man, who had turned white with fear, somewhat after this fashion : " Just listen carefully to me ! I intend to speak to you from my heart and quite candidly ; and I entreat you to be equally candid with me. Your sisters hate me and have done every-thing in their power to turn your parents against me. This is only what you yourself have told me. But your love for me overcame that obstacle. Your parents gave you their blessing, and I made up my mind to marry you in spite of the hatred of the whole family. I hoped to find protection in your love and to endeavour to do my best to dispel the dislike of your family for myself. Now I see that I have made a mistake. You saw for yourself how kindly and politely I received your sisters. Their hostile manners have forced me to keep them at a distance : but I have not uttered a wrong word about them. And what is the result ? Hardly a week has passed since their arrival, and already your manner towards me is changed. You forget, or you daren't keep

your promises to me ; you spend a much shorter time with
me ; you are constrained and embarrassed ; you are much
colder to me. Don't try to deny it and don't try to excuse
it ; you will only be dishonest if you do. I know that you
still love me, but you are afraid to show it. You are afraid
of your sisters, and so you are distant, and even avoid being
left alone with me ! What I say is strictly true. And you
know that yourself. Tell me if I can place any confidence
in the duration of your love ? And is your love worthy of
the name, if it hides itself in terror, because your bride doesn't
happen to please your sisters' taste, as you have already known
for long enough ? And what, pray, will happen to me, if I
don't find favour in your parents' eyes ? Would that make
your love entirely disappear ? No, Alexei Stepanovitsch,
honourable men neither love nor act as you do. As you know
that your relations cannot endure me, their presence ought to
make you redouble your affection and respect for me. Then
they would never have dared to open their mouths against
me. Instead of this, you have permitted them to calumniate
me in your presence. I know everything they have been
accustomed to say against me. All this convinces me that
your love is only empty sentiment which will not last, and
that it is much better for us to part now than to lead a life
of unhappiness together. I will give you two days in which
to consider what I have just said to you. You can continue
your visits ; but for the next two days I will only see you
in the presence of others, and I shall make no allusion to
this conversation. Then I shall demand that you, as an
honourable man, will make it a matter of conscience to tell
me whether you feel prepared to protect me from your relatives
or from anyone else who regards me with hostility, and
whether you will compel your sisters to cease calumniating
me in my absence. To break off an engagement just a week
before the wedding is a great misfortune for any well-bred
girl ; but I would sooner face trouble boldly than have to
endure it for a lifetime. You know that I am not in love
with you ; but I have grown to care for you, and I have no
doubt my love would be more sincere and more lasting
than yours. And now, farewell ! To-day and to-morrow we
are strangers to each other." With these words she quitted

the room, closing the door after her. Alexei Stepanovitsch, whose eyes had long since been filled with tears, and who had several times attempted to speak, was not permitted a moment in which to reply. He stood thunderstruck, unable to collect his thoughts. At length, realising that he was in danger of losing his beloved Sofia Nikolaievna for ever, this feeling of desperation roused the courage and energy which even the weakest and slackest natures can exhibit for a short time. He rushed home, and when his sisters—utterly ignoring the agitated and disturbed appearance of the young man— received him with their usual sneers and jeers, he burst out in fury and reproached them in a way that terrified them. The anger of an ordinarily forbearing and patient man is always terrible. Among other things, Alexei Stepanovitsch informed his sisters that if they dared to utter another insulting word in his presence, whether about his bride or himself, he would leave the house instantly ; would not have anything more to do with them ; and would write and tell his father all about them. This was enough. Alexandra Stepanovna remembered the rebuke administered to her by her father only too well. She knew what a storm any complaint of her brother's would arouse, and what frightful consequences to herself she might expect. Both sisters threw themselves, sobbing, on Alexei Stepanovitsch's neck, entreated his pardon, and, crossing them- selves, swore that nothing of the sort should ever happen again ; that they themselves were really very fond of Sofia Nikolaievna ; and that it was only concern for his own health, and in order to tease him out of running on such a lot of tiresome errands, that they had ventured to make a few silly jokes. That same day they lost no time in hurrying off to Sofia Nikolaievna and treating her with marked civility.

She was aware of what had happened, and very triumphant. In the meantime the bridegroom's state of mind was deplorable. His love—grown more quiet and placid through his daily intercourse with Sofia Nikolaievna by reason of her calm and unaffected kindness towards him and by the immediate prospect of their union, and which, to a certain extent, he had tried to conceal from the ill-natured shafts of his sister's wit—now flamed up with such fire and passion that for the moment he was capable of any sacrifice, any act—even of heroism. All this was conveyed by the expression on his beautiful features and in his sparkling eyes, whenever, during the course of the endless two days, he presented himself before Sofia Nikolaievna. It cost her something to refrain from giving him a word or even a look of encouragement ; but she held fast to her resolve not to shorten the period of probation. She herself was astonished at the compassion and trouble in her heart. Now she realised that she really loved this shy, silent youth, who was so passionately devoted to her that he would inevitably die if she discarded him. But at last the wearisome three days were over. Early on the morning of the third day Alexei Stepanovitsch stood in the Subins' drawing room, awaiting his betrothed. The door opened, and in walked Sofia Nikolaievna, fairer and lovelier than ever, a soft smile playing round her lips, and her eyes so full of love, that, as she came towards Alexei Stepanovitsch, with outstretched hand, he lost control of his senses for the moment, and stood staring at her in silence. Recovering himself but without daring to touch the offered hand, he fell at his bride's feet, and with fiery eloquence and a thousand tears, gave vent to all his repressed love. Sofia Nikolaievna did not allow him to finish. She raised him up and told him that now she felt she had no cause to doubt the sincerity of his love, and added that she believed all his vows and promises and had no hesitation in placing her fate in his hands. She was kinder to him than she had ever been before, and permitted herself expressions of affection which, up to now, she had never uttered.

There now only remained five days before the wedding. All preparations were completed, and the bride and bridegroom could spend the time together without any fear of interruption. Five months had already elapsed since the betrothal, and Sofia Nikolaievna, faithful to her resolve to make a new man of her bridegroom, had neglected no opportunity of instilling into him those moral conceptions which were lacking in him, making what now seemed dark and confused, clear and distinct, and trying to eradicate all the erroneous notions, consequent upon his upbringing and the companionships of his youth. She encouraged him to read numbers of books, and when the conversation turned on literature, she was very apt at correcting errors, resolving doubts, and confirming crude guesses by examples in real life. But all that Sofia Nikolaievna had been able to impart to her bridegroom during these past five months was equalled if not surpassed by what he learnt during these five days of intimacy ; so much had the recent happenings sharpened the young man's intellect, enabling him to grasp things readily and with fresh interest. For my own part I cannot honestly say how all this moral instruction was effected. I can only repeat the assertions of teacher and pupil, who both declared that Alexei Stepanovitsch was duly reborn during this brief period. I willingly accept this statement, but at the same time possess overwhelming evidence that Alexei Stepanovitsch's progress in the realms of social deportment was not great. For instance, it is certain that only the day before the wedding he caused his bride great annoyance, and made her exceedingly angry, by his disregard of the restraining influence of polite manners. And this was how it all happened. Two aristocratic ladies were paying a visit to Sofia Nikolaievna. Suddenly in marched a servant holding a bundle wrapped up in paper, and announced that Alexei Stepanovitsch had just sent this by his coachman, and had likewise sent word that Sofia Nikolaievna must be quick and make it up into a cap for his sister, Alexandra Stepanovitsch. It was barely half-an-hour since Alexei had taken his departure from the house, and Sofia Nikolaievna—who was speechless with astonishment at this extraordinary commission—felt highly insulted. Her two friends, who had at first imagined that the parcel contained a present from the bridegroom, could not conceal their ironical smiles—and the bride, losing her customary self-command, ordered the bundle to be returned to Alexei Stepanovitsch with a message that he could take it to a milliner himself, and that some mistake had been made in bringing the work to her. However the real facts of the case were as follows. On his arrival at home the bridegroom had found his sister in a state of great perturbation : the milliner who had been commissioned to prepare the gala head-dresses for the wedding had suddenly fallen ill, and had returned all the materials. Now Alexei Stepanovitsch, recollecting that he had often noticed how clever his bride was at concocting hats and caps and wishing to oblige his distracted sister, called his servant and ordered him to hurry with the parcel of stuff to Sofia Nikolaievna, and ask her to be so very kind as to make the cap for Alexandra Stepanovitsch. The servant had something else in hand and gave the parcel to the coachman to deliver, and thus it happened that the polite request became an order. Alexei Stepanovitsch hurried off to explain matters to his bride, taking the objectionable parcel with him. Sofia Nikolaievna, who had not yet recovered her temper, was rendered still more indignant at the sight of her betrothed carrying the well-known bundle in his hand, and said a great many violent, bitter, and insulting things. The bridegroom, utterly confounded and disconcerted, made a clumsy apology, and was deeply mortified. Sofia Nikolaievna sent the material to a fashionable milliner. She felt that she had gone too far and was eager to make amends for her hasty utterances. But to her astonishment it was of no avail. Alexei Stepanovitsch was utterly unnerved by the scene she had made, and in spite of all his bride's efforts to console and cheer him, he remained gloomy and aggrieved.

The 10th of May, 1788, the day appointed for the wedding, dawned. The bridegroom arrived early at the bride's abode, and Sofia Nikolaievna, already out of humour as the result of the events of the preceding day, had the mortification of observing that Alexei Stepanovitsch still wore yesterday's unhappy expression. She had accustomed herself to picture him in a state of ecstatic bliss on the day which was to fulfil his fondest hopes, and now he made his appearance with a serious—even careworn—countenance. She rallied him about it, and he grew still more constrained. Of course he protested that he was the happiest of mortals, and so forth ; but all the usual extravagant phrases, which formerly had caused her such pleasure when uttered by him, now fell on her ears in hollow and forced accents. They soon parted, not to meet again until six o'clock in the evening at the church where the bridegroom would await his bride.

The most painful doubts arose in Sofia Nikolaievna's mind. Could she indeed expect any happiness in the future ? Gloomy forebodings harassed her. She reproached herself for her violence, and her insulting remarks : nothing in the episode had warranted such an outbreak of passion ; what was there in this blunder of Alexei Stepanovitsch, for her to seize on it in this way ? Such mistakes were frequent enough on his part, but unluckily it had so happened that her two visitors were ladies who had no love for her ; and that knowledge had caused her to lose all sense of dignity, and had excited her natural irritability to the highest degree. She felt that she had wounded Alexei Stepanovitsch to the quick, recognised her mistake, but could do nothing to mend matters. All she realised in the depths of her soul was, that she was bound to fall into like errors. The immense responsibility of her task— to re-fashion a seven-and-twenty-year-old man according to her own ideas—came afresh to her consciousness. A whole lifetime to be spent in the society of a husband inferior to herself, a man whom, in spite of her love, she could not thoroughly respect ; an endless conflict between dissimilar tastes and opinions ; and the impossibility of any mutual understanding—this was the perspective which stretched before the poor girl, and her strong will began to waver. A hitherto unknown feeling crept into her heart—doubt of her own strength. But what could be done ? Should she dismiss her bridegroom on the very day of the wedding, thereby causing unspeakable anguish to her old father, who was now grown accustomed to the soothing thought that his daughter would be happily settled in life ? Should she give her enemies —and especially the two witnesses of her discomfiture of the previous day—the satisfaction of seeing her expose herself to the gossip, absurd conjecture, and, probably, actual calumny of the whole city ? Should she break the heart of this man who really loved her devotedly ? And all this merely from a fear of not being able to succeed in a design which she had so often contemplated, and whose accomplishment was, to a certain extent, most brilliantly effected ! " No, this shall never be ! God will support me. Our Lady of Smolensk will be my Helper and will give me strength to overcome my sinful passions." So thought Sofia Nikolaievna, and prayer restored her courage and peace of mind.

The Church of the Assumption was close to the Subins' home, and in those days stood in a wide, open space. Long before six o'clock, this space was crowded by all the curious sight-seers of the town. Before the porch of the Subins' house the carriages of the grand personages, who had been invited to accompany the bride, were drawn up ; while the general company assembled in the church. The bride was dressed for the wedding. Her little brother, the three-year-old Nikolinka, whose birth had cost his mother her life, put on his sister's shoes according to time-honoured custom—not entirely without the help of the maids. Shortly before six o'clock the bride's toilette was completed, and after receiving her father's blessing, she made her appearance in the salon. The costly bridal attire gave fresh lustre to her beauty. The road from the bridegroom's house to the church lay past the Subins' residence, and from the windows of her salon Sofia Nikolaievna caught a sight of Alexei Stepanovitsch in the English-built coach, drawn by four superb horses from the Bagrov stud. She even had an opportunity of making a friendly sign to him, as he leant out of the coach when passing and looked into the room. Directly after him came the bridegroom's sisters, with Madame Alakaieva, and the gentlemen who escorted them. Sofia Nikolaievna would not permit her bridegroom to be kept waiting, and in spite of all remonstrances followed him to church without any delay. She entered the building with a calm and dignified demeanour, gave her hand to the bridegroom with a friendly smile, but was provoked by the melancholy expression on his face : and no one present could fail to observe that neither bride nor bridegroom shewed much joy during the ceremony. The church was brilliantly lighted and thronged with spectators. The Episcopal Choir exerted itself to the utmost. From every point of view it was a grand and splendid marriage. At the conclusion of the marriage-service, the young wedded pair were escorted to the Subins' house by all the wedding guests. Dancing instantly commenced, and was continued until an early, but magnificent supper was served. All those guests who had the entry to Nikolai Feodorovitsch's room thronged there to offer him their congratulations. The next few days the festivities proceeded in the following order : a dinner, a ball, visits, and then again a dinner, and another ball ; in short, the usual routine of the fashionable city life of to-day.

MARRIAGE OF THE YOUNGER BAGROV

The shadows which had clouded the young couple's brows when they plighted their troth had long since vanished. They were supremely happy. No one could see them without feeling delight, and frequently their friends would exclaim : "What a charming little pair !" At the end of a week they decided to set off to Bagrovo, whither Alexei Stepanovitsch's two sisters had already betaken themselves three days after the wedding, Sofia Nikolaievna sending an affectionate letter to her parents-in-law by them.

Alexei Stepanovitsch's two sisters had recently grown more circumspect in their behaviour, thanks to their brother's unexpected outburst of wrath : in his presence, at any rate, all signs of hostility, insulting gibes, and equivocal glances disappeared, while their manner towards Sofia Nikolaievna had grown positively affable—a circumstance which in a way led her astray as to its real meaning. Alexei had great hopes of this intimacy between his sisters and his wife. Naturally enough, the former had been forced to play a poor part, both at the wedding and during the ensuing days, and they lost no time in taking their departure. Arrived at home, that is to say at Bagrovo, they kept their resolution to act with caution and to hide their detestation of Sofia Nikolaievna from their father ; but once alone with their mother and their two other sisters, they described all that had occurred at the wedding and in the city with such malignant cunning and skill as could not fail to excite a great feeling of animosity towards the new relative. They took care not to omit mention of the savage rage and threats of their brother over their quite innocent jokes about Sofia Nikolaievna ; but they invariably spoke amiably of her in Stepan Michailovitsch's presence, never saying anything directly bad of her, while they lost no opportunity of machinating against her in any stealthy way. This plotting called for skilful handling, so Jelisaveta and Alexandra Stepanovitsch decided that no one should interfere in the matter and undertook to carry it through themselves. My grandfather was very full of enquiries about the wedding, asking all about the invited guests, the condition of old Subin's health, and above all the general news of the town. The daughters praised everything, but their compliments had a distinctly bitter flavour, which did not escape the old fellow's notice. By way of a joke, and also perhaps by way of a hint to his daughters, he turned to Ivan Petrovitsch Karataiev, and remarked : " Well, what have you to say about your sister-in-law, Brother Ivan ? This backwards-and-forwards talk of my ladies' parlour doesn't help me much, but you, as a man, can explain things better." In spite of all his wife's winks and nods, Ivan Petrovitsch replied with great gusto : " Yes, I can tell you all about her, little father : there's not such another fine lass in the whole world as Alexei's catch. A glance from her is worth a rouble. And, my word, she's a clever girl too ! But I must admit she's proud, and not fond of a joke : if you try to spoon with her, she pulls such a face you have to shut up." " I can easily see, Brother, that she snapped you up pretty sharply," retorted the old man, and then he laughed, and added : " After all there's no harm in that." As a result of this talk, and also from the letter which Sofia Nikolaievna had sent him, Stepan Michailovitsch formed an exceedingly flattering opinion of his unknown daughter-in-law. The news of the approaching visit of the happy pair caused great excitement in the quiet, unpretentious household of these homely country folks. Every thing had to be smartened up, and much thought was given to clothes and such like matters. This Sofia Nikolaievna was a fashionable city dame, who in spite of her lack of fortune had been accustomed to a life of luxury, and naturally she would be very scornful and difficult to please. This was the way everyone thought and spoke of her, with the exception of the old man. There being no spare-room available in the house, Tania was forced to vacate her pretty corner room, whose windows commanded a view of the garden and the clear stream of the Buguruslan beyond, with its banks clothed with green bushes, the home of the silvery-voiced nightingales. Tania had no particular fancy to exchange her room for the bath-house ante-room, but there was no other accommodation for her. All her sisters were at home, and Karataiev and Erlykin slept in the hayloft. The day before the arrival of the young pair, the state bed with its silk hangings and the silk window-curtains arrived at Bagrovo. A servant was sent too who knew how to set up and arrange everything. In a couple of hours Tania's room was quite transformed. Stepan

Michailovitsch admired these elegant appointments, but the women kind bit their lips with envy. At last a mounted messenger brought tidings of the arrival of the bride and bridegroom at the Mordvin village of Noikino, only eight versts from Bagrovo, where they had halted to change their clothes. In two more hours they would be at home! This news made no end of a commotion. The old man had already sent for the priest that morning, but, as the latter had not yet arrived, a man on horseback was sent off in haste to bring the holy man along at once. And meantime a most interesting scene was taking place at Noikino. The newly-wedded pair had sent a servant in advance to bespeak fresh horses, and as all Noikino knew Alexei Stepanovitsch, and Stepan Michailovitsch was venerated there as the benefactor of the whole community, the village population, great and small, men and women, some six hundred souls in all, flocked together outside the house where the grandees would alight. Sofia Nikolaievna, who had never seen any Mordvins before, was delighted with the beautiful and robust girls in their white, red-embroidered shirts, black sashes, and silver coins and bells which decorated their heads, breasts, and shoulders. And when she heard the plain, rough, but hearty congratulations of the crowd and their joyful shouts, she laughed and cried at the same time. " Ei, ei ! " they screamed in their bad Russian, " Ei, ei, Alexei, what a wife God has given you ! Ei, ei, how beautiful she is ! How pleased our father Stepan Michailovitsch will be with her ! God bless you both ! " But when the young wife reappeared, clad in her rich, state attire, and took her seat once more in the coach, such a hubbub of excited and joyous admiration was raised that the horses nearly took fright. The bridal pair bestowed ten roubles upon the community to drink their health, and continued their journey.

And now from behind the stupendous threshing-floor which lay on a high mountain slope a huge coach came into view. " They are coming ! they are coming ! " rang through the house, as the whole of the servants dashed out into the courtyard, where they were soon joined by the field-labourers ; while the children and young people ran to meet the coach. The old Bagrovs and the whole family gathered together on the balcony, Arina Vasilevna wearing a silk gown and jacket with a gold-embroidered silk handkerchief on her head, while Stepan Michailovitsch, arrayed in an old-fashioned coat, newly-shaved, and with a cravat round his throat, stood on the topmost step. He held a picture of the Blessed Virgin, and his wife carried a loaf of bread and a silver salt-cellar. The daughters and sons-in-law were grouped around. The coach drew up, the newly-wedded pair alighted. sank at the feet of their parents, and then kissed them and everyone present. Scarcely was this ceremony concluded, and scarcely had the young wife turned again towards her father-in-law, than he took her hand, gazed in her brimming eyes, embraced her with great affection, and said : " Glory to God ! Come and let us thank Him ! " Still holding her hand, he led her through the crowd into the hall, where the priest arrayed in his vestments awaited them ; and the old man stood beside Sofia Nikolaievna while Father Vasili chanted in loud tones : " Blessed be our God ! Who Is, and Was, and Is to Be ! "

SKETCH IV

THE YOUNG MARRIED PAIR AT BAGROVO

After the thanksgiving service in which my grandfather and his daughter in-law took a fervent part, everyone kissed the Cross. The priest sprinkled the newly-wedded couple and all who were present with holy water. Then the embracing and kissing began all over again, mingled with the usual congratulations and compliments : " I hope to win your love and friendship ! " . . . " As one of the family, I beg to offer you my best wishes." This of course was said by those new relatives as yet unknown to the young wife. Stepan Michailovitsch was silent. He looked with great affection at the glowing cheeks and tearful eyes of Sofia Nikolaievna, listened attentively to what she said to everyone, and observed her manner towards all. Finally, he took her hand, and conducting her to the salon he seated himself on the sofa and motioned to the young pair to sit beside him. Arina Vasilievna seated herself at the far end of the sofa, beside her son. The daughters of the house and their husbands sat in a circle round the group. I must here remark that Stepan Michailovitsch as a rule would never sit in the drawing room, he only entered it on special occasions, and then only remained for a short time. His own room was the only one he liked in the whole house, with its homely old wooden gallery and the stairs leading to the house door. He had grown so accustomed to living in this one room that he felt quite uncomfortable and ill at ease in the drawing room. On this great occasion however, he quite conquered his aversion and was soon deep in a friendly chat with Sofia Nikolaievna. First he enquired after the health of his good friend, Nikolai Feodorovitsch, and expressed his deep sorrow when he was told that the sick man was growing weaker every day, remarking that if that were so he would not keep his dear guests too long at Bagrovo.

It is hardly necessary to remark that the young wife was not at all at a loss in the conversation, and was not merely polite but very winning and affectionate in her manner. Arina Vasilievna, who at heart was quite good-natured, followed her husband's example to the best of her ability and as much as she dared in the presence of her daughters. Aksinia Stepanovna had taken a fancy to her sister-in-law from the first, and was very kind and friendly towards her. The others remained silent, but it was not difficult to guess their thoughts from their expression. At the end of half-an-hour or so, the young wife whispered something in her husband's ear, who rose hastily and went into the adjacent bed-chamber prepared for him and his wife. Stepan Michailovitsch stopped talking, but Sofia Nikolaievna, with ready tact, managed to engage him in such a lively conversation that his attention was diverted, and he was quite surprised when, some minutes later, both folding-doors flew open and Alexei Stepanovitsch entered the room, carrying a great silver tray, so laden with wedding gifts that it positively bent under the load. Up sprang Sofia Nikolaievna, and taking a piece of the finest English cloth and a cloth-of-silver jacket, richly embroidered with gold thread, from the salver, handed them to her father-in-law, observing that the embroidery was her own work, which was indeed a fact. Stepan Michailovitsch cast a doubtful glance at his son, who still stood holding the tray, but accepted the present quite affably and kissed his daughter-in-law. Arina Vasilievna was the recipient of a silk head-kerchief interwoven with gold and a great piece of rich Chinese embroidered silk, an extreme rarity in those days. Each sister-in-law received a piece of silk brocade, and each son-in-law a length of English cloth ; but naturally these last presents were of slightly less value than the first. The presentation occasioned a regular outburst of kissing, hand-kissing, bows, curtsies, and thanks. The doors of the salon fairly cracked with the pressure of the crowd of eager spectators of both sexes, while the greasy heads of chamber-maids were timidly poked from the doors of all the bed-chambers, with the notable exception of the richly decorated apartment of the young pair, into which, so far, none of the household had dared to penetrate. A hubbub now arose in the dining room, where the servants were quite unable to keep out the throng of peasants, who were hindering them from laying the table. Stepan Michailovitsch, hearing what was the matter, rose from his seat, walked to the door, and dismissed the intruders by a look, simply saying : " Begone !"

Dinner took its usual course. The bridal couple sat side by side between the father and mother. The dishes were numerous, each richer and more substantial than the last. Stepan the cook had spared neither cinnamon, pepper, cloves, nor butter. The kindly father-in-law in the most amiable way urged his new little daughter to eat ; and the little daughter ate, while praying Heaven that she might not expire the next day from the effects of the meal. The conversation was of a somewhat limited character, partly because the business of eating left little time for talk, partly because no one had much talent in that line and everyone was more or less nervous. To this must be added the fact that Erlykin, when sober, was remarkably sparing of words a circumstance which had gained him the reputation of being a most gifted and learned individual, while Karataiev never presumed to open his mouth in the presence of his father-in-law unless addressed, and then confined himself for the most part to repeating the last words of anyone's remark, as for instance : " The hay would have been carried very successfully if it had not come on to rain."—" If it had not come on to rain," Karataiev would repeat. Or " The rye has blossomed very well, but this frost was quite unexpected."—" This frost was quite unexpected," Karataiev would echo promptly, and these repetitions were frequently very tiresome. The old folks had quite forgotten to order champagne from Ufa, and the health of the young couple was drunk in a strawberry liqueur, three years old and as thick as oil, whose rich odour filled the entire dining hall. Vanka Masan, wearing boots which reeked of tallow and a new coat which gave him somewhat the appearance of a dancing-bear, marched round the table, presenting to each in turn a glass goblet, decorated with white flowers and a blue spiral right up the centre of the stem. Then came the young couple's turn to return thanks ; and it was indeed a great trial to poor Sofia Nikolaievna to have to drink out of the glass which the thick lips of Karataiev had just touched. But she shewed no disgust, and was preparing to drink off the whole glassfull out of politeness, when her father-in-law checked her, remarking : " You must not drink all that, my dear little daughter, or you will have a sad headache : this liqueur is very sweet and delicious, but you are not accustomed to it and it's too strong for you." Sofia Nikolaievna vowed that such a costly beverage could not possibly harm anyone, and begged permission to have another sip, whereupon the old man playfully handed her the glass for another taste.

It was pretty evident to the whole family that Stepan Michailovitsch was charmed with his daughter-in-law, and delighted with everything she said. Sofia Nikolaievna was quite aware of it, too, though on two separate occasions she had been surprised at signs of momentary displeasure on the part of her father-in-law. During dinner she frequently found him looking at her with an expression of great affection. At last the long—and to Sofia Nikolaievna—wearisome country feast, which she had done her best to enliven by her gay conversation, came to an end. Everyone rose from his or her seat. His son and daughters kissed old Stepan Michailovitsch's hand in turn. Sofia Nikolaievna attempted to do so, but the old man drew his hand away and kissed and embraced her instead. This withdrawal of his hand had already occurred once before, and, true to her impulsive nature, Sofia Nikolaievna exclaimed : " Why do you refuse me your hand little father ? I am your daughter, and entitled to kiss it with love and respect." The old man, looking very seriously and fixedly at his daughter-in-law, replied gently : " Although I love you very dearly, my hand is only given to my own begotten children to kiss. I am not a Pope."[1]

All the company now returned to the salon, and resumed their former seats. Aksiutka served coffee, which the old man did not like and which only made its appearance on festive occasions, although all the rest of the family were very fond of it. Directly after coffee Stepan Michailovitsch rose and said : " It is now high time for us all to go to bed. Our dear guests must be very tired after their long journey." Saying

---

[1] The Popes, as Russian Priests are called, offer their hands to be kissed, after bestowing their blessing. [Tr. S. R.]

this, he went to his own room, accompanied by his son and daughter-in-law. " Here is my nest, little daughter," he said gaily, " sit down, if you have the mind to stay here awhile ! Just once in a way I have sat in the drawing room with you ; nearly strangled by this horse collar, too," (here he tore off his cravat) " Alexei of course knows my ways ; but in future I beg you to come and sit with me here, whenever you feel inclined to do so." He kissed his daughter-in-law, gave his son his hand to kiss, and dismissed them, after which he undressed and lay down to rest himself after the unwonted emotion and fatigue of the day. Almost instantly a deep slumber overwhelmed him, and soon a mighty snoring caused the bed curtains, which Masan had drawn around his old master, to rise and fall in measured waves of linen.

The other members of the family followed the example of the head of the house. The sons-in-law, who had eaten heartily (Karataiev had evidently drunk heartily, too) betook themselves to sleep in the hayloft over the stable. The daughters all assembled in their mother's bedroom. And here arose such an excited whispering and criticising that not one of these ladies had a wink of sleep that afternoon. What had not poor Sofia Nikolaievna to suffer at their hands ! How the sisters-in-law pulled her to pieces ! The evident partiality of Stepan Michailovitsch for his daughter-in-law had put the whole family in a rage. Only one good soul among them, Aksinia Stepanovna Nagatkina, tried to stand up for her ; but she only succeeded in getting herself banished from the room and thenceforward shut out from all family councils, while in addition to all this a fresh and still more insulting epithet was added to her previous nickname of " The Dear Simpleton," which clung to her to her dying day. But in spite of this, and in spite of all persecution on the part of her family, she never ceased to take the part of her cherished sister-in-law.

The young pair withdrew into their richly-adorned chamber. With the assistance of her maid, the nimble black-eyed Parascha, Sofia Nikolaievna set to work to unpack the numerous trunks and chests which had been conveyed in the English coach. Already the lively Parascha had made friends with all the house-servants and knew the names of all the old people in the settlement who were specially worthy of notice. Sofia Nikolaievna had come provided with a rich store of trifling gifts of every description, and she set to work to portion them out according to the future recipients' age, length of service, or the consideration in which they were held by their masters. As neither of the young folks felt in the least tired or in need of sleep, Sofia Nikolaievna, after exchanging her beautiful dress for one of simpler fashion, left Parascha to finish the unpacking and arranging of the room, and, regardless of the heat, went for a stroll with her husband, who wished to shew her his favourite haunts . . . the little birch wood ; the island clothed with linden trees, already green ; the clear current of the encircling stream. And how lovely it was there, at this season of the year, when the freshness of spring blended with the warmth of summer ! Alexei Stepanovitsch, passionately in love and still intoxicated with happiness, was chilled and surprised when Sofia Nikolaievna, without evincing any delight at the sight of the exquisite little wood and the islet, and scarcely indeed paying the slightest attention to them, seated herself beside him in the shade on the bank of the swiftly-flowing river, and promptly engaged him in a long conversation about the family. She chattered away about the reception they had just had, about her sympathy for her father-in-law, adding that from the first moment she had noticed what a good impression she had made upon him. She added that she knew her mother-in-law would like her well enough, if only she were not so frightened of approaching her, and that Aksinia Stepanovna seemed the kindest of them all,though even she was not quite unprejudiced. " I can see and comprehend everything," she concluded," I know exactly who stirs up all the ill-will. Not a word, nor a look has escaped me ; and I know what I have to expect. May God pardon those two sisters of yours—Jelisaveta and Alexandra Stepanovna ! " But Alexei Stepanovitsch listened abstractedly to her remarks ; the shade under the trees was so refreshing, where the tender green branches bowed themselves lovingly towards the water, the river, softly murmuring, hurried so swiftly along with its slily-flashing little fishes . . . his Sofia Nikolaievna, his adored wife, sat at his side with her arm flung round him . . . Heavens ! who could give heed to anything, complain about anything, feel any unhappiness ? At such a moment one can scarcely hear aught, much less understand it . . . and Alexei Stepanovitsch neither heard nor understood a word of all his young wife was talking about. All his longings were so fully and so sweetly satisfied that he fell into a still day-dream and forgot everything around him. Sofia Nikolaievna continued her conversation, grew quite heated and passionate . . . . and at last realised that her husband was not listening and was nearly asleep ! She rose hastily. Then began a repetition of the same painful scene, the same conflict of mutual misunderstandings, which had already taken place on two previous occasions, but which this time was enacted with even greater virulence. All the former insults were repeated, only in stronger terms, and the passionate outbreak ended in tears and the bitterest reproaches for his indifference and listlessness. The confounded Alexei Stepanovitsch, cast thus from Heaven and shaken roughly out of his sweet reverie, vainly sought to pacify his wife by assuring her that all was going as well and smoothly as it possibly could, that she was only fancying injuries and offences, that everyone in the family liked her and it was quite impossible to do otherwise. But for all his agonised appeals and in spite of the boundless love which expressed itself in the look and voice of Alexei Stepanovitsch, Sofia Nikolaievna was incapable of understanding either the mind or heart of her husband, and only discovered fresh evidence of his coldness and indifference in his words ! The discussion was becoming still more heated, and I know not to what a pitch it might have grown, had not Alexei Stepanovitsch caught sight of his sister Tatiana's waiting-maid, running towards them. Guessing that his father was awake and that they were being sought, he drew his wife's attention to the girl. Sofia Nikolaivna regained her composure in an instant, seized her husband by the hand, and hurried towards the house with him ; but Alexei Stepanovitsch followed her in a sorrowful and dejected mood.

Great preparations had been made at Bagrovo for the entertainment of the servants, peasantry, and the neighbouring settlers. The necessary quantity of home-brewed beer had been prepared, and two dozen kegs of brandy purchased.

AKSAKOV'S FAMILY CHRONICLE

Before lying down to rest that afternoon, Stepan Michailovitsch had asked : " Are there many here from Noikino and Kiwazkoie ? " to which Masan replied that everyone had come, including children and the old people. Stepan Michailovitsch smiled, and said : " Well, we must make them all welcome. Tell old Fedosia, the house-keeper, and the steward, Peter, to see that everything is in readiness ! " After a short nap Stepan Michailovitsch woke up in a still better humour than before. " Is all ready ? " were his first words. " Long ago," was the reply. The old man dressed hastily, not in the irksome suit of state but in his beloved old woollen dressing-gown, stepped out on the balcony, and proceeded down the stairs to superintend the preparations in person. Rough trestle-tables made of planks had been set up in the spacious green courtyard, which no hedge or boundary separated from the road. At regular intervals casks of beer and kegs of brandy stood on these tables, with great piles of white wheaten bread between. The house-servants were grouped together nearest the house ; beyond them was the mass of peasantry ; and still farther distant the much larger crowd of Mordvins of both sexes. Stepan Michailovitsch gave a hasty look round, and satisfying himself that all was in order, returned to the balcony. Here he was joined by his family. But he had barely time to enquire what had become of the newly-wedded pair, when Sofia Nikolaievna and her husband appeared. The old man welcomed his daughter-in-law with redoubled signs of affection and treated her quite as if she were his own child. " Now, Alexei," he exclaimed, " take your wife's hand and conduct her to welcome the servants and labourers : these folks all want to see their young mistress and kiss her hand. Come along ! " He headed the little procession, followed by Alexei Stepanovitsch leading his wife by the hand. A short distance behind them came Arina Vasilievna supported by her daughters and sons-in-law. With the exception of Aksinia Stepanovna, the daughters of the house could ill-conceal their mortification. The increasing civility of Stepan Michailovitsch ; this ceremonious installation of the detested Sofia Nikolaievna as the young house-mistress ; her beauty and elegance, her perfections of manner and conversation ; her respectful, enchanting, amiable bearing towards her father-in-law—all served to excite and irritate their jealous dispositions. They felt themselves neglected and supplanted in their paternal home. "It does not matter so much to *us*," whispered Alexandra Stepanovna ; "for after all what are we but lopped-off branches ? But I cannot look at Tania without tears. What more has she to expect in this house ? She is nothing but a maid-servant for Sofia Nikolaievna. As for you, poor mother, no one will have the least respect for you, now. All will be dancing attendance on the new mistress." Her voice trembled, and tears glittered in her big, rolling eyes. Meantime Stepan Michailovitsch had reached the party of servants, and shouted to the peasants : "Why are you standing apart there ? Are you not the children of one and the same mother ? Here," he continued, "is your young mistress, whom your young master has known for a long time. When the time comes, you must serve these two as faithfully and willingly as you have served me and Arina Vasilievna ! And they will always treat you with justice and mercy." At this, the whole assemblage threw themselves on the ground at the feet of the young couple. The young bride stood bewildered and scarcely knew what to do. She was not accustomed to such scenes. Her father-in-law, observing her embarrassment, remarked : "There's nothing in this sort of obeisance ; their heads are not going to fall off. Now kiss your young lady's hand, and then you shall have a bite and sup ! " Everyone rose and advanced towards Sofia Nikolaievna. She turned her head, the sprightly Parascha and her man-servant Feodor (one of her dower serfs) were there with the presents. On a sign from their mistress the two servants promptly handed her a chest and a bundle full of all manner of little articles. Not accustomed to having her hand kissed to such an extent, and at the same time unwilling to stand there like a stock, Sofia Nikolaievna began to kiss each person, who after receiving his or her present, tried to kiss her hand a second time, but was promptly rebuked by Stepan Michailovitsch who remarked that at this rate of proceeding they would not be able to have tea until it was time for supper. "You cannot kiss all of them—only a few of them—twice, little daughter," he said. "There are too many of them here. Kiss the old men and the old grannies ;

I approve of that ; the others must be content with your hand."
But for all this shortening and simplifying, the wearying, tiresome ceremony lasted a very long while. Stepan Michailovitsch enlivened the proceedings considerably by his good
humour, addressing the people by name and explaining their
various callings. Many of the old men and women uttered
simple greetings full of love and devotion ; many even wept ;
and all gazed with affection and reverence on the beautiful
countenance of the new mistress. Sofia Nikolaievna was
deeply moved. " Why are all these good people so ready to
love me, why do they love me so much already ? " thought
she. " What have I done to deserve such love ? " At last,
after all young and old had kissed the young mistress' hand,
after many had received a kiss from her, and after all present
had received rich gifts, Stepan Michailovitsch took Sofia
Nikolaievna by the hand, and together they walked towards
the crowd of Mordvins. " Good-day, neighbour folk ! " he
cried gaily : " I am pleased to see you all assembled here.
This young lady is your new neighbour. You must be very
kind to her ! Now I must beg you to drink her good health,
and to accept my fullest hospitality." Loud and joyful
shouts arose by way of answer : " Many thanks, Stepan
Michailovitsch ! God be praised ! What a beautiful wife
He has given Alexei ! How beautiful, how beautiful she
is ! This is your reward for your goodness, Stepan Michailovitsch ! "

The feast began. Stepan Michailovitsch, accompanied
by his whole family, returned to his favourite seat on the
balcony. He observed that the time for tea, which they usually
drank at six o'clock, was long since past. As a matter of fact
it was considerably after seven. Already the long shadow of
the house was verging more towards the South, and resting
on the storehouse and stables. For long enough the samovar
had hissed and bubbled on the big table set out near the balcony
with Aksiutka in waiting. All took their seats round the table.
Only old Stepan Michailovitsch could not tear himself away
from his balcony, and still remained in his favourite perch, over
which he had carefully spread his faithful old felt coverlet.
On this occasion Tania served the tea, with Aksiutka as her
assistant. Sofia Nikolaievna begged permission to sit beside

her father-in-law on the staircase, which was granted with evident signs of pleasure. The daughter-in-law sprang up nimbly, her half-empty tea-cup in her hand, and in an instant seated herself beside the old man. He caressed her fondly, and had another rug spread for her, lest her dress should be soiled. They chatted merrily together. Angry glances were cast at them by the party at the tea-table and malicious remarks were exchanged in whispers, without however causing the young husband to pay any attention to them. Of course he could not but help hearing them, but *they* were not the cause of his dissatisfaction and unhappiness. The loud voice of his father broke in upon his gloomy meditations : " Come here, Alexei ! It's much cosier up here." Alexei joined the couple, sat down beside his father, and grew a little more cheerful. After tea, all remained sitting in their places, and chatted together until supper-time, which to-day was served later than usual—towards nine o'clock. At intervals the loud songs and ringing laughter of the merry crowd could be heard from the distance, where the shadows were growing thicker and darker. The company separated immediately after supper. Each crawled into his hole, as Stepan Michail-ovitsch was wont to say. When Sofia Nikolaievna bade the old man Good-night, she asked him to give her his blessing and make the sign of the Cross upon her, and this her father-in-law did gladly, and kissed her with fatherly affection.

The mother-in-law and the eldest sister-in-law, Madame Nagatkina, accompanied the young couple to their bed-chamber, and remained a little while with them. On leaving the room they were accompanied by Alexei Stepanovitsch. Sofia Nikolaievna hastened to dismiss her maid, and seated herself beside the open window, which looked out over the river, gliding along between its banks of willow and alder. The night was magnificent : the sunset after-glow lingered yet, as if resolved to blend with the red light of the dawn. The coolth of the neighbouring river and the fresh scent of the young leaves were wafted into the room together with the thrilling song of the nightingales. But Sofia Nikolaievna's mind was busied with other matters than these. Being a girl of great intelligence, she had known from the first what awaited her in her husband's family, and had made her plans accordingly. But her life having always been spent in a city, she had no clear conception of the life of a none-too-rich country nobleman, such as dwelt scattered sparsely over the extent of the wide province. Everything was unpleasing to her : everything made a bad impression on her : the house, the garden, the little birchen wood, the islet. She was accustomed to the beautiful scenery of the rocky banks of the Bielaia as it flowed past Ufa ; and this little village in the valley, the old wooden house weather-stained and time-worn, the mill-pond with its swampy banks, the endless clatter of the stamping mill—all this she found positively hateful. She liked no one in the place—beginning with the family and ending with the peasant children—with the exception of one person—Stepan Michailovitsch. If he had not been there, she would have given herself up to despair. She had met him with a pre-conceived good opinion : just at the first blush of the moment his somewhat rough exterior had shocked her—but the next minute his intelligent glance and his friendly smile had re-assured her, the very accents of his voice had convinced her that this old man had great sympathy of heart and feeling, and she had resolved in her heart to love and be loved by him. She had known, quite early in her engagement, that all her future peace and happiness rested with her father-in-law, and had been fully prepared to spare no effort to win his approval : but now she had ended by actually falling in love with him herself ; and this satisfactory part of the situation was balanced against the oppression in her heart. In this one respect Sofia Nikolaievna was perfectly content with herself —she had attained her goal, and very easily too. On the other hand, she was pained by the thought that in a moment of passion she had wounded her good husband : she waited for him in great anxiety and with impatience, but he made no sign of returning to her. Had she only known where he was, she would have lost no time in hastening to his side. She longed to fall weeping on his neck, and to murmur : " Forgive me," and to wash the last lingering traces of displeasure from his heart in a torrent of tender words and caresses. But still Alexei Stepanovitsch did not return. These salutary instants of repentance, the enthusiastic love, the ardent desire to make full amends for the past . . . . all were in vain. Such exaltation of the feelings can never be of long duration, and after some minutes Sofia Nikolaievna first felt astonishment, and finally anger, at her husband's continued absence. When at last he made his appearance, melancholy and ill at ease, instead of throwing herself into his arms and whispering : " Forgive me ! " . . . . almost before he crossed the threshold, Sofia Nikolaievna challenged him in an excited and far from amiable tone with the words : " In God's name where have you been ? Why did you leave me alone like this ? I have been in a fine state of mind, waiting here for you for two mortal hours ! " " I have scarcely spent a quarter of an hour with my mother and sisters," replied Alexei Stepanovitsch in a low and miserable voice. " And they have been saying nothing but evil of me, blaming and slandering me, and no doubt you believed every word they said. Why do you look so downcast and unhappy ? " Sofia Nikolaievna's face expressed the liveliest agitation and her beautiful eyes filled with tears. Her young husband grew still more uneasy and more alarmed. Her tears terrified him. " Sonitschka," he pleaded, " calm yourself : no one has spoken ill of you : who would think of doing such a thing ? You have done nothing to merit it." Here, Alexei Stepanovitsch said what was not strictly true. Certainly no one had criticised his wife openly, nor had anyone actually said anything wrong about her ; but by hints and allusions he had clearly been made to understand that his wife had evidently made up her mind to ingratiate herself with her father-in-law in order to domineer over and humiliate all the other members of the family ; that it was easy enough to see through her tricks, that Alexei Stepanovitsch would think the same, in time, though just now he was her abject slave. Alexei Stepanovitsch paid no heed to all these hints and whisperings ; but the anguish of mind, which he had endured since the scene on the island, was increased by this backbiting and ill-will, and his affectionate heart was sorely wounded. He merely replied : " I do not agree with you, dear mother," and left the room, not to return to his wife however, but to pace to and fro awhile in the dark and empty hall. The seven windows stood open, and he peered out, gazing towards the rookery, now wrapped in shadow . . . the bosky river banks, so often the scene of his childish games . . . . he heard the throbbing notes of the nightingale . . . . the distant rattle of the mill . . . . the cry of the night bird. His heart grew comforted, and he returned to his room without a suspicion of what was in store for him. Luckily, Sofia Nikolaievna recollected herself in time ; remorse awoke in her heart, perhaps not quite with its former energy, but enough to change her tone. She turned, full of love and compassion, towards her husband, and implored his forgiveness with kisses and caresses. In terms of the sincerest affection she told him how happy she felt to have gained the sympathy and regard of his father ; besought him to always treat her with candour and trust ; proved to him the absolute necessity for mutual confidence . . . . and the soft heart of her husband was won. He was calmed and comforted, and told her a great deal that he had made up his mind never to repeat, lest he should set his wife at variance with the rest of the family. After he had thus relieved his overwrought heart, he lay down and instantly fell asleep. Sofia Nikolaievna however could not sleep, and lay awake in earnest meditation. At length she recollected that next day she had to rise very early, having resolved to visit her father-in-law at daybreak on his balcony, long before the rest of the family were astir, intending to please the old man and to take the opportunity of having a private conversation with him. She tried to sleep, and at last succeeded in doing so, but with difficulty and not until the greater part of the night had passed.

Sofia Nikolaievna awoke next morning with the first sunbeam. Though she had slept little, up she sprang, refreshed and cheerful. She dressed herself hastily, kissed her husband, told him that she was going to talk with the old man, but that he might sleep for another two hours yet—and hastened to her father-in-law. Stepan Michailovitsch had slept rather longer than usual, and had only just stepped out on the gallery. Morning—the glorious enchanting May morning in the full splendour and pomp of spring-tide, with the joyful thousand-tongued choir of all living things, and the long shadows where the misty and fragrant dews of night were absorbed by the triumphant rays of the sun—all this magic whispered in the soul of Sofia Nikolaievna, although, as yet, she and Nature were strangers. The sudden apparition of his daughter-in-law was a joyful surprise for the old man. Her rosy cheeks, sparkling eyes, carefully curled hair, and charming morning-gown proved that no sooner had the daughter-in-law been awakened than she had made haste to dress and be ready to pay her respects to her father-in-law. Stepan Michailovitsch had a great liking for lively, brisk, clever folk. As Sofia Nikolaievna possessed all these qualities, she found great favour in his sight. " Why have you got up so early ? " he asked, as he embraced her. " You have not had nearly enough sleep You are not accustomed to these early hours, and you will have a bad headache ! " " No, father," replied Sofia Nikolaievna, returning his embrace warmly, " I am quite accustomed to rise early. Ever since I was a child I have had a great many duties and much responsibility. I have had to look after a whole family, and a sick father too. It is only quite recently that I have begun to rise rather later. But this morning I woke very early. Alexei . . . ." (the old man frowned). . . . " told me that you must have been up and about a long time, and so I have come in the hope that you won't drive me away, but let me stay here and make tea for you." This simple speech was uttered with such warmth and such genuine feeling, that the old man was quite touched, and kissing Sofia Nikolaievna on the brow, replied : " Well, if that's the case, many thanks to you, little daughter ! We will have a cosy chat together and you shall make the tea." Asiutka had already set the samovar on the table. Stepan Michailovitsch gave orders that no one was to be awakened, and Sofia Nikolaievna set to work to prepare tea. This she did as skilfully and gracefully as if she had been accustomed to do it all her life. The old man watched this beautiful young woman with delight, she had so little in common with his own familiar women-kind, who never touched a thing but it slipped out of their clumsy hands. Everything was prepared just as he liked it : that is to say the tea was strong ; the tea pot, wrapped in a napkin, was set on the samovar : the cup was filled to the brim, and Sofia Nikolaievna handed it to him without letting the least drop overflow into the saucer ; the fragrant liquor was so hot that it scalded his lips. " You are a real enchantress," said he, astonished and delighted, as he took the cup from her and tasted the tea. " You know exactly what I like. If you are like this with your husband, he will be a happy man ! " In an ordinary way the old man drank his morning tea alone, and only when he had finished were the family allowed to drink theirs ; but this day, as he accepted his second cup from his daughter-in-law, he invited her to pour out a cup for herself and to sit down beside him. " I never drink more than two cups, but to-day I have a fancy for a third," he said in his hearty voice ; " and I really think I never tasted such good tea before ! " In fact Sofia Nikolaievna behaved with such affectionate consideration towards him that her influence upon so susceptible a nature as Stepan Michailovitsch's was irresistible and could not fail to put him in a still better humour. He made his daughter-in-law take another cup of tea and eat one of the home-made rusks, for which the Bagrovo ovens were famous. The tea-things were then cleared away, and the father-in-law and his daughter began to talk in the most friendly and intimate way. Sofia Nikolaievna displayed such a depth of feeling and such bewitching charm that she quite won the heart of Stepan Michailovitsch. In the middle of their pleasant chat he suddenly asked : " And where is your husband ? Is he still asleep ? " " Alexei was awake when I got up," replied Sofia Nikolaievna ; " but I told him he had better go to sleep again." The old man drew his brows close together and was silent. " Listen to me, dear little daughter-in-law," he said, after a pause, not speaking with anger, but with gravity. " you are so sensible, that I can speak the truth to you without mincing matters, and it is my practice to speak out and not keep things at the back of my mind. If you take my advice, well and good. If you reject it, you must please yourself—you are not my own child. I do not like your way of addressing your husband as ' Alexei.' It is only right for you to add his father's name : you are not his father, nor yet his mother. A servant is called plain ' *Alexei*.' A wife must treat her husband with respect if she desires his to be respected by others. And I was far from pleased yesterday, when you sent him off to bring in the presents, and made him stand holding the tray exactly as if he had been a servant. And just now you tell me that you have *ordered* him to remain in bed. A wife must never presume to give her husband orders : that leads to no good. Perhaps these are some of your city customs, but they are no good to us with our old country ways." Sofia Nikolaievna heard him with great respect, and replied in such earnest and sincere tones that each word went straight to the old man's heart : " I am grateful to you, father, for not hesitating to tell me if my behaviour has annoyed or vexed you in any way. Not only will I cheerfully do exactly as you wish, but I see for myself how wrong I have been. I am only young, father, and I have had no one to guide me or advise me. My father has been a bed-ridden invalid for the last six years. I have treated my husband as I have seen other women treat theirs ; but in future you shall never see anything to complain of in this way, nor will I change my manner when no one is by to criticise me. Oh, father ! " she added, and great tears like pearls filled her eyes, " I love you with a daughter's love, and will you not accept me as your own child ! Blame me, chide me when I do wrong, and forgive me afterwards : but never cherish any anger against me in your heart ! My youth and my passionate heart may, any moment, lead me into making a false step : only recollect that I stand alone in a family of strangers, I know them not and they know not me : do not you forsake me ! " With this she threw herself upon her father-in-law's neck, embracing him like an affectionate daughter, and kissing his breast and hands. The old man, whose eyes, likewise, were overflowing with tears, did not withdraw his hand this time, and replied : " So be it then." As we have already noted, Stepan Michailovitsch possessed unerring instinct. Bad people invariably repelled him, while the good as unfailingly attracted him. At the first sight of her he had been very much drawn towards his daughter-in-law; but now he fully comprehended and appreciated her worth, and thereafter never ceased to love her. This feeling was fated to undergo much test and trial in the future, but it neither failed nor faltered to his dying day. . . .

Soon after this little scene Alexei Stepanovitsch appeared, and after him, the whole family. For quite a long time the daughters had been pressing and urging their mother to join their father outside in the gallery ; but she had not the courage to take their advice, as Stepan Michailovitsch's previous order that no one was to be awakened, amounted to a command that he was not to be disturbed by any of them. She only made her appearance now, because the old gentleman had sent his servant Masan to summon his wife and daughters to his presence. All traces of tears had disappeared from Sofia Nikolaievna's countenance, and she greeted her mother and sisters-in-law with especial politeness and amiability. Neither was there anything specially to be noted in Stepan Michailovitsch's manner, but the obvious joy and happiness of Sofia Nikolaievna struck the same note of alarm in the jealous breasts of the second and third sisters-in-law, who knew what it betokened . . . . Stepan Michailovitsch now directed that the newly-married couple should pay their round of formal visits to relatives, taking each in order of seniority. According to his arrangement it was decided that their first visit should be paid next day to Aksinia Stepanovna Nagatkina, who left the house that afternoon in order to make her preparations. With her went Jelisaveta Stepanovna, to help her sister to get all ready to entertain the young pair at dinner. The Nagatkina estate was fifty versts away, but the good Bagrovian horses could easily cover this distance without fatigue, and six o'clock the next morning was fixed for the hour of departure.

Stepan Michailovitsch made no effort to conceal his affection for his daughter-in-law. He would not let her leave his side, and seemed never to tire of her conversation. Soon he began asking her all about her family history and her life in the city. He listened to all she had to relate with the greatest interest and sympathy, and frequently uttered terse and pithy comments of his own. Sofia Nikolaievna was much impressed by the weight and significance of his remarks, and saw plainly that he had not merely assumed pretended interest in her, but had formed a just estimate of her worth. For his own part Stepan Michailovitsch acquainted Sofia Nikolaievna with the minutest details concerning the present and future circumstances of her new family. He told all in such a simple and scrupulous way, and with such candour and good feeling, that Sofia Nikolaievna—the sole one there capable of understanding and valuing his true worth—was quite enraptured.

She had never met a man of his type before. Her own father was a clever and amiable old man, of slightly irritable temper and upright disinterested character, but weak, a slave to the rigour and formality of those days ; a smooth servile official, who had worked his way up from a mere government clerk to the rank of vice-regent. But here, on the contrary, she recognised a man who, however uncultured and rough his exterior might appear, and whatever his recorded acts of violence might be, still possessed intelligence, good nature, a love of truth, and the most steadfast adherence to all moral laws. A man who not only acted honourably in every relation of life, but who never spoke anything but the truth. And from these traits, the vivid imagination of the noble young woman formed an ideal of masculine worth and dignity, quite new to her, which appeared loftier than any she had as yet encountered. On him depended her position in her new family, probably her whole future happiness.

Dinner was a much more lively meal than on the preceding day. The young wife was again seated between her husband and father-in-law : Arina Vasilievna however had resumed her usual seat opposite her husband. Directly after dinner Aksinia and Jelisaveta left for Nagatkino. As the old man was preparing to lie down for his customary nap, he said to his wife : " Well, Arischa, it seems as if God had given us a splendid daughter-in-law. It would be a sin not to love her." " It would indeed, Stepan Michailovitsch," replied Arina Vasilievna ; " if Sofia Nikolaievna pleases you, she pleases me." The old man grimaced, but said nothing, and the old lady hurried off as quickly as possible, in order to avoid any further discussion on the subject, as well as to communicate this weighty observation of their father to her daughters, which they all instantly recognised as a command to be obeyed, and not, at any rate openly, set at nought.

Although Sofia Nikolaievna had slept but little the night before, she could not rest that afternoon. Once more she accompanied her husband for a walk, as he suggested, in the old birch forest and beside the river. This expedition brought no uncomfortable developments in its train. Filled with joyful confidence in the future and overflowing with love and admiration for her father-in-law, she tried to impart her own delight and rapture to her husband. As is so often the case with excitable and enthusiastic characters, she realised to a certain extent how her own youth and beauty had enchanted the old man, and at that moment loved him even more dearly than before. Alexei Stepanovitsch listened to his charming wife's lively conversation with great pleasure and surprise, and said to himself : " Thank God that she and my father get on so well together : everything will be all right now." He kissed her hand, and vowed again that he was the happiest man in the world, that in her he possessed a jewel whose like was not to be found in the whole of creation, and to whom everyone must needs pay homage. All the same, he could not fully understand his wife, nor appreciate the subtlety of mind which recognised the worth and nobility of Stepan Michailovitsch's character. For his own part he held to his original conception of his father as a man to be respected, certainly, but more feared than liked. But to-day Sofia Nikolaievna paid no heed to trifling vexations. She even shared her husband's feelings in admiring everything around her—the rugged birch wood, the deep river. . . . She actually spoke of her sisters-in-law quite affectionately !

Immediately on awakening from his after-dinner sleep, Stepan Michailovitsch had his daughter-in-law and her husband, as well as the other members of the family, summoned to his presence. For long enough he had not been known to be so cheerful and good-tempered. Was it his sleep that had done him good, or was his heart extra light ? . . . . Be all that as it might, everyone was agreed that the old master was quite exceptionally amiable and jolly. Ever since hearing about her father's very significant utterance, Alexandra Stepanovna had made up her mind to behave with more affability, while Arina Vasilievna and Tania were only too pleased to. be allowed to make friends, and talk with the bride : even Karataiev at a sign from his wife began boldly to repeat the concluding words of any remark; whether addressed to himself or not : only the General preserved his deep and portentous silence. The whole family circle was extraordinarily lively and talkative. The old man had a fancy to drink tea earlier than usual, of course in the shadow of the house and near the balcony staircase ; and the daughter-in-law was invested with the dignity of making the afternoon tea. Tania was quite content to resign this office to her. After tea Stepan Michailovitsch ordered two carriages to be got ready, and made his daughter-in-law sit beside him, while the whole party drove to the mill. You may recollect that my grandfather had a great fondness for this mill, and understood the working of it thoroughly. His mill-stones and crushing gear were in excellent order, even if the mill buildings were dilapidated and neglected and overgrown by sedges. He loved to explain all the mechanism of the mill, and had an especial fancy to shew every detail to his daughter-in-law. He was delighted with her utter ignorance and curiosity, frequently with her terror, as when he suddenly released a torrent of water from all four conduits and everything around her began to shake and rumble and rattle, while the mill stones began to revolve swiftly, growling and buzzing, the floor trembled, and all the objects near disappeared under a cloud of flour. All this was quite new to Sofia Nikolaievna, but not particularly delightful. In order to gratify her father-in-law, however, she pretended to be interested, asked questions about everything, and admired all that was shewn her. The father-in-law was honestly delighted with her sympathy ; he kept her a long time examining the mill, and when at last he conducted her to the verge of the mill-dam, where the young husband and his two sisters were busy with their fishing-rods, a great outburst of laughter greeted them. The old gentleman and the young lady were literally covered with flour. Stepan Michailovitsch, accustomed to this powdering, had shaken and dusted off some of his floury bloom at the door, but he could not help but laugh himself when he saw his daughter-in-law, who had been perfectly unconscious of her ghostly appearance. Naturally, she laughed and jested more than anyone, when she discovered what was amusing them all, and only regretted she had no mirror to show her how becomingly she had been powdered for a ball. As the others were quite absorbed in their angling, the old man took his young miller's-wife, as he styled her for the rest of the evening, for a walk beside the dam, over the bridge, along the banks of all the creeks and inlets of the expanse of water, and back again along the dam to where the fishers were still angling in the lock, and where the portly Arina sat and watched their performance. Wherever the carriage took them it was damp and dirty. It was almost impossible to cross the rickety wooden bridge in safety, and still more difficult to get along in the slush of the dam banks. All this disgusted the young wife in the highest degree ; but, naturally, of this Stepan Michailovitsch observed nothing. The dirt and puddles were quite indifferent to him, and he neither noticed the evil smell of the stagnant pond nor the effluvium from the dung-plastered dam. He had made the place himself, and everything about it suited him exactly. The sun sank below the horizon, the night air was growing chill, and all betook themselves gaily home, the anglers laden with booty, fine perch, roach, and chub.

The steward was waiting for his old master beside the balcony, to discuss sundry agricultural matters with him. The bride rearranged her disordered dress. Meantime the fish were cooked and fried in sour cream, the largest perch being baked without any scaling, and at supper-time all were voted most excellent.

So ended the second day. They all went early to bed, for next morning the young pair were to rise betimes, and set out on their round of visits. . . . No sooner was Alexandra Stepanovna alone with her mother and younger sisters, than she threw off her irksome mask and gave free rein to her long-controlled rage and poisonous tongue. She saw only too well that all was lost ; that her father was infatuated with his daughter-in-law ; that her prophecies had been only too-well fulfilled ; and that the sleek, sly intriguer had bewitched the old man. There was nothing to be done now but to get the young couple packed off to Ufa, and then to make new plans. She utilised the occasion to abuse Arina Vasilievna and Tania for their friendliness : " If I had not been on the alert," scolded Alexandra Stepanovna, "this fashionable madam, this beggarly granddaughter of a Cossack, would have befooled you, too."

Punctually at six o'clock the next morning the newly-wedded pair set out for Nagatkino in the English coach, to which six mettlesome Bagrovo-bred horses had been harnessed. Sofia Nikolaievna had managed to find time to prepare her father-in-law's tea, and he had parted from her in the most loving manner, even blessing her for the journey, as the young pair would be absent for a night. At first the road lay down-wards, along the river bank, then crossed the river and went uphill towards the circuit town of Buguruslan. Without halting here, our travellers crossed the bridge over the great Kinel, and then rolled gaily along the water-meadows, following the summer-track which lay through the high grass of the steppes ; not stopping to alight at any of the scattered villages. The horses kept up a brisk trot, ten versts an hour. It was long since Alexei Stepanovitsch had visited this side of the Kinel, and the fragrant, verdant, flower-starred steppe enchanted him. Terrified bustards flew before the carriage every minute ; while the crested snipes accompanied it, circling around, and then alighting on the ground some dis-tance in advance, only to start up again when it drew near, while the air echoed with their sonorous cries. Alexei Stepan-ovitsch regretted not having brought his gun with him. This wondrous, teeming, thousand-tongued steppe—in those days rich in game of every variety—distracted his mind or, to speak more justly, absorbed his attention to such a degree that he listened to his wife's intellectual conversation without having the slightest notion of what she said, and for the most part without even hearing her. It did not take her long to discover her husband's absorption, and she was silent, then grew angry, then began to talk to Parascha who accompanied them. After crossing a flat table-land they arrived at Aksinia Stepanovna's little country house, at about twelve o'clock. This was much smaller than the Bagrovo house, and rather resembled a town-dwelling. It stood on the level banks of the Little Kinel, merely separated from the river by a kitchen garden, where for the moment a couple of sunflowers and the white peeled sticks supporting the rows of sugar-peas were the sole objects of interest. How well I remember this poor, solitary little dwelling, which I saw for the first time ten years later, and can well imagine how it charmed Alexei Stepanovitsch and horrified his wife. There it stood in brightest sunlight, a barren desolate spot on the flat river bank, and all around the level steppe pierced by the holes of the *bobacs*[1] . . . . no tree, no bush ; a placid deep river, fringed with reeds and rushes. How should it find favour in

[1] The bobac is a species of marmot. [Tr. H. R.]

anyone's sight ? Nothing here that was beautiful, splendid,
or picturesque ! And yet Alexei Stepanovitsch loved this
place so dearly that he preferred it to Bagrovo. I cannot say
I agree with him in this, but I too loved that quiet little house
on the banks of the Kinel—the limpid ripple and waving masses
of rushes in the stream, the wide extent of the green steppe,
even the ferry boat, into which you could almost step from the
house-door, and cross to the farther bank of the Kinel, where
a still more desolate plain stretched towards the South losing
itself in seemingly interminable distance.

The house-mistress, her two little boys, and her two-year-
old baby daughter, together with Jelisaveta Stepanovna and
the latter's husband, greeted their dear guests at the door. In
spite of its poverty-stricken exterior this little country house
was very pretty and neat indoors, far neater and prettier than
Stepan Michailovitsch's house. Every corner of it bespoke
the refinement of the " dear simpleton " as her sisters de-
risively called her, which, in spite of her widowhood and her
young children, produced the simple and peaceful home
atmosphere peculiar to women of extreme delicacy of feeling.
I have already told you that Aksinia Stepanovna was very
good-hearted, and genuinely fond of her new sister-in-law.
Small wonder then, that she was the kindest of hostesses
towards her newly-married visitors. This partiality had been
so evident at Bagrovo that Jelisaveta Stepanovna had been
sent along with the culprit, in order that her (Jelisaveta's)
intellectual and social superiority (she had married a General)
should act as a curb on the too-affectionate zeal of the amiable
Aksinia Stepanovna. But the latter good soul was not influenced by the crafty and malignant Madame General, and
replied simply and briefly to the latter's insolent admonitions :
" The rest of you may please yourselves, and may abuse and
hate Sofia Nikolaievna if it suits you to do so, but I am quite
satisfied with her conduct. I have only received good and
kind treatment from her, and I am determined that she and
my brother shall be made welcome in my house." Thus she
spoke and thus acted, inspired by genuine affection and good
feeling ; she looked after the young bride with the greatest
solicitude and entertained both her and her husband most
hospitably. The haughty Jelisaveta assumed a much colder

and more distant attitude here than at Bagrovo, and her husband followed her lead. He, however, got so tipsy towards evening that he had to be locked up in the empty bath-house. Sofia Nikolaievna took not the slightest notice of the couple's rudeness, but was excessively amiable towards her hostess and the children. In the afternoon, after a short rest, they all went for a row on the Kinel, crossed to the other shore, and then returned home. After drinking tea almost at the water's edge, they proposed that the new sister-in-law should try her luck at fishing, but she hastily replied that she could not bear this sort of occupation and would far sooner chat with the sisters. Alexei Stepanovitsch on the contrary, who was delighted to note the good understanding between his eldest sister and his wife, gave himself up to his favourite sport with the utmost complacency, assisted by all the household and the two boys. There he sat, among the rushes, until supper-time, and caught numbers of the great bream which were once so plentiful in the placid Kinel. It had been arranged that they should start on the return journey at six o'clock the next morning, but the young pair decided to leave at a still earlier hour, in order not to keep Stepan Michailovitsch waiting for his dinner. The hostess, however, and her sister, the General's lady, were to leave towards evening, stopping at Buguruslan for the night, where the horses could be duly baited and rested, and arriving at Bagrovo the day after that. Sofia Nikolaievna felt somewhat piqued by her husband's behaviour. In spite of all her intuition, she failed to comprehend how it was possible for a man, loving her as he did, to be so fond of his horrid damp Bagrovo, with its dirty mill dam, foul pond, and rugged birch-wood ; how he could be so completely absorbed by the dreary steppe and the stupid snipe ; and whatever on earth could he find to attract him in that hateful fishing and those disgusting fish with their moist, offensive smell—that he could forget his wife for whole hours at a time ? She could not understand it at all, and felt positively insulted when Alexei Stepanovitsch described his delight in nature and in field sports to her. On this occasion however she had the prudence to abstain from all discussion or criticism : the recollection of the scene on the island was too recent in her memory.

AKSAKOV'S FAMILY CHRONICLE

Alexei Stepanovitsch and Sofia Nikolaievna slept in state in Aksinia Stepanovna's own bed-chamber, which she resigned to them for this night ; and which she had adorned to the best of her ability, without paying any attention to the sneers of her sister, the General's wife. The young pair took their leave—a good half hour before the appointed time next day, and started for home. Nothing worthy of note occurred on the return journey, unless it was that Alexei Stepanovitsch was not *quite* so wrapped up in the steppe and the snipes ; that he didn't think it necessary to shout whenever a bustard started up before the coach : and that, as the result of this abstention he was somewhat more interested in his wife's conversation and looked at her more tenderly. They arrived at Bagrovo some time before they were expected. The servants were busy laying the table, and Alexandra Stepanovna had just uttered the remarkable prophecy : " To-day the little father will have to wait for his dinner. City folk can't keep up this early-rising business day after day." The old man understood the hint perfectly well, and replied cheerily : " Well, what of that ? We can very well wait a bit for our dear guests." This speech had a petrifying effect on all present. Stepan Michailovitsch had never, in the whole course of his life, sat down to dinner later than twelve o'clock : nay, when his appetite was especially hearty, the meal was served even earlier, and the slightest hitch or delay would cause an outburst of wrath. " This is all that Sofia Nikolaievna's doing," whispered Alexandra Stepanovna to her mother and younger sister in the adjoining room." It's a pleasure to be kept waiting by her ! But if ever you have happened to be a bit late for dinner when you have been coming back from Neklyudovo, what sort of an uproar has been made for you, and all the rest of us, too ! " She was still whispering away, when the coach dashed up to the balcony staircase, the wearied horses panting and sweating . . . . the old man kissed his daughter-in-law, and congratulated the young folks on their punctuality, and then roared : " Masan ! Tanaitschenok ! Bring in dinner ! "

The day was spent in the usual way. After tea Stepan Michailovitsch, whose good-will towards his daughter-in-law seemed to increase every hour, enquired if she had ever seen a herd of horses, such as roamed the steppes, half wild and in great numbers. On hearing that she had not seen but would much like to see such a herd, he had all his horses collected and driven into the courtyard. He then himself led his daughter-in-law into their midst, and pointed out all the finest mares to her with their sucking foals ; the one and two-year-old stallions ; and the young geldings which during the summer were allowed out at pasture with the herd in the rich, nutritious steppe grass. He presented her with a pair of the most beautiful mares, and added that he hoped his daughter-in-law would breed a fine stud of horses from them. Sofia Nikolaievna was delighted with the young foals, their capers, and their affection for their dams : and she thanked her father-in-law most heartily for his present. " And take great care, Spirka," added Stepan Michailovitsch to the head groom, " that the young mistress's mares are thoroughly well looked after ; her two foals must be specially marked. You had better slit their ears a little deeper, and later we'll have them branded with her name. I only wish you had a fancy for horses, my little girl ! " he added, turning to Sofia Nikolaievna : " Alexei takes no interest in them ! " The old man had a veritable passion for horses, and in spite of his limited means had managed, through his own energy and exertion, to establish a considerable stud, and to breed a fine race of strong draught-horses, which was the envy of all the neighbouring connoisseurs and fanciers. He was enchanted with the interest which Sofia Nikolaievna took in his horses. It must be admitted she only did it to please him, but he believed it in all seriousness, and marched her into the stables to shew her the coach-horses being fed.

I fear I shall be wearying my reader with all these details of how the days were passed, and must briefly add that the next day—the fifth since the arrival of the bridal pair at Bagrovo—was spent in the same manner as the four preceding ones. By claim of seniority in age, the next visit of the young couple should have been to the Erlykins, but the estate of the latter was situated a hundred-and-seventy versts distant from Bagrovo, much nearer to Ufa, so it was arranged to visit them in the course of the return journey to the city. Add to this that Jelisaveta Stepanovna's spouse, the sullen and taciturn General Erlykin, after getting drunk at Nagatkino, had indulged in one of his regular outbursts of drunkenness, which never lasted less than a week, and that his wife had been compelled to leave him in the care of friends at Buguruslan, under pretext of his being ill. Hence it came about that the next day was fixed for the visit to Alexandra Stepanovna, who left a day in advance for her estate of Karataievka accompanied by her Bashkir husband, first obtaining her father's permission to include her youngest and eldest sisters in the invitation. Thus Jelisaveta Stepanovna remained in possession at Bagrovo, ostensibly because her husband was supposed to be lying sick at Buguruslan, but in reality to watch the old people. The road to Karataievka, which was about the same distance from Bagrovo as Nagatkino—that is to say, rather over fifty versts—lay in a quite opposite direction —directly to the north For half of the way, the district was mountainous and wooded. The newly-married pair set out after an early breakfast, and the road being very bad and seldom used, they had only proceeded about half-way on their journey, when they were forced to come to a halt in the open country between Old and New Mertovschtschina, and wait a couple of hours to rest and feed the horses. It was tea-time when at last they arrived at Karataievka. The residence of this lover of Bashkir customs was much more poverty-stricken in appearance than the little house at Nagatkino. At the first glance one was struck by the dismal, narrow little windows ; the floors were all uneven, as if laid in steps, full of big holes gnawed by the rats, and so dirty that it would have been impossible ever to scrub them clean. Sofia Nikol- aievna entered this uncomfortable and inhospitable dwelling with some trepidation and the utmost reluctance. Alexandra Stepanovna received her with the extremest insolence and quite surpassed herself with hints and taunts, somewhat after this fashion : " Welcome, dear guests, come indoors, and make the best of things ! You, dear brother, will not criticise us, I know ; but I fear that Sofia Nikolaievna will not like to put up with our poor cottage, after being accustomed to her father's grand palace in the city. We are only poor folks of the lowest rank, and must cut our coat according to our cloth. Salaries and revenues are not for the likes of us." Sofia Nikolaievna, without being in the least disconcerted, replied that each one's manner of life depended more on his or her own tastes than on means ; moreover it was none of her business how and where her husband's relatives chose to live. After supper, the young couple were installed in the so-called drawing room for their sleeping apartment, and no sooner were the lights extinguished than a most hideous clatter, rattling, and jumping-about began, and they were attacked with such boldness by a legion of rats, that poor Sofia Nikolaievna, between her terror and her disgust, had not a wink of sleep. Alexei Stepanovitsch was forced to relight the lamp, and armed with a bar used for propping the window open, he held the bed against the onsets of the obnoxious rodents, some of which had actually sprung on the quilt as soon as the light went out. Alexei Stepanovitsch experienced neither disgust nor fear : this was no new experience for him ; and just at first he was highly amused at the comical leaps, spirited attacks, and wild squeaks of the enemy. Eventually he fell asleep, lying across the bed, still clutching his weapon : but Sofia Nikolaievna had constantly to rouse him, and it was only at dawn, when the foe had withdrawn to his subterranean camp, that the poor woman was able to sleep at all. She awoke with a racking headache : her hostess only laughed when she heard how the wretched rats had terrified Sofia Nikolaievna, and remarked that rats always disliked strangers, but treated the owners of a house with due respect. However, Aksinia Stepanovna and Tania could not observe their sister-in-law's wan and worn countenance without feeling compassion, and they both sympathised with her and took her part. Madame Nagatkina reproved her sister Alexandra for not having made the usual arrangements, that is to say, not having placed the bed in the middle of the room, with the curtains hung round so as to be easily tucked in under the mattress. To this Alexandra only replied with a malicious smile, and the remark : " It's a pity the rats didn't bite off our dear relative's nose ! " " Take care," retorted Aksinia Stepanovna ; " if our father gets to hear of this, it will be the worse for you ! "

The village of Karataievka was scattered on a hill bordered by a little river which took its rise in a number of purling springs and brooks. At the far end of the village the stream was enclosed by dykes and worked a little water-mill. The district in itself was far from ugly ; but the proprietor and his manner of life were so utterly repulsive, that nothing in his neighbourhood could possibly be agreeable. Karataiev, in awe of Stepan Michailovitsch at Bagrovo, was terrified by his wife when at home. Many a time he longed to shew some kindness and civility to Sofia Nikolaievna, but dared not brave his wife's wrath. However he took advantage of the latter's occasional absence to beg permission to kiss his sister-in-law's hand, while making his usual remark that she was the most beautiful woman in the world. On requesting this favour a second time, it was refused.

Karataiev led a weird life. During the greater part of the summer he spent his days with the Bashkir tribes in their pasture lands, drinking koumis with them. He spoke their language like one of themselves, and would remain whole days in the saddle, never alighting even for a moment, so that his legs were as bowed as any Bashkir horseman's. He could shoot with a bow and arrow and could split an egg at an enormous distance. The rest of the year he dwelt in a room containing a stove, which communicated directly with the hall. There he would sit the whole day long, wrapped in furs staring through the open window, regardless of the biting cold. From time to time he would whistle a Bashkirian melody, and then refresh himself with a sup of stomach bitters or a drink of Bashkirian mead. Why Karataiev stared out of this window, which looked out on the desolate courtyard, crossed diagonally by a rough footpath—what he saw—what he kept under observation—what that head set on those athletic shoulders was thinking about—are secrets which no psychologist can unriddle. It is true that the meditations of the philosopher were sometimes interrupted—as when, for instance, some buxom wife or lass would cross the yard on her way from the kitchen to the stable. Then would Karataiev nod and wink to her, receiving similar nods and winks by way of answer. But the female form would vanish like a ghost round the corner, and he would resume his staring into the empty distance.

Sofia Nikolaievna could hardly wait for the moment of departure from this dismal den ; and after an early breakfast, eaten while the horses stood at the door, the newly-married pair took a hasty leave and set off. By way of farewell the hostess kissed her sister-in-law on each cheek and on the shoulder, and thanked her heartily for her kind visit, while the latter returned equally warm thanks for her hospitable reception.

No sooner was Sofia Nikolaievna seated with her husband in the coach than she gave way to her ill-humour. The good-hearted Aksinia Stepanovna, without any idea of making mischief, had let out to her that the hostess had deliberately neglected taking the necessary precautions against the rats, and the young bride, who had restrained her anger while in her enemy's house, now lost all control over herself. She forgot that Parascha was seated in the carriage with them ; she forgot that Alexandra Stepanovna was Alexei Stepanovitsch's sister, and was unsparing in her abuse and epithets. Alexei Stepanovitsch, with his straightforward disposition and kind heart, could not believe it possible that his sister had been guilty of such malice, and attributed the neglect entirely to oversight on her part ; he was seriously annoyed by Sofia Nikolaievna's furious attack, which, to tell the truth, was not entirely justified. For the first time the young man grew angry with his wife, told her that she ought to be ashamed of herself to speak in such a manner, turned his back on her, and kept silence. In this frame of mind they arrived at Old Mertovschtschina, where just then old Maria Michailovna Mertvaia[1] resided, whose daughter Katerina Borisovna (a great friend of Sofia Nikolaievna) had quite recently married P. J. Tschitschagov, who had been banished to Ufa where his first wife had died. Katerina and her husband had just arrived on a visit to the former's mother, and the meeting between her and the young Bagrovs was quite un-expected. Sofia Nikolaievna, who was not less attached to Tschitschagov than to his wife, was so agreeably surprised by this rencontre, that her ill-humour all vanished, and she was quite gay and excited. Alexei Stepanovitsch, on the contrary, remained so sad and silent than no one could fail to remark it.

[1] In later years her sons obtained the permission of the authorities to adopt the surname of Mertvago.

AKSAKOV'S FAMILY CHRONICLE

Tschitschagov's history is a romance in itself, which I will try to relate as briefly as possible. I do this, because we shall meet with this family later in the course of our story, and their influence on the fate of the younger Bagrov was not inconsiderable. P. J. Tschitschagov was an exceedingly clever or, more strictly speaking, quick-witted man, who had received what in those days was considered a most liberal education. He spoke several languages, was a good draughtsman and architect, and wrote both in prose and poetry. In his passionate youth he had fallen in love, while in Moscow, with a Mademoiselle Rimsko-Korsakova, and in order to gain her hand, had committed an unpardonable fraud, which was only discovered after the marriage had taken place, and in consequence of which he was banished to Ufa. His wife died soon afterwards; and, at the end of a year, he was so far consoled as to fall in love with Katerina Borisovna, who fell a victim to his merry wit, amiable disposition, and cultured mind. At any rate, she cannot have been fascinated by his personal appearance, for he was hopelessly plain-looking. Katerina Borisovna was a mature girl of strong character. Her mother and brothers could not get on very well with her, and gave her to Tschitschagov to wife. Eventually he was pardoned, but was not permitted to leave Ufa. Sofia Nikolaievna cherished a two-fold affection for this man, first as the dearly-loved husband of her friend, secondly and principally, as an intellectual and cultured companion. Old Maria Michailovna had made up her mind to end her days in the country, and Tschitschagov and his wife had come to assist her with the building of her house and a church. Sofia Nikolaievna, who had already spent a whole week with her husband's relations, was as delighted with the Tschitschagovs' company as if she had received a Christmas present. Once more she breathed freely, her sprightly spirit was refreshed, and she laughed and chatted gaily until nearly midnight. Alexei Stepanovitsch might have sat the whole evening in silent isolation, if the considerate old mistress of the house had not taken him in hand and encouraged him to talk by dint of skilful questioning. As it was, as soon as supper was over, he wished them all Good-Night, and went off to the hastily-prepared guest chamber. Sofia Nikolaievna found him fast asleep, and the next day they left at a very early hour for Bagrovo, without rousing the family from their slumbers.

On the way home Alexei Stepanovitsch continued sulky and silent. To Sofia Nikolaievna's direct questions he only replied in monosyllables and in the coldest tones ; and after awhile she grew silent too. This was a great trial to one of her impatient and irritable disposition, but she had made up her mind to have no more disputes in Parascha's hearing, and postponed all discussion until the hour for the after-dinner siesta, when she expected to be alone with her husband. She began chatting with Parascha about the old days in Ufa, while Alexei Stepanovitsch squeezed himself into a corner of the coach, and either slept or pretended to sleep. They reached Bagrovo two hours before dinner time. Stepan Michailovitsch was visibly delighted to have his daughter-in-law home again, and told her he had felt very lonely without her. " No," he went on, " it would never do for you to remain here much longer ; for I should grow so fond of you, my little daughter-in-law, that in the end I should always be longing for you." He made Sofia Nikolaievna give him a full account of the round of visits. He knew Maria Michailovna, of whom he spoke with great respect, remarking that he would send word to her next day, inviting her, her daughter and son-in-law to take bread and salt[1] with the newly-wedded pair, and to extend their visit for four days including the Sunday. " The day after to-morrow you must go and see the Kalpinskis and Lupenevskis, and invite them too for Sunday. After Sunday you must stay another three days here, and then return home, and God be with you. Gossip Nikolai Feodorovitsch has never been parted from you before," he went on, turning to Sofia Nikolaievna, " and will be longing for you, and you for him—poor, suffering invalid ! "

Stepan Michailovitsch very soon guessed that something unpleasant had occurred during the journey. In the course of the conversation he asked his son and daughter-in-law how they had been received at Karataievka. Naturally he was told that they had had a most hospitable reception. Sofia

---

[1] Symbols of hospitality, an expression which is understood to be an invitation to dine. [Tr. S. R.]

Nikolaievna however mentioned among other matters that she had not slept at all during the night because of the rats. Stepan Michailovitsch expressed great astonishment at this. He had only visited Karataievka once, and that was some time ago, but he had noticed nothing of the sort then. " Oh, yes, it's quite true, Stepan Michailovitsch," interrupted Arina Vasilievna innocently. In vain did Jelisaveta Stepanovna wink and grimace, the old lady never noticed her, for which blunder she got finely scolded by her daughters later. " There are such dreadful rats there," she went on, " that you can't sleep without bed curtains." " And you were put to sleep without curtains ? " asked the old man in an altered and ominous tone. They were compelled to reply that this was the case. " A hospitable hostess ! " said he, and gave his wife and his daughter, the General's wife, such a look that they felt cold all over.

Karataiev, Madame Nagatkina, and Tania had not yet arrived, but were expected by tea-time. Dinner was not a cheerful meal. All were nervous, and not without good reason. Arina Vasilievna and Jelisaveta Stepanovna felt the storm approaching, and dreaded the bolt that would inevitably descend upon them. For a long time past Stepan Michailovitsch had had no outburst of fury, and they feared his rage all the more from being less accustomed to it. Sofia Nikolaievna noticed that her father-in-law was in a very bad temper. It would have been only right if he had given his daughter—her own avowed enemy—a severe reproof ; but she was afraid that some evil consequences would fall upon herself. She had mentioned the rats quite inadvertently, without ever dreaming that her father-in-law would attach so much importance to the circumstance. Besides this, she had another anxiety weighing down her heart, she did not know how to conciliate her husband, who for the first time in his life had been angry with her for her abuse of Alexandra Stepanovna. Should she wait for him to make the first step towards a reconciliation, or should she herself make the advance in order to bring the present painful situation to an end, begging his forgiveness and obliterating all recollection of her passion and temper with kisses and caresses ? Most certainly she would have chosen the latter plan, for she loved her good, gentle, affectionate husband most truly and tenderly. She reproached herself bitterly. She might have foreseen all that would happen. Well she knew that while Alexei Stepanovitsch had been ready to lay down his life for her sake, still it was useless to expect him to comprehend and realise her mortification over the various petty annoyances of daily life. And what should she do to quell her own hot blood, her excitable finely-strung nerves, her lively imagination, and the incurable sensitiveness of her disposition ? These thoughts distracted the poor girl, walking to and fro in her chamber whither she had escaped after dinner, where she awaited her husband, who had been waylaid by his mother and called into her room. The moments passed like hours to Sofia. The thought that Alexei Stepanovitsch was intentionally keeping out of her way, in order to avoid any farther discussion with her—the thought that she might probably have to meet him in the presence of his relations, without having been reconciled to him or having relieved her aching heart of its heavy burden—the prospect of having to keep up an appearance of gaiety and composure during the whole evening—these thoughts pressed upon her and threw her into a fever of anxiety. Suddenly the door opened, and Alexei Stepanovitsch entered the room—no longer timid and depressed, but resolute and even forbidding—and began to reproach his wife for having complained about his sister, Alexandra Stepanovna, to his father. " They are all trembling and weeping now, and God knows what is going to happen," he exclaimed, primed by the hints and suggestions of his mother and Jelisaveta Stepanovna. " It is mean and disgraceful to bring nothing but quarrelling and dissension into your husband's family. I told you my father had an ungovernable temper when roused, and, although you knew that, you took advantage of his fancy for you to . . ." Here Sofia Nikolaievna lost all patience. The blood rushed to her head ; her better feelings, together with all consciousness of guilt or sentiments of remorse, vanished ; and the unfortunate bridegroom realised that Stepan Michailovitsch was not the only person who could fly into a passion. A breathless torrent of complaints, reproaches, and accusations descended upon him ; and Alexei Stepanovitsch was attacked, annihilated proved inexcusably guilty of everything, and well nigh convinced that he must be an utter scoundrel . . . . and there she was—lying at his feet, dissolved in tears, and entreating his pardon ! Many a braver man than Alexei Stepanovitsch might well have quailed before such a fiery onslaught of mind, heart, conviction, and marvellous gift of speech ! And many a justly-angered man, of far stronger character than Alexei Stepanovitsch, at such a moment would have freely admitted himself in the wrong to such a young, charming, and beloved wife. And Alexei Stepanovitsch was decidedly in the wrong.

The storm in the newly-married pair's room was lulled ; but at the other side of the house it was just breaking in Stepan Michailovitsch's chamber. The old gentleman awoke. His slumbers had not calmed his temper, nor banished the frown from his lowering brow. For a short while he remained sitting gloomily on his bed, and then shouted : " Masan ! " Masan had been stationed outside the door for long enough, peeping through a crack. He had been placed there as a sentry by the family, who were gathered together in a state of the greatest perturbation in the hall. Masan, bawling : " What's your will ? " burst noisily into the room. " Is Alexandra Stepanovna there ? " " She has deigned to be present." " Call her here ! " The next instant Alexandra Stepanovna entered the room, as an instant's hesitation at these times might have most serious consequences. " So you provided rats for the entertainment of your brother and his wife, my lady ? " began Stepan Michailovitsch in his well-known ominous voice. " Forgive me, father ! " faltered Alexandra Stepanovna, whose knees trembled and whose natural malice had given way to terror. " I had my drawing room prepared for my visitors, and quite forgot to provide bed-curtains.- It was purely joy and excitement which caused me to forget them." " Pure joy, indeed ! As if I didn't know what you are ! How dare you offer me and your brother such an affront ? How dare you disgrace your father in his old age ? "

Probably the matter might have rested here and have passed off with a certain amount of scolding and abuse—with perhaps a couple of cuffs thrown in by way of conclusion—but

Alexandra Stepanovna could not endure the thought that she owed this humiliation to Sofia Nikolaievna. Believing the storm had passed harmlessly away and quite forgetting that in a case of this sort any retort would only make matters worse, she grumbled : " So I am to be treated in this unjust way, just to please *her* ! " On this a fresh and still more violent fit of anger seized Stepan Michailovitsch (whose rage, when it took possession of him, never failed to produce some disgraceful scene). Scarcely, however, had a frightful epithet escaped his lips, when Arina Vasilievna, the widow Nagatkina, and Tania rushed into the room from their ambush behind the door, and flung themselves at the old man's feet, uttering loud cries for mercy. Karataiev, who had been listening behind the door with the ladies, dashed away into the birch grove, where he struck about him right and left like a madman, breaking down the harmless twigs with his stick to relieve his helpless rage at this treatment of his wife. Jelisaveta Stepanovna had not ventured to put in an appearance, as her conscience was far from clear in the matter and she knew that her father guessed as much. " Little father Stepan Michailovitsch ! " wailed Arina Vasilievna, " your will is law here ; do as you please, for we are all in your power ; but save our honour and do not disgrace your family in the eyes of your daughter-in-law ; she has only just arrived and you will frighten her to death ! " Evidently these words brought the old man back to his senses. He was silent awhile—then kicked Alexandra Stepanovna from him, and shouted : " Out with you ! " No one waited for farther orders : in a trice the room was empty, and all was silent around Stepan Michailovitsch, whose blue eyes remained gloomy and troubled for a long while, whose breast heaved convulsively, and whose breath came with difficulty. For he had restrained himself, and his furious passion was far from being exhausted.

The samovar had been hissing and bubbling for quite a long time on the drawing-room table, for tea was not to be served in the gallery as the weather was cold and damp. It had only just ceased raining, and it would seem as if Nature sympathised with the stormy atmosphere of the Bagrovo household, for since dinner-time two thunder-clouds had gathered in the sky, each blacker than the other. Lightning flashed, and the hollow firmament shook with the rumbling of the thunder. But finally the storm dissolved in a shower of rain, the clouds rolled off towards the East, and the dazzling sun appeared in the West in full splendour. Forest and field were fresher and more fragrant, birds sang more lustily and joyfully. Different—how different are the traces of the storms of human passion ! . . . .

Arina Vasilievna and her daughters, with the exception of Alexandra Stepanovna—whose absence was accounted for on the plea of illness—her son-in-law Karataiev (Erlykin was still at Buguruslan) all gathered together in the drawing-room. Stepan Michailovitsch gave orders that his tea was to be served in his own room, and refused admittance to all. The door of the young couple's bed-chamber was still closed, and at last it was decided to summon them to tea. They appeared at once, and although Sofia Nikolaievna looked more cheerful and Alexei Stepanovitsch was actually more cheerful than before, it was not difficult to guess from their faces that something unusual had taken place between them. So far, they had heard nothing of the scene in Stepan Michailovitsch's room. Whatever *had* happened to Arina Vasilievna and her daughters, it is certain that they presented the appearance of folks who had just been rescued from flood or fire—or both. It is a pity that no one was present to observe the interesting expressions of the various countenances and the assumed composure of the assembled company. Conversation was constrained and languid. The absence of Stepan Michailovitsch and Alexandra Stepanovna was so *very* suspicious that Sofia Nikolaievna seized the earliest opportunity of retiring to her own room, where she summoned Parascha, and the mystery was solved. Everyone knew about the affair in the maidservants' hall. In the first place Masan and Tanaitschenok had overheard the whole of the uproar ; and in the second place the old lady and Mademoiselle Tania were accustomed to confide everything to their maids. Hence it happened that Parascha was able to give her mistress a full and circumstantial account of the frightful scene. Sofia Nikolaievna was terribly upset. She had never dreamt of such dire consequences arising, and blamed herself anew for having mentioned the unlucky rats to her father-in-law ;

while she felt the utmost compassion for Alexandra Stepanovna. She returned to the salon, and asked her mother-in-law's permission to go and see the sick daughter : she was informed, however, that Alexandra Stepanovna was asleep. While Sofia Nikolaievna was in her room with Parascha, Alexei Stepanovitsch had heard the whole story from his mother and sisters. At nine o'clock supper was hastily eaten, and immediately afterwards everyone went to bed. No sooner was Sofia Nikolaievna alone with her husband than she flung herself, weeping, on his shoulder, and again entreated his forgiveness with the deepest contrition ; taking, indeed, more blame upon herself than was her just due. Alexei Stepanovitsch was unable to appreciate the exquisite source of this sincere regret and heartfelt compunction. He was only distressed that she should be so unduly pained ; and tired himself out with his efforts to console her telling her that, thanks to God, all had ended well ; that they were only too well accustomed to this sort of thing at home ; that tomorrow his father would wake up quite good-tempered, forgive Alexandra Stepanovna, and everything would go along better than before. He begged Sofia Nikolaievna not to be drawn into any discussion with the family, and not to carry out her intention to ask pardon for her unpremeditated blunder, and advised her in future not to pay early-morning visits to his father, but to wait until the old man sent for her himself. Sofia Nikolaievna realised more clearly than ever before exactly what type of man she had married—her dreary forebodings for the future were only too well fulfilled. Her husband slept peacefully, as was his wont ; she lay awake the whole night through.

His attack of rage had greatly shaken old Stepan Michailovitsch ; he was ashamed of his savage behaviour, when he reflected that his daughter-in-law might possibly get to hear of it. But all base and malicious tricks were utterly detestable to his honest and upright mind ; and his daughter's behaviour had appeared in the light of an act of defiance against his fatherly authority. He ate no supper, never took his usual seat on the balcony, even declined to see his steward, sending the latter his orders by a servant. But the soothing hours of darkness, wherein our better instincts are aroused, and finally Sleep—that bringer of Peace and consoler of the Spirit—produced their much-desired effect. Next morning Stepan Michailovitsch had Arina Vasilievna summoned to his presence at a very early hour, and ordered her to communicate the following instructions to her daughters, which evidently were intended specially for Alexandra Stepanovna, and in part for Jelisaveta Stepanovna. No one was to appear in the least upset or disturbed, nor to act in any way that might lead the daughter-in-law to suspect that anything was amiss. Shortly after this the samovar was brought out, and the whole family summoned. By the greatest good fortune Arina Vasilievna had already found time to send a message to her daughter-in-law by Alexei Stepanovitsch, entreating her to do her best to cheer up the old gentleman, who, so she said, was not very well that morning and rather low-spirited. The daughter-in-law, although she had not slept a wink during the night, and was not especially cheerful herself, exerted herself to the utmost to fulfil this request of her mother-in-law, which was not only the old lady's, but the whole family's and, in particular, her own desire.

Sofia Nikolaievna had a marvellous personality ! Her sprightly, susceptible, easily excited nature was so swayed by the swiftest variation of thought or sentiment, that, in an instant, she could transform her whole being to suit her mood. In consequence of this peculiar versatility she was frequently suspected of dissimulation—which suspicion was a great error and an injustice to her. Rather was it a special gift of sympathetic insight, which enabled her to transport herself into any sphere and situation whatever—to abandon herself unreservedly to a new idea or a fresh desire—and to be irresistibly carried away on the wings of her own ardent fancy. And now the wish and desire to calm the agitation of this poor old man, whom she loved so dearly, who had taken her part, who had flown into a passion on her account, and whose health had suffered in consequence—combined with the wish to comfort her husband and the rest of the family, who were suffering from the effects of her thoughtlessness—took such utter and exclusive possession of her entire being, that she seemed as if transformed into someone almost supernatural. Soon everything and everyone was subject to her spell. She poured out the tea herself, and even handed round the cups, first serving her father-in-law, next her mother-in-law, and the rest of the party in due order. She talked and chatted with everyone, and was so unconstrained, so amiable, and so cheery, that her father-in-law was quite satisfied that she had heard nothing of yesterday's uproar, and grew more cheerful himself. His good spirits were highly infectious, so much so indeed that by the end of an hour every trace of the miserable affair had vanished.

Directly after dinner the bridal pair sallied forth on a fresh round of visits, this time wending their way towards Neklyudovo to the Kalpinskis ; and to Lupenevka (two versts beyond Neklyudovo) to our old acquaintance, Flena Ivanovna Lupenevskaia. Ilarion Nikolaievitsch Kalpinski and his wife, Katerina Ivanovna, dwelt at Neklyudovo. The former was, in his way, a somewhat remarkable man ; without any scientific training it is true, but intellectual and well-read ; who, in spite of his humble origin (it was said he was a Mordvin by birth) had risen by his own efforts to the rank of Privy Councillor, and had prudently bettered his position by marrying the daughter of a land-owner of the ancient nobility. He had quite recently devoted himself to agriculture, and was making money very fast. Kalpinski claimed to be a free thinker and philosopher ; and having heard of such a person as Voltaire, called himself a Voltairean. He led an isolated and solitary life apart from his family, and devoted himself solely to his own pursuits and interests. Sofia Nikolaievna had heard of him before, but had never met him, as he had formerly resided in Petersburg, and had only quite recently come to Orenburg. She was very much astonished to meet an intelligent and, for those times, cultured man, arrayed in fashionable and well-cut city clothes. Just at first she was agreeably surprised ; but later, noting the godlessness and cynicism with which this man strove to exhibit the worse side of his moral life before the fashionable beauty, she contracted a great dislike for him, which she never quite overcame. His wife, so far as the laws of honour and morality were concerned, was in no way different from her sister Lupenevskaia, though a much cleverer woman. After spending an hour with the Kalpinskis, the young pair proceeded to Madame Lupenevskaia's and spent another hour in her company. At each house they were offered tea and preserved fruit, spiced with conversation which was exceedingly offensive to Sofia Nikolaievna. Both families were invited to dine at Bagrovo on the following Sunday. And here an unaccountable phenomenon of psychological character must be recorded—to wit that Flena Ivanovna felt herself irresistibly attracted towards Sofia Nikolaievna, and to such an extent indeed; that when the latter took her leave, the old lady overwhelmed her with such a torrent of exaggerated endearments and compliments that her guest was forced to blush and laugh at the same time. The young pair reached home an hour before supper time, and there— seated upon the familiar old balcony—was Stepan Michail- ovitsch, who received them with great pleasure. He was vastly entertained by the account of Flena Ivanovna's sudden affection for his daughter-in-law, and how she had kissed and caressed the latter, greeting her as a kindred soul and her " best-beloved cousin." When supper was finished, the whole family gathered together, according to their custom, on the balcony, and talked long and confidentially in the evening's cool, beneath the starlit canopy of heaven, which still shim- mered with the reflection of the dying after-glow of sunset—so especially dear to Stepan Michailovitsch, although the old man could not have told you why.

The two days still remaining before Sunday passed without any event worthy of recording. Erlykin returned from Buguruslan yellow and depressed, as was the case after his fits of drunkenness. Stepan Michailovitsch was quite aware of this unfortunate failing or disease of his son-in-law, and undertook to cure him himself with doses of some particularly nauseous medicated wine, but without any visibly good results. When sober, Erlykin felt a positive disgust for all spirituous liquor, and could hardly raise a glass of wine to his lips without a shudder. But about four times a year a species of periodic passion for intoxicating drink seized him ; if it were refused him he fell into a condition of absolute depression and misery ; kept up a perpetual maundering, scolded and wept, threw himself at folk's feet, begging for a taste of wine : should this still be refused, he flew into a rage, raved and blustered, and even tried to commit murder. Sofia Nikol- aievna had heard all about him, and felt exceedingly sorry for her poor brother-in-law. She treated him with the greatest friendliness, and tried to engage him in cheerful conversation, but all in vain. The haughty, gloomy, and sullen General persisted in his obstinate silence. Jelisaveta Stepanovna, far from feeling grateful, considered herself insulted by her sister-in-law's attentions to her husband ; and very pointedly gave the latter to understand this. Observing which, Stepan Michailovitsch gave his gifted daughter such a severe rebuke, that in future she forebore from sneering at her sister-in-law.

Twice did Stepan Michailovitsch escort Sofia Nikolaievna through the winter-and-summer-sown wheat fields towards the enclosed forest lands and his beloved mountain springs. The old man fondly imagined that his darling daughter-in-law was interested in and pleased with all around her : but she detested everything. Only one thought sustained Sofia Nikol-aievna's endurance, the desire to quit Bagrovo as soon as possible and never to set eyes on it again. Had anyone told her then that she would spend nearly the whole of her future life there, and die there too, she could not have believed the prophecy, and would have declared that she preferred death to such a fate. Thus man deems himself unable to bear an unaccustomed load, little guessing that God Himself will place that burden on his shoulders hereafter !

Sunday arrived. The guests assembled. Maria Michail-ovna arrived from Old Mertovschtschina ; from Lupenevha and from Neklyudovo came the Lupenevskis and Kalpinskis ; and two old bachelors, the magistrate and chief of police, came from Buguruslan. In addition to these guests, an old neighbour, a little, meagre, talkative being of the name of Afrosinia Andreievna (I forget her surname, for no one ever addressed her by it) arrived on the scene from her estate. She was a matchless liar, and her wondrous inventions used to afford Stepan Michailovitsch the same entertainment that adults sometimes find in fairy tales.

But it was worth while to make Afrosinia Andreievna's acquaintance, if only for a short time. She had once spent ten years in Petersburg during the hearing of a law suit, which was eventually decided in her favour, and ever since had resided on her own little property. She had brought home such a marvellous string of adventures which had happened to her while in Petersburg that Stepan Michailovitsch used nearly to die of laughing when she solemnly recounted them. Amongst other things she used to vow that she had been on the most intimate footing with the Empress Katerina Alexeievna ; adding, by way of explanation, that when folks lived together for ten years in the same city, it was but natural that they should get acquainted with one another. '' I was in church on one occasion,'' remarked this gifted liar ; '' mass had just come to an end, when the Empress stepped to my side ; I curtsied low, and ventured to congratulate her in the name of her patron saint, but Her Majesty was pleased to reply : ' Good-day, Afrosinia Andreievna ! How are you getting on with your law suit ? Why do you never bring your knitting along, and come and sit with me of an evening ? We could have a nice little chat together.' After that, I visited her every evening. The Court servants got to know me quite well ; and everyone in the palace knew me, and liked me too. Whenever anyone of the household was sent into the city to make purchases, they used to come and see me and tell me all the Court news. Naturally, I always had a little glass of brandy ready for these occasions. One fine day, towards evening, I was sitting at the window ; suddenly a Court lackey galloped past, all dressed in red, embroidered with the Imperial arms ; after a while a second rode past, and then a third. Then I couldn't contain myself any longer, but opened the window, and called : ' Filip Petrovitsch ! Filip Petrovitsch ! Where are you off to in such a hurry that you can't stop to see me ? ' ' No time for that, little mother,' replied the lackey : ' it's a cursed nuisance ; but we have no lights in the palace, and we shall soon be wanting them ! ' ' Stop ! ' I screamed, ' I have five pounds of candles in stock, and you are welcome to them ! ' How pleased my Filip Petrovitsch was ! I carried those candles out to him myself, and did him that service. Oh, yes, Stepan Michailovitsch, that was how I managed matters. It was only natural that folks should be fond of me ! ''

Stepan Michailovitsch, among his many peculiarities, took an especial pleasure in listening to the harmless lies of good-natured folk. Although a sworn foe to all calculated deceit, and even to the least deviation from the truth, nevertheless he was always highly amused at the marvellous flights of fancy of innocent beings like Afrosinia Andreievna, whose too vivid imagination ran away with them to such an extent that they really believed all they said was true. He loved to talk to Afrosinia Andreievna, and not only in company either ; but when he was in a good humour he enjoyed a tête-à-tête with her, and would listen for hours while she entertained him with the greatest eloquence with stories of her ten-years' residence in Petersburg, all more or less in the style of the foregoing specimen.

But let us return to our party of guests at Bagrovo. What a coat was that worn by the magistrate—what a uniform that of the chief of police ! And there, between that couple of scarecrows in female array—that's to say between his wife and her sister—behold Kalpinski in a French embroidered coat of dandified cut, two watchchains displayed on his waistcoat, countless rings glittering on his fingers, and glorious in silk stockings and gold-buckled shoes ! Even Stepan Michailovitsch had thought it necessary to make something of a toilette, and the whole family had arrayed themselves in their very best. The witty, sarcastic Tschitschagov could hardly conceal his amusement at the varied selection of costumes, especially that of his friend, Kalpinski. He was able to give free rein to his tongue, as his wife and Sofia Nikolaievna, to whom he whispered all his comments, were seated together somewhat apart from the others. Sofia Nikolaievna only restrained her laughter with great difficulty : she tried not to listen to what he said, and begged him earnestly either to be silent or to address himself to the worthy Stepan Michailovitsch. He did as she bade him, and soon grew to regard the old man with great respect and affection, which was reciprocated. The master of the house, on the contrary, could not endure Monsieur Kalpinski, first, because he was a parvenu, and secondly because he was a drunkard and an unbeliever.

You may well imagine what a noble feast had been prepared. On this occasion Stepan Michailovitsch denied himself his favourite dishes, sausages made from pigs' chitterlings, and roast chine of pork with green groats. A skilful cook had been procured from some place or other, and the materials from which the various dishes were concocted left nothing to be desired. A choice six-weeks' calf, a pig fattened to the verge of monstrosity, poultry of every description, and fat mutton—everything was provided in the greatest profusion in honour of the great day. The table literally groaned under the weight of dishes ; and room could not be found for some of these, it being the fashion of those days to place everything on the table at once. The banquet opened with cold viands : ham and smoked pork with garlic : then came the hot dishes : green cabbage soup and cray fish soup, accompanied by various wheaten pastes : next came an iced beetroot soup, followed by freshly-salted sturgeon and a whole pyramid of shelled crawfish tails. Of entrées there were but two : marinaded quails with cabbage ; and stuffed ducklings, served with a sauce composed of plums, peaches, and apricots. The entrées were a concession to fashion. Stepan Michailovitsch utterly despised them and described them as " muck." A colossal turkey next made its appearance, flanked by a fillet of veal garnished with salted melons, marinaded pippins, and salted mushrooms preserved in vinegar. The meal concluded with a variety of sweet pastry and an apple cake served with thick cream. The accompanying beverages were fruit liqueurs, home-brewed March beer, iced kvass, and foaming mead. The guests ate steadily through the menu, without missing a single dish, and the heroic stomachs of our grandparents were fully equal to the mighty task ! They ate slowly and seriously, and dinner was a long affair. Add to the multitude and solidity of the dishes the fact that none of the servants— neither those of the house nor those brought by the guests—had the slightest notion of how to wait at table, and were continually colliding with each other, whereby the ladies' gowns ran considerable risk of being besprinkled with sauce and gravy.

Nevertheless the meal was a very pleasant affair : on the host's right hand Maria Michailovna was seated, and on his left, Tschitschagov, (whom Stepan Michailovitsch liked better and better as time went on), and who in himself was able to enliven the dreariest company. Next to Maria Michailovna came the bridal pair ; and Sofia Nikolaievna's friend, Katerina Borisovna sat on her right. Kalpinski placed himself beside Katerina Borisovna, and paid assiduous court to both young ladies during the feast; and also found time now and again to exchange a jest with Alexei Stepanovitsch, besides devouring a double portion of everything on the table, to compensate for the strict fast that he voluntarily imposed upon himself at home, out of pure avarice. Tschitschagov's neighbour was Erlykin, who, alone of the whole company, ate but sparingly, drank nothing but cold water, and remained sunk in the gloomiest and most profound meditation. Around the hostess were grouped her daughters, nieces, and the rest of the guests. After dinner all adjourned to the drawing room, where a couple of tables were set out with all manner of dainties. On one of these tables stood a circular confectionery service, made of Chinese porcelain and set on a base of gilded and painted bronze. The service consisted of a number of oblong compartments, each provided with a china lid, and containing severally, preserved raspberries, strawberries, cherries, red white and black currants, and the like. In the centre was a raised china dish, filled with conserve of rose leaves. This comfit service, which in those days was a costly novelty, was a gift from old Subin to Stepan Michailovitsch. The other table was covered with little plates filled with dried plums, peaches, dates, figs, walnuts, shell almonds, pistachio nuts, cedar nuts, and so forth. Stepan Michailovitsch was so lively after dinner that he would not hear of taking his usual nap. It was obvious to everyone present that he regarded his daughter-in-law with the utmost affection and devotion, and wished to make it plain that he did so; while she, for her part, sincerely loved and respected him. All during dinner he was constantly turning towards her, and asking her to perform all sorts of little services for him, to reach him this or hand him that, or to cut him a slice of meat just as she liked it herself. "I and my little daughter-in-law have the same taste in everything," he declared. Then he would ask her to repeat what he had said to her the day before; and to tell the company what she had said to him on this or that occasion —as he had quite forgotten what it was. It was the same after dinner. She must arrange this or bring that; and all these trifling behests, coupled with his devotion and his affectionate words—which were uttered with such homely simplicity and clumsy eloquence—left no doubt in his hearers' minds as to the old man's infatuation for his daughter in-law. It is not necessary to relate with what grateful affection Sofia Nikolaievna responded to the slightest—to many present quite unnoticed—utterances in which the partiality of her rugged old father-in-law found expression. In a sudden fit of caprice Stepan Michailovitsch turned towards Madame Lupenevskaia, and enquired bluntly : " Well, Flena Ivanovna, what do you think of my daughter-in-law ? " Flena Ivanovna, whose enthusiasm had been raised to the highest pitch by her generous potations of beer and kindred liquors, began protesting, and swore by the Cross that, from the first moment of setting eyes on Sofia Nikolaievna, she had loved the latter better than her own daughter, Lisanka, and that Cousin Alexei Stepanovitsch was indeed the happiest of mankind. " So you can lie to this tune too," said Stepan Michailovitsch in a meaning tone : " take care that you don't fall into the old tune again ! " Here he was interrupted by Sofia Nikolaievna (who had no desire to have this sort of conversation carried on any farther) who now entreated him to go and rest if only for a little while, to which he readily consented. His daughter-in-law escorted him to his chamber, where she arranged the curtains round his bed with her own hands, and then hastened back to the guests, to carry out the old man's request that they should be hospitably entertained. Some of them likewise retired to rest ; while the others had repaired to the island, and were now reposing in the shade beside the clear stream. Sofia Nikolaievna recalled her ungovernable outbreak of rage in this very spot some days before, and recollected the bitter words which had so saddened and cast down her husband, and her heart smote her. Although Alexei Stepanovitsch was just then in the highest spirits, laughing outrageously at one of Kalpinski's questionable stories, she could not resist the impulse to draw him aside ; and while embracing him, with her eyes swimming in tears, to murmur : " Forgive me, my dearest husband, and forget for ever all that happened here on the day of our arrival ! " Alexei Stepanovitsch, who was very much put out at the sight of her tears, returned her embrace, and kissed his wife's hands, adding cheerily : " Do not distress yourself over such a trifle, my little heart ! " and then rushed back to Kalpinski in order not to miss the end of the interesting anecdote. To speak truly, Sofia Nikolaievna had no ground for dissatisfaction. Nevertheless she remained sad and thoughtful awhile.

But soon the old gentleman awoke, and the whole party were summoned to tea. Before the balcony, in the wide shadow of the house, the samovar was already humming. Tables, easy chairs, and all sorts of seats were awaiting the guests. The bride poured out the tea, while splendid, thick scalded cream, baked until its surface was quite brown, and the most excellent cakes and pastry were handed round, all of which found a resting place in the visitors' stomachs. After tea the Kalpinskis and Lupenevskis went home, as they only lived fifteen versts away and there was no accommodation where they could spend the night at Bagrovo. The guests from Buguruslan took their leave at the same time.

Early the next day Maria Michailovna and the Tschit-schagovs took their departure; and after dinner the Erlykins set off to make the necessary preparations for receiving the newly-wedded pair on their return journey to Ufa. The evening of that same day Stepan Michailovitsch informed the remaining guests, with scant ceremony, that it was time for them to be thinking of going, as he wished to spend the last days of his son's and daughter-in-law's visit solely in their society. Naturally, the visitors lost no time in departing the next day. Alexandra Stepanovna bade her sister-in-law farewell as amiably as she could, and Sofia Nikolaievna took leave of her with unaffected joy. It really seemed as if her father-in-law had divined her secret wish to spend a couple of days quite alone with him, without his daughters' company. How she blessed the sharp-sighted old fellow! She parted from her sister-in-law, Aksinia Stepanovna, with feelings of the warmest gratitude and sincerest regard. The old man did not fail to notice this. Her mother-in-law and Tania did not irk her in the least; first, because they were kindly by nature and moreover felt no hostility towards their new relative; and secondly, because they had the praiseworthy habit of taking themselves off, when they observed that their company was not wanted.

The young couple remained three days longer in Bagrovo —a period of tranquillity, free from the wearisome supervision of hostile witnesses and from hypocritical pretence of friendship and venomous hints. Sofia Nikolaievna's sensitive nerves were relieved, and she was able to make a calmer survey of the peculiar sphere which she was henceforth fated to occupy, and to comprehend and value it at its true worth. She was also enabled to make a juster and more forbearing estimate of the characters of her mother-in-law and Tania, who were both possessed of qualities as yet quite unknown to her, and to observe her father-in-law with much circumspection. She observed and understood the environment in which her husband's youth had been spent with the utmost clearness, realising how impossible it was that he should have developed into anything different than what he actually was ; and she could not fail to realise farther that she would have to be prepared for eternal mutual misunderstanding, even perhaps in questions of conscience. But this last was but a fugitive thought, and once again her earlier and delicious dreams of transforming and regenerating her Alexei took possession of her lively imagination. And what so frequently befalls the majority of young wives happened inevitably in the case of Sofia Nikolaievna : her consciousness of her husband's intellectual inferiority, even his lack of comprehension and sympathy, in no wise hindered her from resigning herself to him in a passionate abandonment of boundless love . . . . but already a dim feeling of unrest had begun to dawn in her soul, she felt that he did not love her as she had a right to be loved . . . . that even in her company he had eyes only for the mill-pond and the islet, for the steppe and the quail, for the river and the fish that she detested so heartily. This feeling of jealousy, at first dimly and vaguely felt, was already developing in her fervent heart ; and the gloomiest forebodings arose within her as she contemplated her future. Stepan Michailovitsch, who, in like manner, had been distracted by being forced to keep a constant eye on his daughters' behaviour, was now able to observe his daughter-in-law, and his son too, more closely. He was so clever, in spite of his lack of education, and possessed such unerring delicacy of feeling, in spite of his rough exterior, that it did not take him long to discover the inequality of these two so-different natures. By this, I do not mean to insinuate that he was not pleased and touched by their mutual affection and by the growing and pathetic devotion of Sofia Nikolaievna towards her husband. No, he delighted in it, but always with a lurking presentiment of evil, and without any steadfast belief in the durability of this satisfactory condition of affairs. He spoke long and earnestly with the young couple, both together, and singly. He wished to say things, to point out things, to give useful advice. But when he began to talk, he found himself quite incapable of giving adequate expression to his own half-defined and half-understood thoughts and feelings ; and was forced to fall back on the homely, well-worn, but sage precepts which old folks in those days were wont to instil into their children's minds as sure guides for a future life of honour and rectitude. His own lack of eloquence pained him, as he candidly admitted to his daughter-in-law, who, however, could always guess exactly what he had in his mind, whatever difficulty he found in expressing himself. To his son he remarked : " Your wife is a sensible woman, but now and then too hasty. If she lets her tongue run away with her, don't hesitate to rebuke her ; but forgive her directly afterwards, and don't sulk or bear malice. Take care you always speak out when she does anything to annoy you, for you can rely upon her good heart, and she will never put anyone before you." Speaking in confidence to Sofia Nikolaievna, he said : " My dear little daughter-in-law, God has withheld none of His gifts from you, but I have one word of advice to offer you : restrain your hot blood. Your husband is a good and honourable man : his disposition is mild, and he will never do anything to hurt your feelings. Now, for your part, never do anything to grieve him ! Honour him, and treat him with respect ! When the wife has no respect for her husband, there is but a poor prospect of happiness. If he acts or speaks contrary to your mind, you will do well to keep silence and not to make a fuss over trifles. I love you with all my heart and can read you like a book. Most earnestly I entreat you to keep a tight hand over yourself. Moderation is best in everything, even in devotion and reverence."

His son accepted his father's counsel with his customary awe and respect ; Sofia Nikolaievna, with the warm and loving gratitude of a daughter. Many other matters were discussed :

the future life in Ufa, Alexei Stepanovitsch's coming career in the service of the Government, the necessary means for the young pair's life in the city. Every point was minutely examined and considered, and on all points all were finally and unanimously agreed.

At last came the day of departure. The silk curtains and bed-hangings had all been taken down, the satin and muslin slips with their wide lace borders had been removed from the pillows, and all these fine things had been packed up and despatched to Ufa. All sorts of provisions for the journey were cooked and baked. Spiritual aid was not forgotten, and old Father Vasili was summoned to offer up prayers for travellers. Horses had been bespoken, not in Noikino this time, but at Korovino, forty versts from Bagrovo. Thus far the spirited home team were to convey them—those same six matchless horses that had brought them to the old home. For the last time they sat down to table together : for the last time Stepan Michailovitsch pressed his daughter-in-law to taste his favourite dishes. The coach stood ready at the door. All rose from the dinner table and went into the salon, where they seated themselves, and a silence fell on them. Stepan Michailovitsch rose from his chair, crossed himself, and commenced to utter the parting Farewell.[1] Everyone, except Stepan Michailovitsch, was in tears, and he himself could scarce refrain from weeping too. While blessing and embracing his daughter-in-law, he whispered in her ear : " Rejoice my old heart with a grandson ! " Sofia Nikolaievna blushed, and bending down, kissed the old man's hands, which this time were not withdrawn. Outside the house all the household and the greater part of the peasantry were assembled round the balcony staircase. Some of them ventured to approach to bid their young master and mistress Farewell, but Stepan Michailovitsch, who disliked these parting scenes, called out to them : " Don't intrude ! Make your obeisance, and then be off ! " Only Fedosia and Peter were permitted to kiss Sofia Nikolaievna. The young travellers sprang nimbly into the coach, and like a feather it was whirled away by the lusty team. For awhile Stepan Michailovitsch remained

[1] It is the custom in Russia to take leave of travellers setting out on a long journey in this fashion. [Tr. S. R.]

standing silent, shading his eyes with his hand from the blinding sun, and trying to distinguish the coach through the fleeting clouds of dust upon the highway. But soon it vanished behind the hill where the threshing-ground lay, and the old man returned to his room and lay down to sleep.

SKETCH V

LIFE IN UFA

For the first few moments following her departure Sofia
Nikolaievna could only feel the pain of the parting with her
father-in-law ; she could only think of this old man, whom
she had learnt to love so well, and who was now grieving over
her absence. But soon the regular swaying of the coach, the
pleasant sight of field and forest flying past the windows, the
shady mountain spurs round which the road was winding—all
these had a soothing influence on her spirit, and she felt the
most intense joy at the thought that now she would never
set eyes on Bagrovo again. This joy increased to such a pitch
that it was impossible for the young wife to entirely conceal
it, although she was conscious that such a feeling must needs
be unwelcome to her husband. It seemed to her as if Alexei
Stepanovitsch were gloomier than the occasion warranted, and
probably this might have given rise to some unpleasantness ;
luckily the presence of Parascha prevented this catastrophe.
The coach rolled rapidly through Noikina, accompanied by
the joyous shouts of the Mordvins who ran out to meet it ;
over the rickety bridge, where the bank of the Nasiagai joins
a tributary of the Bokla ; sped past Polibino, and, crossing
the Nasiagai for the second time, arrived at Korovino, where
the relay of horses was awaiting the travellers. Here the
Bagrovo horses were to be baited and rested, and sent back
home early the next day. Sofia Nikolaievna had brought
writing materials, and wrote a warm letter of thanks to her
father and mother-in-law, which, sooth to say, was solely
intended for Stepan Michailovitsch. The latter guessed as
much and treasured the letter in a secret drawer of his little
old writing table, where it was safe from any prying eyes ;

and where it was accidentally found by Sofia Nikolaievna herself, eight years later, after the old man's death.

The fresh horses were harnessed to the coach, and our travellers continued their journey, after bidding adieu to the coachman and postillion, the latter rôle being filled on this occasion by the long-shanked Tanaitschenok. Fate seemed determined to shew especial favour towards Sofia Nikolaievna, for it was found quite impossible to pay the appointed visit to the Erlykins. The bridge across a deep river, which it was necessary to cross in order to reach their estate, had collapsed. To wait until it had been repaired would have taken too much time, so the newly-married pair decided to travel direct to Ufa. What dreary and wretched hours was the young wife spared, by this toward event ! The nearer they approached Ufa, the warmer grew the fount of her filial affection. The image of the suffering father (from whom she had already been separated for more than two weeks) surrounded only by neglectful servants, was ever present to her vivid imagination. The passage of the Bielaia in a dilapidated ferry boat, which delayed the travellers for more than an hour, in addition to the exceedingly toilsome ascent of the mountainous shore—all this strained Sofia Nikolaievna's nerves to the utmost degree, and wrought upon her impatient and irritable temper. At last, arrived at home, she hastened in a feverish state of anxiety to her father's room, and opened the door softly. The old man lay in bed as usual, and beside him, in the armchair which hitherto had been sacred to Sofia Nikolaievna, sat his servant—the Kalmuck Nikolai !

I must now tell you all about this Kalmuck. In former times it was quite a common thing in the Government of Ufa for folks to buy Kalmuck and Kirghiz children of both sexes from their parents or other relations, and the children so purchased became the absolute property of the purchaser. Some thirty years before the already-recorded events, Nikolai Feodorovitsch bought two little Kalmucks, whom he caused to be baptised and of whom he had grown very fond, treating them with the utmost indulgence. As the boys grew older, he had them taught to read and write and installed them as his personal attendants. Both were clever, active, and apparently full of zeal. But as soon as the Pugatschevian revolt broke out, they ran away and joined the rebels. One of them was killed almost immediately ; the other, Nikolai, formerly his master's favourite, ingratiated himself with the notorious agitator, Tschika, who was in high favour with Pugatschev. As everybody knows, a great number of mutinous serfs were encamped for a long time on the far shore of the Bielaia, directly opposite Ufa ; among these was the Kalmuck Nikolai, who occupied a responsible position. It was said that he had been the worst brigand in the district, and had uttered specially menacing threats against his master and benefactor, Subin. The tale went that each time the rebels prepared to cross the Bielaia in order to seize the defenceless city, a great army of troops appeared on the crest of the precipitous opposite shore, headed by an old man mounted on a snow-white steed, bearing a lance in his right hand and the Cross in his left. And each time the cowardly crew of rascals was too terrified to carry out their design. While they hesitated and delayed, the news arrived of the capture of Pugatschev. This was the signal for the dispersal of the base camp. The Pugatschev revolt was subdued, and the fugitive serfs were, for the most part, captured and brought to justice. Among these was the Kalmuck Nikolai, who was tried and condemned to be hanged. I cannot vouch for the truth of the story, but I have been solemnly assured that Nikolai, who had been tried in Ufa, had the rope actually round his neck, when Subin, exercising his right of ownership, granted a pardon to his former favourite, and took him back into his own service on his own bail and responsibility. The Kalmuck professed great repentance for his misdeeds, and sought to rehabilitate himself by zealous service. By degrees he found means to insinuate himself afresh into his master's confidence ; and when Sofia Nikolaievna took over the control of the house after the death of her stepmother, she found the fellow already installed as head-servant and her father's favourite, principally owing to the fact that he had been in high favour with his late mistress. The Kalmuck, who had inflicted innumerable insults and injuries upon the young lady during her period of humiliation, was cunning enough to perceive the altered situation, and played the part of penitent sinner with great adroitness, attributing all his insolence to the defunct stepmother, and pleading that he had been compelled to carry out her tyrannical orders. The magnanimous, fourteen-year-old mistress, who, by uttering a single word, could have had him banished for ever from the house, believed in the sincerity of his repentance, and herself entreated her father to let him remain in his situation. Eventually, things turned out very unsatisfactorily, for she was greatly annoyed by his arbitrary attitude and the suspicious way in which sums of money confided to his keeping disappeared; while she could not fail to observe that he was secretly growing more familiar with her father than she approved. Still, in consideration of his indefatigable care of her father (in whose room he always slept) and his excellent service as house-steward, she contented herself with rebuking him gently, and left the wretch free to make his footing in the house still more secure. After Sofia Nikolaievna was betrothed, she had to busy herself with the preparation of her trousseau and the rest of her dowry furnishings; she was compelled to spend considerable time with her bridegroom, and consequently less time with her father; and could give but superficial attention to household matters. The Kalmuck made the most of this favourable opportunity, and each day strengthened his influence over his old and sick master.

In anticipation of getting rid of his mistress and of becoming sole master in the house, he grew bolder and bolder, and made no attempt to conceal his arrogance. Sofia Nikolaievna would not have hesitated to put him in his place with prompt severity, but, to her infinite distress, she found her father growing more and more absolutely dependent on the Kalmuck's services, and becoming more and more influenced by him. The final days before, and the early days after, the wedding, and now the two weeks' absence of the young pair, had sufficed the astute Kalmuck to gain full control of his half-dead master; and the first sight of this lackey seated in her chair (a thing he had never dared to do before) opened Sofia Nikolaievna's eyes to the true state of affairs. She threw such a look at the favourite, as quite abashed him, and he slunk out of the room. The old man evinced none of the joy at the sight of his daughter that she had expected, and he hastened to inform her that he himself had frequently requested the

Kalmuck to sit beside him in the armchair. Sofia Nikolaievna replied briefly : " You are making a great mistake, father ; you will spoil him, and then will be obliged to get rid of him. I know him better than you do," and hastened to change the unpleasant subject by expressing her great joy at finding her beloved invalid no worse. Alexei Stepanovitsch came into the room, and the old man who was much affected by the tender concern of his daughter and the sympathetic kindness of his son-in-law, as well as by their mutual love, listened affectionately to their account of their visit and blessed God for their happiness. Sofia Nikolaievna promptly set to work to make the necessary arrangements for her new position ; selected three adjacent rooms for herself ; and at the end of a few days was able to receive visitors without in the least disturbing her sick father. She then determined to resume her place as head of the household, and to take over the care of her father, relegating the Kalmuck to his former subordinate position ; but the fellow, who had always hated her, considered himself sufficiently strongly established to engage in open warfare with his young mistress. While redoubling his attentions to old Subin, he managed, with incredible audacity, to insult the daughter, and especially her unassuming husband, in every possible way, until Alexei Stepanovitsch, for all his forbearance and easy-going disposition, lost all patience and told his wife that such a state of things was simply intolerable. For some time Sofia Nikolaievna refrained from troubling her invalid father, and herself attempted to keep Nikolai within the bounds of decency. She counted upon his prudence, and, farther, upon his knowledge of her firm character, believing that he would not risk driving her to extremity. But the wily Asiatic (as everyone in the house called him) was assured of victory from the first, and did his utmost to irritate Sofia Nikolaievna, in the hope of driving her into a furious rage. Long ago he had succeeded in convincing his old master that the young mistress could not endure him—the faithful Kalmuck—and that she had made up her mind to drive him out of the house. This information had greatly agitated and disturbed the sick man, and he had sworn by all that was sacred that he would sooner die than be parted from his Nikolai. Sofia Nikolaievna, speak-

ing in the mildest and most forbearing tone, tried to make
her father comprehend that the Kalmuck conducted himself
with the greatest insolence towards her and her husband,
carrying out her orders so negligently that it was not difficult
to see that his intention was to annoy her. Nikolai Feodorovitsch grew terribly excited on hearing her complaints ; he
refused to listen to her, assured her that, for his own part,
he was perfectly satisfied with the Kalmuck, and begged her
to leave the man in peace, and commission one or another of
the servants to carry out her orders. It cost the haughty
young woman many and bitter pangs to submit to the will
of a base slave in her own father's house, where she had been
accustomed to rule absolutely. Still, she loved her father so
devotedly and felt such an urgent longing to tend his sick
bed and to ease his sufferings so far as lay in her power, that
for long enough it never even entered her mind to leave the
house, and thereby abandon her father wholly to the influence
of the infamous Kalmuck and the rest of the servants. She
restrained her anger and her injured pride : her orders were
henceforth given to other servants, but it was impossible not
to see how persistently the Kalmuck interfered and prevented
them being carried out as she wished. She entreated her
father to forbid the Kalmuck his room, while she was in it :
but this prohibition was very soon infringed. Nikolai was
always finding fresh pretexts to sneak into the old man's
room ; and the invalid himself gave the man every occasion
for so doing, by continually calling for his services. And this
wretched state of things continued for some months.

Sofia Nikolaievna had arranged her social life in Ufa
entirely to suit herself : she saw a great deal of her personal
friends, entertaining them and being entertained by them in
turn. She was merely on formal and polite terms with the rest
of the citizens. Alexei Stepanovitsch had formerly been known
to everyone in Ufa, but now was treated with much greater
intimacy by Sofia Nikolaievna's friends, who learnt to value
his sterling, good qualities ; and he was very well pleased with
these new friends, who formed his wife's especial social circle.

Very shortly after her return from Bagrovo Sofia Nikolaievna experienced a peculiar indisposition, the news of which
filled the heart of Stepan Michailovitsch with joy. The

continuation of the ancient line of the Bagrovs, the coming descendant of the illustrious Schimon,[1] became the dearest object of his hopes and ambitions ; and secretly caused him much solicitude and care. No sooner had his son communicated the joyful tidings to him than Stepan Michailovitsch cherished the hope—nay the conviction—that a grandson would be born. Later, the family declared that his temper had been extraordinarily amiable during the months of anticipation. He immediately ordered prayers to be offered up in church " for the health of the noble Sofia." Many a fault and many a debt was overlooked or remitted to his serfs or neighbours. Everyone was expected to offer him congratulations ; and beer and brandy were most liberally bestowed upon these well-wishers. In the midst of all this joyous tumult, it suddenly occurred to him that he ought to reward his tea-and-coffee handmaiden, Aksiutka, whom, Heaven alone knows why, he had always regarded with especial favour. Aksiutka was originally an orphan peasant child, who had been admitted into the household when seven years old, solely because no one else would give her a home or a situation. She was very ugly, carroty-haired, her face was covered with freckles, and her eyes were of a doubtful hue, while her dress was invariably untidy and her temper atrocious. Was it possible indeed, that anyone could be attracted by such a being ? But in spite of all, Stepan Michailovitsch had a great regard for her, and not a day passed without him sending her something good from the family dinner-table. As soon as she was a grown-up lass, Stepan Michailovitsch appointed her to serve him with his early cup of tea, and utilised these occasions to chat with her for hours at a stretch. Aksiutka was now well advanced in the thirties. One fine morning, a couple of days after receiving the happy news from Ufa, Stepan Michailovitsch said to her : " You stupid girl, why do you always go about in that dirty old smock ? Be off, and dress yourself decently : put on your holiday clothes, and I will find you a husband ! " Aksiutka shewed all her teeth in a grin, thinking that the master was making game of her, and replied : " Who wants to have a poor orphan like me ? At the best, only the shepherd, Kir-

---

[1] A traditional Varangian (or Slavic Russian). [Tr. H. R.]

sanka ! " The shepherd was noted for his plain looks and stupidity. This retort appeared to irritate Stepan Michail- ovitsch. " If I choose a husband for you, you shall have the best lad that can be found ; so be off, and smarten yourself up, and come back as soon as you are ready ! " Aksiutka departed in a state of joyful astonishment, and Stepan Michailovitsch sent for Ivan Malisch,[1] to whom we have already been introduced. He was a youth, four-and-twenty years old with ruddy cheeks ; slim, yet strong of build, and a smart fellow in all respects. He was a son of the faithful old retainer, Boris Petrov Chorev, who died during the Pugatschev revolt, worn out, as everybody knew, by the responsibility of looking after the New-Bagrovian serfs,who had been committed to his charge, when the family fled to Astrachan for safety. Ivan had acquired the nickname of *Malisch*,[2] as he had an elder brother also called Ivan, who had inherited his father's nickname of *Chorev*.[3] Ivan Malisch made his appearance before his master, who observed his good looks with great satisfaction, and addressed him in such a kind and friendly tone, that the young man's heart fairly throbbed with joy : " Malisch, I am going to have you married." " Your gracious will be done, little father Stepan Michailovitsch ! " replied the young man, who was devoted, body and soul, to his master. " Run away and dress yourself nicely and come back to me as quickly as you can ! " Off dashed Malisch to do as he was told. Aksiutka, however, was ready the first : she had plastered her red hair with butter to make it lie smoothly, and had put on her Sunday skirt and bodice, and forced her big feet into a pair of shoes ; and, with all this preparation, was not a bit more beautiful ! She could not prevent her mouth twisting into a permanent smile of delight, which she bash- fully attempted to conceal by covering her face with her hand. Stepan Michailovitsch was highly diverted. " Ah," said he, " how pleased she is to have caught a husband ! " Up ran Malisch, and turned cold with horror when he perceived the bedizened scarecrow, Aksiutka. " Here is your bride," said Stepan Michailovitsch, gaily, " she serves me faithfully :

---

[1] See Sketch III. [Tr.] [2] *Malisch* means the Little One. [Tr. S.R.]
[3] *Chorev* signifies The Pole Cat. [Tr. H.R.]

your father served me faithfully, too : you can always rely upon my protection ! " " Arischa," he continued to his wife who had just arrived on the scene, " the bride must have her wedding dower prepared : I shall give her a cow too, and the wedding shall be celebrated with plenty of beer, brandy, and good cheer." No resistance was possible. The wedding took place immediately. Aksiutka was madly in love with her good-looking husband ; but Malisch contracted a downright hatred for his repulsive bride, who was ten years his senior. Aksiutka persecuted her husband from morning to night with her jealousy, for which she had only too good cause ; while Malisch thrashed his wife early and late, and not without cause too, for the stick alone—and that only for a few minutes at a time—could make her stop scolding. Alas, alas, Stepan Michailovitsch had made a sad mistake ; and in the joy of his own heart had prepared an evil lot for others !

The intense joy of the old man at this period was revealed to me—not so much by the accounts given by relatives—as by a letter written by him to Sofia Nikolaievna about the same time. It is scarcely credible that this rugged man (although, as we have already seen, capable of true and sincere affection) should have been able to express his feelings so exquisitely. The whole letter breathes the tenderest solicitude, and is full of entreaties and admonitions to her for the care of her health. I can only recall a few words of the letter. " If you were but here with me," wrote the old man, " I would not let the least breath of wind blow upon you, nor let a speck of dust defile you."

Sofia Nikolaievna valued this affection of her father-in-law at its true worth (although she was perfectly aware that at least the half of it was on account of the expected heir) and dutifully promised to observe all his directions and commands. She belonged to that order of women who pay for the bliss of motherhood by a nervous indisposition, which is worse to endure than downright illness. In addition to this, her mental suffering was intense : her relations with her father became more strained each day that passed, and the insolence of the Kalmuck more unbearable. Alexei Stepanovitsch was content enough on hearing that his wife's condition was quite natural under the circumstances, that nothing dangerous threatened her, and that her indisposition would soon pass away. He was sorry, certainly, that his wife suffered so much, but did not shew any special concern ; and this indifference helped to make Sofia Nikolaievna ill. As far as Alexei Stepanovitsch's life in his father-in-law's house was concerned, he had made up his mind to avoid any intercourse whatever with the Kalmuck ; he fulfilled his duties in the Supreme Court most zealously, having every expectation of being shortly appointed State Agent. Meanwhile he tranquilly awaited a better condition of affairs at home, and annoyed his wife by his composure. And so some more months passed away without bringing much satisfaction to anyone.

But the Kalmuck was by no means disposed to let matters rest here : he was determined to bring about a crisis. As he could not fail to perceive that Sofia Nikolaievna was putting the utmost restraint on her just indignation, he resolved to exhaust her patience. He hoped to irritate her and to force her to complain about him to her father, having previously warned his old master that the young mistress intended to have him turned out of the house. Without waiting for any special opportunity, the fellow made such insolent and out-rageous remarks about Sofia Nikolaievna and her husband to his fellow servants—speaking in an audible tone, and selecting an occasion when his young mistress was standing at the open door of the adjacent room, not a couple of steps distant—that Sofia Nikolaievna was for the moment paralysed by his audacity. Recovering herself quickly, without uttering a word to the Kalmuck, she rushed into her father's room, and, nearly breathless with rage, told him how his favourite had treated her. The Kalmuck instantly followed her. Pulling a most lamentable face, and crossing himself before the sacred picture, he interrupted her by protesting that the whole story was a slander, that he had never said anything of the sort, and that Sofia Nikolaievna was guilty of a grievous sin in trying to ruin a poor man ! " Do you hear what he says, Sonitschka ?" asked the sick man in an agitated voice. Sofia Nikolaievna, wounded to the very depths of her soul, forgot all her mag-nanimous resolutions, forgot that any excitement was very injurious for her father, and denounced his favourite with such vehemence that the latter was fairly driven from the

room. At length she said to the old man : " After such
insults, father, I cannot remain any longer in the same house
with this Kalmuck. You must choose which of us you will
banish—him or me ! " and she rushed out of the room like one
possessed. The invalid fell into a swoon, and the Kalmuck
hurried to his assistance. After the application of the
necessary restoratives the old man recovered, and had a long
and private conversation with his favourite, at the end of
which he sent for his daughter. " Sonitschka," said he, with
as much firmness and composure as he could summon, " in
my deplorable condition I find it impossible to part with
Nikolai. My life is dependent on his services. Take this
money and buy the Veselovski house ! " Sofia Nikolaievna
sank unconscious to the ground and was carried from the
room.

And this was the end of the mutual and tender affection
between father and daughter ! This love, so immeasurably
strengthened by the estrangement contrived by the step-
mother, by the remorse and gratitude of the guilty father,
by the warm and great-hearted magnanimity of the injured
daughter, who condoned all the evil treatment she had
suffered ! This daughter, who had devoted herself so entirely
to the sick old man, and who had only married on the understanding that she and he were never to be separated ! And
at what a moment was she bidden to leave him ! Just when
the doctors had declared that they could not answer for his
living another month ! However the doctors were mistaken
in their prophecy, as is frequently the case to-day. The
invalid survived for more than a year.

When Sofia Nikolaievna came to herself again and saw
the pale and shocked countenance of her Alexei Stepanovitsch,
she felt that there yet remained in the world one being who
was devotedly attached to her. She flung her arms round
her distressed husband, and a flood of tears relieved her over-
laden heart. She related all that had passed to him ; and the
telling of the tale renewed all the bitterness of the humiliation
she had suffered, and placed the hopelessness of the situation
in a still clearer light. Most assuredly she would have
collapsed in utter despair, had she not been sustained and
encouraged by her husband. Mild in character and vastly

inferior to his wife intellectually, Alexei Stepanovitsch was superior to her in that he never failed in case of need and never lost his presence of mind in the face of a crisis. It may appear strange that it was Alexei Stepanovitsch who infused courage and self-command into his wife : but this notable woman, in spite of all her mental gifts and apparent strength of character, possessed the unfortunate peculiarity that, whenever subjected to unexpected trials which wounded her in her *affections*, she became utterly helpless and disconcerted. As an impartial recorder of verbal communications, I must add that she was wont to attach far too much importance to the opinion of the world, and was far too much influenced by it ; in spite of the fact that she herself was of much higher rank than the other members of the circle in which she moved. The thought of what society in Ufa would say about the matter, especially women of fashion and position—what her husband's family would think, and, above all, what her father-in-law would think of her deserting her dying father—these harassing ideas tormented her haughty, sensitive spirit, and caused her almost as great agony as the pangs of her injured filial affection. She dreaded lest anyone should blame her father for his ingratitude towards his own child, quite as much as she feared being accused of heartlessness towards her dying parent. It was quite impossible to conceal the rupture ; in some way or another everyone in the city would get to know all about it, and would blame either father or daughter. A feeling of the deepest compassion, mingled with astonishment, overwhelmed Alexei Stepanovitsch at the sight of his wife's distress. It was a hard business to console and reassure his Sofia Nikolaievna. Her excited imagination conjured up all sorts of frightful prospects, and she painted her future in the blackest colours. She utterly refused to believe in any possible chance of escaping from her present overwhelming difficulties ; and flatly declined to try to make the best of the situation. But love and a simplicity of nature, which latter quality was utterly wanting in Sofia Nikolaievna, prompted Alexei Stepanovitsch to act for the best ; and after he had checked the first uncontrolled outburst of passionate lamentation, he began to reason with his wife in his homely but loving way, until she gradually became, if not quite consoled, at any rate more calm and sensible. He assured her that, hitherto, she had conscientiously fulfilled her duty as a loving daughter should ; that the same sense of duty now bade her defer to the wishes of her sick father ; that it was perfectly obvious that Nikolai Feodorovitsch had long since made up his mind that she was to have a house of her own ; that it would be a terrible blow for him—a sick and dying man—to have to part with the Kalmuck, and to be deprived of his skilful and devoted nursing ; that his father, Stepan Michailovitsch, should be made acquainted with the true facts of the case ; and as for their friends, well, they could explain that it had always been Nikolai Feodorovitsch's wish to see his daughter and son-in-law settled in their own house during his own lifetime. Sofia Nikolaievna could visit her father twice daily, and to all intents and purposes look after him as well as ever ; that everyone in the town would learn the real truth in time, and already had heard rumours of it, and would lay all the blame on the Kalmuck and entirely ex-onerate her. " Besides," added he, " it is possible that your father spoke in haste, and, when it comes to the point, will not wish to be separated from you. You must see him again and talk things over with him ! " Sofia Nikolaievna made no reply, and was silent awhile fixing an earnest and enquiring gaze on her husband : she felt revived and comforted by the sincerity and simplicity which breathed in every word of his plain and unaffected speech, and this in a manner hitherto unknown to her complex nature. She wondered that she had not thought of all this before, and embraced her Alexei Stepanovitsch with love and gratitude. And thus they made up their minds that Sofia Nikolaievna was to go to Nikolai Feodorovitsch and persuade him to reconsider his decision, and to permit her and her husband to remain in his house—on the understanding that they lived quite to themselves and never came in contact with the Kalmuck—at least until the time when Sofia Nikolaievna, with God's help, should have completely recovered after her confinement. This proposal was based on the plea that for a woman in Sofia Nikolaievna's state of health, it would be exceedingly dangerous to con-tinually jolt over the badly-paved streets of Ufa ; while it was quite certain that nothing would deter her from visiting her invalid father daily. But the conference with her father led to nothing. The old man told his daughter quietly, but firmly, that his decision was not the outcome of a momentary fit of temper, but the result of much earnest deliberation. " From the very first I have known, my dear Sonitschka," said Nikolai Feodorovitsch, " that it would be absolutely impossible for you and Nikolai to live in the same house together. You have an antipathy for him, for which I do not blame you, for he behaved very badly to you in the old days. You forgave him, but you forgot nothing. I know that he occasionally causes you dissatisfaction, but you are determined to look at matters in the worst possible light " . . . . " Father ! " interrupted Sofia Nikolaievna ; however the old man would not give her time to finish, and went on : " Wait ! and listen until I have said all I have to say ! Admitted that the Kalmuck is as much to blame as you say, then so much the more inadmissible for you to remain under the same roof with him, for you know it is impossible for me to part with him. Have some pity for my miserable and helpless condition ! I can scarcely breathe, I am a living corpse—and you know that the man has to lift me up twenty times a day, to turn me, and to lay me down again. No one can supply his place—only one thing is needful to me now : peace of mind ! Death stands at my door ! Each instant I must be prepared to enter Eternity ! The thought of this Kalmuck embittering your life robs me of all peace. There is no other way out of the difficulty ; and we must part, my dearest child. Go, and dwell in your own home ! Whenever you come to see me you shall not be troubled by the sight of this obnoxious man ; and he will be only too pleased to keep out of your way. He has now attained his object, has forced you to leave the house, and can plunder me to his heart's content. I am perfectly aware that he does so ; but I forgive him on account of his devoted care of me by day and night. The way he exerts himself for me almost passes the limit of human strength. Don't distress me by refusing to do as I desire you ; but take the money, and buy yourself the house in Golubinaia Street ! "

I shall not attempt a description of the multifarious uncertainties, doubts, inward combats, fits of passion, and torrents of tears which succeeded each other with Sofia

Nikolaievna. Briefly, she was forced to accept the money; the house was purchased, and two weeks later Alexei Stepanovitsch and his young wife took possession of their new abode. It was a pretty, plainly-built little house, which had never before been occupied. Sofia Nikolaievna set to work to make her domestic arrangements with her wonted zeal and energy. But her health, affected by her condition and still more by her recent excitement and emotion, was badly shaken, and would not stand this fresh fatigue : she became seriously ill, was compelled to keep her bed for two weeks, and nearly a month elapsed before she was able to go and see her father.

The first meeting of Sofia Nikolaievna and her father, after her recovery, was both sorrowful and affecting. The old man had grown much weaker ; he had yearned after his daughter, reproaching himself with having caused her illness ; and had been terribly afflicted by the utter impossibility of visiting her. But now at least they were reunited and shed tears of joy. Nikolai Feodorovitsch was greatly shocked to observe how emaciated and disfigured his daughter had become, which, however, was less the result of her illness and grief than of her special physical condition. There are certain women whose appearance at these periods undergoes a great change, they even grow ugly, and this was the case with Sofia Nikolaievna. In a very short time the most perfect agreement and most amicable relations were re-established between father and daughter. The Kalmuck kept most religiously out of Sofia Nikolaievna's sight. . . . Stepan Michailovitsch, alone, did not approve of Sofia Nikolaievna being separated from her dying father. Sofia Nikolaievna had foreseen this, and, before she fell ill, had written a very frank letter to her father-in-law, in which she strove to explain away and excuse her father's decision. But all her trouble was wasted. In this affair Stepan Michailovitsch considered that Sofia Nikolaievna, and not Nikolai Feodorovitsch, was to blame, and was of opinion that it was her duty to have borne her troubles in silence, and not to have permitted even a trace of discontent to be seen, whatever rascally tricks the base Kalmuck had played. He wrote to Alexei Stepanovitsch, rebuking him for permitting his wife to leave her father " in the hands of a knave." The idea of a separation being necessary for the sick man's tranquillity of mind, was utterly incomprehensible to Stepan Michailovitsch, and he was equally incapable of understanding that in certain cases a wife is justified in acting without her husband's sanction. But in this case both husband and wife were in perfect accord.

In order to complete the domestic arrangements of her little house more quickly and comfortably, Sofia Nikolaievna called in the assistance of one of her intimate friends, a widow and a burgess of Ufa, Katerina Alexeievna Tscheprunova. This was a simple and worthy woman, who lived in a little house of her own in a distant suburb, where she earned a scanty living by the sale of the produce of her little orchard. In addition she carried on various little bits of trades in order to support herself and her darling Andrei, her crippled and only son, even selling cakes in the market. The principal branch of her business was, however, the sale of Bokhara woollen goods, to purchase which she made a journey to Orenburg each year. On her mother's side Katerina Alexeievna was related to Sofia Nikolaievna, but the latter was weak-minded enough to conceal the fact, which, nevertheless, was known to every soul in the city. Katerina Alexeievna was devotedly attached to her distinguished and aristocratic cousin ; and during the late stepmother's reign of persecution and humiliation, she used to secretly visit and comfort Sofia Nikolaievna, in spite of being forbidden the house. Since Time had wrought the great change in her position, the grateful girl had constituted herself the special benefactress and patroness of the poor cake-seller. In private, Sofia Nikolaievna lavished kindnesses upon her faithful and disinterested relative, and treated her with the utmost respect ; but in public she was the vice-regent's daughter, and her cousin was only her humble protégée. But the good-natured Katerina Alexeievna never took the slightest offence, and had even suggested this plan herself : she loved her beautiful cousin with simple adoration, regarding her in the light of some beneficent being of a higher sphere, and could never have forgiven herself, if she had, in any way, marred the splendour of Sofia Nikolaievna's position. It was but natural that the young husband, Alexei Stepanovitsch, should be made a party to the little secret ; and, in spite of his ancient and aristocratic descent, of which his family were so inordinately proud, he accepted the poor little shopkeeper as a cherished and honoured relation of his wife, and never failed to treat her with regard and respect. He would even have kissed her toil-worn hand, but she would never consent to his doing such a thing. Only by the most pressing entreaties did Sofia Nikolaievna prevent him from openly acknowledging the relationship to his family and friends alike. And what fervent devotion was awakened in the simple soul of Katerina Alexeievna by his kindly demeanour ! With what zeal and energy she strove to straighten out all domestic differences and troubles in days to come ! Assisted by this good woman who knew exactly where anything was to be found, or where anything was to be had cheaply, Sofia Nikolaievna was very soon able to regulate her household affairs to a nicety.

Of course there was a great deal of gossip and scandal in the city, when it became known that the young Bagrovs had bought a house and had gone to live in it by themselves. Much that was exaggerated, and much that was false was circulated ; but Alexei Stepanovitsch had not been mistaken. Soon enough the true facts of the case were known, and principally through the Kalmuck's own agency ; for he was continually boasting in his own circle of how he had driven the supercilious young mistress out of the house, while he never lost an opportunity of abusing and slandering her. And so the evil rumours soon ceased altogether.

In those early days, this was the manner of life led by the newly-married pair. During the earlier part of the morning Alexei Stepanovitsch was engaged on his work in the Supreme Court. When he set out there he was accompanied by his wife, whom he dropped at her father's house. On his return journey, he called for his wife, spent some time with his father-in-law, and then the young couple went home, where a plain dinner awaited them. This tête-à-tête meal in their own house, paid for with their own money, had a special homely charm ; but custom and Time worked their inevitable will, and the novelty very soon passed away. In spite of her delicate health and the moderate means at her disposal, Sofia Nikolaievna had succeeded in making her little house very attractive. Good taste and attention to details can compensate for lack of money to a certain extent ; and many of the Bagrovs visitors considered the establishment quite splendid. The most difficult part of the domestic arrangements was allotting their duties to the servants. Two of the servants included in Sofia Nikolaievna's dower, her footman, Feodor Micheiev, and her abigail, the black-eyed Parascha, had made a match of it : while the young servant from Bagrovo, Yefrem Yevseyitsch, an upright faithful youth, who loved his young mistress from the depths of his true heart (which could not be said of the rest of the servants) had Sofia Nikolaievna's young laundress, Annuschka, bestowed upon him for a wife. The young mistress was very fond of her trusty Yefrem, and with good reason. This jewel of a man proved the depth of his attachment to her throughout his life. [1]

Time went on, and life in Ufa gradually sank into a regular and monotonous groove. By reason of her poor health and depressed spirits, Sofia Nikolaievna very rarely went into any company. And even then, however, she only received or visited her intimate friends ; and this narrow circle still lacked the best friends of all, namely the Tschitschagovs, who only arrived in town with their mother in the late autumn. The continued ill-humour of Sofia Nikolaievna, which might justly be attributed to her disturbed nervous system, was at first very disturbing and

---

[1] Yevseyitsch (as he was called for short), later became the guardian or body-servant of her eldest son, whom he tended with the most affectionate solicitude. I knew the worthy man well. It is now some fifteen years since I last saw him. It was at the estate of one of Stepan Michailovitsch's grandsons in the Government of Pensa, where he, a blind, old man, was spending the last years of his life. That summer I spent a whole month at the place, and every day I went to fish in the early morning, in the fine lake formed by the mouth of the rivulet Kakarma where it joins the charming Insa. The hut, where Yevseyitsch lived, was built close at the water's edge, and each day as I approached the lake, I perceived the bent, white-haired old man leaning against the wall of his cottage, facing the rising sun ; his withered hands clasped round a staff which he held pressed against his breast ; while his sightless eyes were raised towards the Eastern sky. He could not see the light, but he enjoyed the warmth, which comforted him in the chilly dawn ; and his countenance was at once serene and melancholy. His hearing was so acute that he could hear me approaching from a great distance, and he would greet me patronisingly as an old fisherman a young one, although at that time I was over fifty years old. " Ah, so you are there, my Falcon ! " (this was his name for me) " God give you good sport ! " . . . . Two years later he expired in the arms of his son, his daughter, and his wife—the last surviving him some years.

alarming to Alexei Stepanovitsch. He simply could make nothing of such a state of things. Suffering without any definite illness—misery without any cause—or rather illness as the result of groundless melancholy, and melancholy as the result of a non-existent or imperceptible illness—nothing of the sort had ever occurred in the course of his previous life. But as he gradually realised that his wife's condition was neither critical nor dangerous, he grew accustomed to it and reconciled himself to the situation. He made up his mind it was all imagination. This, in fact, had been his own explanation of Sofia Nikolaievna's earlier outbursts of passion and emotion, whenever he had been at a loss how to account for them. He ceased to worry himself over her, and began to feel very much bored. This was but natural. For all his love for his wife and for all the pity he felt for her continual depression of spirits, it became very irksome to be compelled to listen for hours to a string of lamentations over a state of things which was only natural ; and to endless ominous forebodings of the appalling consequences which her enceinte condition was bound to produce. Each day in the week Sofia Nikolaievna discovered some new and sinister symptom in herself, which she sought to explain in the most scientific way, by referring to one or other of her medical books. When she had discovered exactly what was the matter with her, that would be the cause of fresh distress. So long as she had imagined Alexei Stepanovitsch to be a man utterly incapable of deep feeling or fervent love, she had actually been much easier in her mind. " What God has denied a man," she was wont to say, " that will He not demand from him ! " Unluckily Alexei Stepanovitsch in the first days of their marriage had proved to her by his passion and ardour that he *was* capable of the deepest love, and now she was quite convinced that he had already grown cold towards her. This dismal idea entirely dominated her too-fertile imagination. Her ingenious mind soon found a thousand good grounds for suspicion. First and foremost, she placed the hostile influences of his own family, her own ill health, above all the loss of her beauty, for her mirror shewed her only too plainly how changed she had become. Another reason was the utter indifference shewn for her gloomy misgivings by the cold-hearted Alexei

Stepanovitsch ; and then he never shewed due interest in her
condition, and never tried to amuse or pacify her : he was
beginning to take more pleasure in the society of other women
. . . . and like a spark in a powder magazine, up sprang
what until now had lurked unsuspected in the depths of her
heart—that agonising, keen-sighted and yet blind passion—
jealousy ! From that moment on—fresh uproars, reproaches,
tears, quarrels—and reconciliations ! And Alexei Stepanovitsch was innocent of the slightest offence against her. He
never paid the slightest attention to any of his sisters' innuendoes. The sole authority to which he ·deferred at home was
his father's, and that had only served to heighten his love and
regard for his wife. His wife's sufferings distressed him
considerably, if not overwhelmingly. The loss of her good
looks he regarded as a misfortune of a quite temporary
nature, and looked forward to the time when she would regain
her beauty. He could not feel very cheerful when she was
always so melancholy ; but it was quite impossible for him
to take all her presentiments and forebodings in earnest, as
he considered them merely empty delusions. Like a great
many other men, he understood very little of what was expected of him in the way of attention ; besides it was a very
wearisome and ticklish task to try to pacify or amuse a woman
of Sofia Nikolaievna's type ; it was so easy to make some
faux pas, and put her into a still worse humour A great deal
of skill and tact was necessary for the job, and Alexei Stepanovitsch possessed neither. It is quite possible that he *did*
feel more comfortable and happy in other women's society,
because there he was not in continual dread of arousing a
storm of temper and irritability by some quite harmless
remark. But Sofia Nikolaievna looked at the matter from a
quite different point of view ; this was the inevitable result of
her sensitive and extravagant disposition. What could be
expected when one possessed sound, strong, blunt nerves,
and the other's nerves were irritable, delicate, and diseased ?
Sofia Nikolaievna's whole being was affected by emotions
not even guessed at by Alexei Stepanovitsch It was only
the Tschitschagovs who knew the real grounds of the trouble
which existed in the the home of these young married people ;
and as Sofia Nikolaievna —far less Alexei Stepanovitsch—

made no allusion to the very delicate subject, they took the most kindly interest in the situation ; and by their affectionate attentions, frequent visits, and sensible and sympathetic conversation, managed to pacify the unreasonable young wife, proving themselves at this juncture the truest friends of the newly-married pair.

And so matters remained between the young folks until Sofia Nikolaievna became a mother. In spite of all the commotion in her mind, her health was appreciably better during the last months of her pregnancy, and she was safely delivered of a daughter. It is true that Sofia Nikolaievna, and especially Alexei Stepanovitsch, would have preferred a son. But when the mother pressed her child to her heart, there was no distinction in that love between son and daughter. The feeling of maternal love possessed her entire soul, spirit, and being. Alexei Stepanovitsch thanked God for sparing his wife's life, was rejoiced that she was doing so well, and never gave the hoped-for son another thought.

But the news was very differently received at Bagrovo ! Stepan Michailovitsch had desired a grandson so earnestly that at first he positively refused to believe that a granddaughter had been born. However when he had seen the news in his son's letter with his own eyes, and convinced himself that there could be no possible doubt of the fact, he was greatly out of humour, would not permit the promised feast to be given to the peasantry, and would not write himself either to his son or to his daughter-in-law. To the latter he merely sent congratulations on her accouchement, and requested that the child should receive the name of Praskovia in baptism, in compliment to his beloved cousin, Praskovia Michailovna Kurolesova. As it happened, this wish of his had been anticipated, the little one having already had the name of Praskovia bestowed upon her when the prayers for her mother's safe delivery were offered. Stepan Michailovitsch's anger was both distressing and comical. Even his family laughed at him behind his back. The old man had the sense to see that he was quite foolish to make such a fuss about the matter, and yet he could do nothing else during the first days of his disappointment, so much had he accustomed himself to the delightful prospect of soon having a grandson, and thereafter resting assured of the continuation of the noble line of Schimon. He had the genealogical tree removed and locked up, which for a considerable time past had been ready spread out on the table, on whose page each day he had hoped to inscribe the name of his grandson. He forbade his daughter, Aksinia Stepanovna, to go to Ufa to stand as the child's godmother. " Why should you go to the baptism of a girl ? Such an event can happen any time and why should a fuss be made about it ? " . . . . However time and reflection worked their will, and at the end of a few days the frown disappeared from Stepan Michailovitsch's brow (on this occasion it had alarmed nobody) and the thought that his daughter-in-law might possibly have a son the following year pacified the old man. He wrote a very affectionate letter to Sofia Nikolaievna, scolding her playfully for disappointing his hopes and begging her to find a grandson the next year.

Sofia Nikolaievna was so completely absorbed in her new emotions and was so ravished by this new Heaven into which maternal love had admitted her, that she heeded nothing of her father-in-law's displeasure, and never even noticed that Aksinia Stepanovna was not present at the baptism. It was only with the greatest trouble that the young mother could be persuaded to remain in bed for the usual nine days after her accouchement. She felt so well that by the fourth day she declared she could dance. But she had no desire to dance, only to be always beside her child, denying herself sleep and rest in order to tend it day and night, for the little Praskovia had come into the world weak and ailing, as might well have been expected after all the sorrow and suffering which her mother had endured during the time of her pregnancy. The physicians would not permit Sofia Nikolaievna to nurse the child herself. To speak more correctly, the physician, Andrei Yurievitsh Avenarius, a highly intelligent, cultured, and amiable man, an intimate friend of the Bagrovs, would not allow it. As soon as ever it was possible Sofia Nikolaievna took her little one to the grandfather, that is to her father, Nikolai Feodorovitsch. She hoped that the sight of the little creature would please him, and that he might trace a likeness between the child and his first wife, Vera Ivanovna. It is probable that no such likeness existed, and according to my belief it would be a most remarkable thing if any likeness could be found between a newly-born infant and an adult person : but Sofia Nikolaievna was always wont to declare that her first-born daughter resembled her grandmother as much as one drop of water resembles another. Old Subin was rapidly approaching his end, his mind and body were undergoing swift dissolution. He gazed listlessly at the child, which he was scarcely able to bless, and merely murmured : " I congratulate you, Sonitschka ! " Sofia Nikolaievna was much distressed, both at the desperate condition of her father, whom she had not seen for more than a month, and at his indifference towards her angelic little Praskovia.

But the young mother soon forgot the whole world beside the cradle of her daughter. All interests, all possible pursuits and pleasures, paled before the mother's love, and Sofia Niko-laievna surrendered herself to this new passion with the most feverish ardour. No hand but hers was to lull the child to rest. She herself gave the child to the nurse, herself held it to the breast, and not without jealousy and grief did she witness a strange woman giving nourishment to her child. It may sound incredible, but it is a fact which Sofia Nikolaievna later con-fessed sorrowfully, that it was so intolerable to her to permit her child to remain for long at the nurse's breast, that she frequently took the half-suckled child out of the arms of the stranger and rocked and sang it to sleep herself. Sofia Niko-laievna now never found time to see anyone, not even her best friend Katerina Borisovna Tschitschagova. Naturally, everyone considered this very strange and ridiculous, and her intimate friends were very much vexed about it. After a while she re-sumed her daily visits to her father, always hurrying home in a state of the greatest apprehension, and enquiring if her daughter was all right. Her husband was left entirely to his own devices and might do exactly as he pleased, and Alexei Stepanovitsch, after spending a few days at home, did not fail to observe that Sofia Nikolaievna took not the slightest notice of him, except to order him out of the little nursery, on the plea that too many people in the room would exhaust the air—herself, of course, never quitting the place. So he began to visit his friends and acquaintances, at first occasionally, and then more and more frequently, and last he got into the habit of leaving his own house every evening and going wherever he could have a game of boston or rocambole. Certain among the ladies of Ufa interested themselves in the neglected young husband, and joked and flirted with him, protesting that it was a work of charity to console the grass-widower ; and they vowed that they hoped to receive Sofia Nikolaievna's due thanks in the event of her ever releasing herself from her miraculous devotion to her little daughter and making her re-appearance in society. Sofia Nikolaievna heard all about these pleasantries later , and was very much put out by them.

Katerina Alexeievna Tscheprunova, who came daily to visit her relative, observed the latter's conduct with mingled astonishment, pity, and vexation. She herself was a most affectionate mother, and deeply attached to her one afflicted child ; but this maternal passion of Sofia Nikolaievna, which involved complete oblivion of everything else in the world, struck her as a species of insanity. She would sigh, groan, smite herself with her fist on breast and stomach (as was her wont in moments of great excitement) and protest that such exaggerated love was a crime against God, and that He would surely punish it. Sofia Nikolaievna took great offence at this, and ordered her to keep out of her nursery in future. Avenarius was the sole person who had the regular entrée of this sanctum. Sofia Nikolaievna of course discovered the symptoms of some fresh disease every day, and would then experiment with some cure according to Buchan's instructions ; and the result usually proving unsatisfactory, she would then have recourse to Avenarius. He was quite puzzled how to deal with the poor mother, who would not be persuaded to give up her faith in her own physicking. So he prescribed various remedies, mostly of a simple, but sometimes of a more active, character, as the child was really in very poor health.

It is difficult to say where all this folly and delusion would have ended, if Providence had not struck an unexpected blow at Sofia Nikolaievna. Her cherub, her Praskovia, died suddenly. It is an open question whether excessive coddling, too much physic, or congenital weakness was the cause of death. Briefly, the fragile creature surrendered her life at the end of four months, as the result of an ordinary fit, such as nearly every young infant experiences. While sitting beside the cradle of her Praskovia, Sofia Nikolaievna noticed a slight convulsion pass across the tiny face. She took the child in her arms. It was dead . . . .

This woman must have had a strong, nay an iron, constitution to have survived the shock. The doctors took it in turn to watch beside her. Sanden, Avenarius, Klauss—all friends of hers—for several days feared that her brain would give way, as she recognised no one. But with God's help her young and strong organisation triumphed over the threatened danger. The bereaved mother recovered her senses and her love for her husband (who likewise had felt the loss of his child deeply) a love which regained its old supremacy every moment that passed. It was her salvation. Sofia Nikolaievna regained consciousness for the first time during the fourth night after the baby's death, and heard an account of what had happened. When she recognised Alexei Stepanovitsch, whom at first she did not know, so changed was he by sorrow, and perceived her faithful friend, Katerina Alexeievna, a heart-rending cry burst from her strained breast and a flood of salutary tears flowed from her eyes . . . . Until that moment she had not wept. She embraced Alexei Stepanovitsch and sobbed for a long time on his breast without uttering a word ; he, for his part, cried like a child. The danger to the brain was now past ; but a new peril threatened—death from complete physical exhaustion. The poor young woman had not been able to take any nourishment for four days ; and now could not manage to eat a mouthful of food, nor take any medicine, nor even a drop of water. The situation was one of such danger that the physicians did not refuse the invalid's entreaty to be permitted to make her confession and receive the last Sacraments. The accomplishment of this Christian rite was beneficial to Sofia Nikolaievna : she slept naturally for the first time, awaking at the end of two hours, when, with a countenance beaming with joy, she told her husband that she had seen a picture of the Iberian Virgin, similar to that in their own parish church, in a dream ; and added that if she were permitted to pray before the picture and kiss it, she knew that the Virgin would save her. The holy picture was at once brought to the house. The priest recited the prayers, " for the Health and Recovery of a Sick Person." At the words : " Pitifully behold, Oh, most Blessed Virgin, my grievous bodily sufferings," all present fell on.their knees, repeating the words. Alexei Stepanovitsch was sobbing loudly. The sick woman also wept during the service, but these were tears of healing and consolation ; she kissed the holy portrait, and felt so much better that immediately afterwards she was able to swallow some water, and then took medicine and food. Katerina Borisovna Tschitschagov and Katerina Alexeievna Tscheprunovna remained with their friend, who was very soon quite out of danger. The racked heart of Alexei Stepanovitsch at last was eased. The physicians worked with fresh ardour for her complete recovery, which, however, presented peculiar difficulties and dangers, as the learned trio really took the condition of their patient too seriously, owing to their great personal regard for her. This one feared consumption, that meningitis, and the third dreaded the possibility of an aneurism. Luckily, all three were of one mind in recommending a stay in the country, where the patient would be able to enjoy forest air and take a koumis cure at the same time. It was now the beginning of June, the herbage was in full luxuriance, and the mares' milk had not yet lost its spring-time, health-restoring properties.

Stepan Michailovitsch received the news of his grand-daughter's death with apparent indifference ; and remarked that it was foolish to make so much ado over the loss of a girl, as they were always plentiful enough. But shortly afterwards, when news was brought of Sofia Nikolaievna's dangerous condition, the old man was seriously disturbed and uneasy. When the third despatch arrived, stating that the patient was out of danger but very weak, and that the doctors had decided that the only hope for her lay in a koumis cure, Stepan Michailovitsch flew in a great rage, and denounced the doctors as persecutors of mankind, who knew nothing and strove to pollute human souls by persuading folks to swallow heathenish drinks. " If it is forbidden by orthodoxy to eat horse-flesh," said he, " it seems it's no sin to drink the milk of the unclean beast ! I see what will happen," he continued, as he heaved a deep sigh, " it's possible that my daughter-in-law may survive the stuff ; but she will never be healthy again, nor have any more children ! " Stepan Michailovitsch was very much upset, and remained in a very depressed state of mind for a long time.

Nine-and-twenty versts South-West of Ufa, on the road to Kazan, the little Tartar village of Usytamak (or Alkino, as the Russians are accustomed to call it, after the name of its owner) is situated where the little Usa flows into the superb Djonia, all surrounded by magnificent forests. The huts are clustered together in picturesque confusion in a luxuriant valley, and creep up the slopes of the Bairam-Tau, which shelters them from the North wind. To the West rises another mountain, the Sein-Tau.[1] To the South-East the rivulet of the Usa meanders, bordered by shady groves, through the blossoming meadows full of fragrant and succulent herbage. The mighty forests of oak, lime, elm, maple, and other trees of richest foliage waft refreshing purity and vivifying perfume on every breeze that blows. To this enchanting spot Alexei Stepanovitsch brought his feeble, emaciated, faded wife, who looked like a shadow of her former self : the devoted Avenarius accompanied them. The patient had been greatly fatigued by the short journey. The hospitable head of the village received the new-comers in the friendliest manner ; his house was a good-sized one with out-buildings. Sofia Nikolaievna however preferred not to live in this house, and chose one of the adjoining buildings. The head man's family were so profuse in their attentions and so pressing in their hospitality, that the doctor deemed

---

[1] Tau means mountain, Bairam feast or festival. This name, according to the legend, was given to the mountain, because it was here the Bashkirs used to hold their solemn festival of prayer which concludes the *Urasa*, or fast. Sein-Tau means the mountain of the Assembly. The word Sein signifies a gathering or feast of the community, on which occasions races and various sports used to take place. The mountain was called by this name on the occasion when it was sold by the Bashkirs on the banks of the Usa to its purchaser Alkin. As soon as the bargain had been concluded, Monsieur Alkin gave a magnificent banquet to the Bashkirs upon the mountain side. Tamak means mouth : hence the village at the mouth of the Usa, where it joins the Djoma, is called Usytamak. What the words Usa and the hereafter-mentioned river named Kurkal-Dauk signify, I have not been able to ascertain.

it necessary to keep his patient somewhat apart, so as to
escape their friendly importunities. These good folks were
Mahometans, speaking very fair Russian. Their mode of
existence was a quaint mingling of Tartar and Russian habits
and customs ; but koumis was their universal beverage from
morning to night. This wholesome drink was prepared for
Sofia Nikolaievna after a somewhat more dainty fashion than
that employed by the natives. Hers was not fermented in
the usual dirty horse-skin bag, but in a nice new little barrel
made of linden wood. The Alkins declared that koumis made
in that barrel would be less efficacious, and would not taste
nearly so good ; but the patient had such a strong objection
to the bag of raw horse hide that they agreed to prepare the
beneficial drink for her in her own clean way. The doctor
gave the necessary directions for the carrying-out of the cure,
and returned to Ufa ; Alexei Stepanovitsch however, as well
as Parascha and Annuschka, remained with the invalid. The
fresh air, the koumis, at first only taken in small quantities,
the daily expeditions taken with Alexei Stepanovitsch through
the magnificent forests in the neighbourhood, on which occasions Yefrem, who had grown to be a great favourite of
Sofia Nikolaievna, drove them ; the charming solitude of the
woods, where the patient reposed for hours, lying on a leathern
mattress, her head supported by pillows,breathing the aromatic
breeze, while she listened to some simple tale being read aloud
or drifted into a sweet slumber ; all this produced the most
pleasing results, and at the end of a fortnight Sofia Nikolaievna
quitted her couch, and even attempted little walks. Her
doctor paid her a visit, was delighted at the excellent effects
of the cure, increased the doses of koumis ; and, as his patient
was, at that period, unable to take the increased amount of
the milk, he said she must take more exercise, and suggested
riding. This sort of exercise was at that time unheard-of
among the Russian aristocracy. Alexei Stepanovitsch disliked the idea very much ; and Sofia Nikolaievna herself did
not think it seemly. In vain did the daughters of the house
set her an example, by scouring the enchanting district for
miles around, mounted on their Bashkirian steeds. For long
enough Sofia Nikolaievna resisted all entreaties, even her
husband's, to whom the doctor had confided the urgent

necessity for this sort of exercise. But the Tschitschgovs came on a visit to Alkino, and so it happened that Sofia Nikolaievna found it impossible to withstand the united solicitations of her friends. Her consent indeed was largely influenced by the self-sacrificing example of Katerina Borisovna Tschitschagova, who, like the true friend she was, conquered her own prejudices and took to riding, at first alone, but soon accompanied by her convalescent friend. This exhilarating motion was followed by a fresh command, to wit the daily consumption of fat mutton, which Sofia Nikolaievna disliked very much indeed. Evidently Avenarius was modelling his cure on the daily life and diet of the Bashkirs who, during the koumis season, exist exclusively on fat mutton, which they eat without any accompaniment of bread or vegetables ; from early till late they ride far and near across the wide steppes, leading this life from the days when the heath grass displays its earliest green, and only quitting the plains when its slender feathery tufts are glistening in silvery autumnal waves. The cure continued to work well, and the riders were joined by the sons and daughters of the owner of the land, and became quite a cavalcade. Frequently they made excursions to the potash works, which were situated in the middle of the forest, two versts from Alkino beside the pretty little stream of the Kurkul-Dauk.[1] Sofia Nikolaievna observed the iron cauldrons full of boiling potash, the wooden tubs in which the crude crystals were congealing, and the smelting-ovens from which the potash finally issued in the form of a white porous salt, with great interest. She was particularly pleased with the nimble and dexterous Tartar labourers, so active in their pointed caps and their long smocks which in no way impeded their movements. The hospitable proprietors of the works spared no efforts to entertain their visitors with all sorts of pleasant diversions.

---

[1] This manufactory was closed in 1848. In the year 1791 the preparation of potash was not very general in the Province of Ufa. Later it caused the destruction of a gigantic number of trees of the greatest beauty. Huge forests of limes, elms, and maples were felled. These species of trees grew in such abundance in this district at the time of which we write that at first they were utilised solely for the production of potash, as their ashes are specially rich in this alkali. In those days the potash industry was the principal business in the district which we have striven to pourtray for the reader.

Having this end in view, they arranged native dances, races and wrestling matches among their Mahommedan retainers.

At first Alexei Stepanovitsch took part in all these jaunts and merry makings ; but as he observed that his wife's health improved daily and that she had plenty of company and distraction, he began to enjoy these delicious hours of freedom in his own way. This rural life, the beautiful weather, and the irresistible charm of Nature roused all his old fancies : he prepared his fishing tackle and set to work to try to beguile the wary trout from his watery abode in the plentiful and clear mountain streams of the Alkino district ; while he frequently snared quails with nets. Feodor Micheyev, Parascha's young husband, assisted him in this latter sport, being an adept at it, besides being most skilful with the bird-call. Amateurs of other varieties of sport regard this sort of fowling with the utmost disdain. I must confess that I see no reason for this scorn. To lie in the scented meadow grass, the net extended before you over the lofty blades, mimicking upon your pipe the sweet, melodious cry of the little lady quail ; to listen for the reply of the misguided little lovers ; to watch them arrive from every side, flying and fluttering in the greatest haste ; to observe their amusing antics, and finally the excitement of dropping the net over the lucky or unlucky capture : all this, I confess, afforded me great pleasure in my early days, and the recollection of it is still delightful. Sofia Nikolaievna, however, saw nothing attractive in such occupations. Meantime, her condition improved visibly, and at the end of two months her face had filled out and a fresh colour bloomed in her cheeks.

Avenarius came to Alkino for the third time, and was delighted at his patient's good progress. He was proud, and justly so, of the result of his cure. He was the first to recommend koumis, and had laid down all the rules for the application of the remedy. He had always been very fond of his patient, but after succeeding in restoring her to health and strength, he felt the love of a father towards her.

Each week Alexei Stepanovitsch sent his father a detailed account of the state of Sofia Nikolaievna's health. Stepan Michailovitsch was overjoyed on hearing of his daughter-in-law's recovery (naturally, he utterly refused to believe that it

was in any way due to the koumis) and was very much
horrified on hearing about the riding, which little secret his
son had inadvertently betrayed in one of his letters. The
family did not fail to use this favourable opportunity to the
best advantage, and by their skilful manipulation of hints
and pointed innuendoes, they worked up the old man into
such a temper that he sent a very surly letter to Alexei
Stepanovitsch, which wounded Sofia Nikolaievna's feelings
deeply. But as soon as her health was fully restored and her
former bloom and beauty returned, his first delightful hopes
filled the old gentleman's head and he ceased abusing the
koumis and the riding on horseback.

It was autumn when the young pair returned to Ufa.
Old Subin was in a hopeless condition, and the marvellous
recovery of his daughter made not the slightest impression
on him. For him all earthly things were at an end, all cords
were loosened, all threads severed that had attached him to
life. His soul barely tarried in its fragile prison. The further
development of the conjugal life of the young Bagrovs had
been entirely interrupted by the manifold events just
chronicled : first by the birth of the baby daughter, and the
boundless and passionate love bestowed upon the child by her
mother : then by the death of the little one, which had reduced the mother to the verge of insanity and nearly killed
her : and finally by the long cure and the life in the Tartar
village. During the period of her agony of mind and bodily
suffering, Alexei Stepanovitsch had devoted himself to his
wife in the most loving and self-sacrificing way. There had
been no opening or occasion for any collision between these
two most opposite characters. When life's capital is being
spent, who pays heed to the petty cash ? Times of great
anxiety and cases of especial significance are only paid for in
great sums ; while the trivial round of daily life costs but
little. Alexei Stepanovitsch had large reserves of capital,
but very little small change. When a man is confronted with
peculiar danger or sorrow, such as when the life and well-being
of an adored wife are threatened, he suffers in the depths of
his soul—he denies himself sleep, rest, nourishment ; he
forgets himself entirely ; and, with quivering nerves and
exalted soul lives but for another. At such times life has

no room to spare for little airs and graces. But the time of portentous events passes, life resumes its old placid track ; the mind is at rest, the nerves relaxed ; common affairs regain their ancient and dreary supremacy ; old habits reassert themselves—and now is the time for the little things at which we have hinted—the time for trifling attentions and kindnesses, for complaisance and yielding, and the thousand insignificant and trifling actions which unite to make up our daily life. The periods of trial, of lofty self-sacrifice, and of supreme self-denial are but rare—between them Life perpetually flows in its daily channel ; and these trifles lend it peace, joy, and charm ; in short, all that we call happiness. And so it came about that, as Sofia Nikolaievna grew strong and well and Alexei Stepanovitsch ceased to feel any anxiety for her life and health, gradually the old claims and pretensions of the one and the inability of the other to satisfy these claims, revived anew. Tender reproaches and exhortations bored the husband ; his awe of solemn and serious interviews was rapidly vanishing ; with his awe, his complete and unreserved candour disappeared ; and the loss of candour in marriage, especially in that partner who is inferior in strength of character, infallibly leads to the wrecking of wedded happiness. The return to Ufa, to an idle, monotonous life in a city would probably have produced the inevitable discord sooner, had it not happened that the painful condition of Sofia Nikolaievna's father, who was now actually face-to-face with death, absorbed all her attention and demanded her filial love to the complete exclusion of any other feeling. This circumstance caused a further postponement in the evolution of her home relations with her husband, while she remained day and night in her father's house. The Kalmuck continued to nurse his sick master with the utmost devotion and skill, and with untiring constancy. He was most careful to keep out of the daughter's way, although he had plenty of opportunity for annoyance, unchecked and unchallenged. Sofia Nikolaievna was conciliated by this behaviour. She summoned the man and made up her quarrel with him, and thereafter permitted him to assist her to attend to her dying father. In spite of his apparent detachment from all that took place around him, Nikolai Feodorovitsch observed his daughter's action, and tried to press her hand, while he whispered almost inaudibly : " Thank you ! " From this instant Sofia Nikolaievna never quitted her father.

I think I have already told you that the joyous hopes of yore had bloomed anew in Stepan Michailovitsch's head in consequence of the welcome news of his daughter-in-law's restoration to good health. Nor were his hopes disappointed : very shortly afterwards he received a letter from Sofia Nikolaievna herself, in which she announced that, God willing, she hoped soon to present him with a grandson to console his old age. In the first moments Stepan Michailovitsch was transported with joy, but soon composed himself and would not betray any of his hopes before his family. Perhaps he feared that Sofia Nikolaievna would produce another daughter, or possibly that the newcomer might likewise succumb to the united coddling and physicking of the mother and doctor. Probably, however, he was only acting as many others do, when they persist in prophesying evil in order to provoke Fate into bringing about the exact opposite, and it may well be doubted if Stepan Michailovitsch was really so cold and incredulous as he pretended. Said he : " This time no one shall have the better of me : I will not again give credence to the statement, or rejoice over it as if it had really come to pass ! " The family were greatly astonished at such an attitude, but made no comment on it. But the old man secretly believed that a grandson *would* be born after all, and once more ordered Father Vasili to offer up prayers " for the health of the pregnant handmaiden of God, Sofia " ; fetched the banished family-tree from its retirement, and kept it in his own room.

Meanwhile Nikolai Feodorovitsch's last hour was slowly approaching. After so many years of intense suffering, the conclusion of such a miserable and unhappy existence (which, so to speak, was only unnatural in such a shattered body) could not really cause anyone any grief. For her part, Sofia Nikolaievna prayed Heaven for an easy and peaceful death for her father. Calmly and peacefully, even joyfully, the sick man expired. In the act of death a bright smile played on his features and, in spite of the closed eyes, the rigid corpse long preserved this expression. The funeral ceremony was solemn and pompous. In earlier days old Subin had been a

great favourite in the town, but his public services had gradually been forgotten ; even compassion for his long martyrdom
had to a certain extent grown blunted. But as soon as the
news of his death spread through the city, the ancient regard
for him was revived in all hearts, mingled with pity for his
recent great sufferings. Every house was empty, and the
entire population of Ufa thronged the pavement between the
Church of the Assumption and the cemetery, on the day of
the funeral. Peace to thine ashes, worthy man ! To human
weakness thou didst unite human kindness !

After Nikolai Feodorovitsch's death two trusteeships were
formed for the children of his two marriages. Alexei Stepanovitsch was oppointed trustee for Sofia Nikolaievna's brothers
by the same mother. These youths had both been obliged
to enter a regiment of Guards in Petersburg, before either of
them had completed his studies at the school for the nobility
at Moscow. I have omitted to mention the fact that shortly
before the death of his father-in-law, the latter had used his
interest to get Alexei Stepanovitsch appointed a State Agent
of the General Court.

Long did Sofia Nikolaievna weep and lament, and Alexei
Stepanovitsch wept and lamented with her : but these were
quiet tears and quiet prayers which did not affect Sofia
Nikolaievna's barely-restored health. Obedient to the wishes
of her husband, the advice of her friends, especially that of the
prudent Avenarius, she was careful to avoid all agitation and
gave all needful heed to her situation. It had been made
quite clear to her that the well-being, nay the life, of the
coming child depended upon her own health and peace of
mind. Bitter experience confirmed this declaration of friends
and physicians ; and the young wife was quite resolved to
act as she was advised in every particular. To a letter from
her father-in-law, in which he expressed his sympathy for his
daughter-in-law in her bereavement in his plain way and
farther expressed his fear lest her health should suffer thereby,
she sent a most reassuring reply ; and indeed she strove most
earnestly to keep her mind and body in health and repose.
The arrangement of the young pair's daily life was at once
regular and full of variety. Avenarius and Klauss (the latter
also was an intimate friend of the Bagrovs) had ordered Sofia

Nikolaievna to take a daily drive or preferably a walk. Each evening a little party of affectionate friends either met at the Bagrovs' house, or the young pair visited one or other of these, most frequently going to the Tschitschagovs'. Madame Katerina Borisovna Tschitschagov's brothers had grown very friendly with Alexei Stepanovitsch and his wife, especially the younger one, D. B. Mertvago, who had requested the honour, in advance, of standing godfather to the expected child. Both brothers were frequent visitors at the house in Golubinaya Street and were quite at home there. They were young men of the highest integrity, and highly educated according to the standard of those times. The favourite evening's entertainment at the Bagrov parties was for one of the company to read aloud. But as one cannot read aloud, nor even listen, for ever, Sofia Nikolaievna was instructed in the art and craft of card-playing. This task was undertaken by Klauss, and each time that the Bagrovs were at home of an evening, he found means to arrange a game of cards. Avenarius took no share in this diversion, for all his life long he never could distinguish between an ace and a five.

An early and profusely-blossoming spring had followed the winter, the ice of the Bielaia had suddenly broken, and the waters spread over the plain for a stretch of seven versts. The beauty of the noble scene could be fully enjoyed from the windows of the little house in Golubinaya Street. The fruit trees planted round the house were in leaf and bloom. The sweet fragrance of apple and cherry blossom filled the air. The drawing-room was exchanged for the garden, and the life-giving warmth invigorated and refreshed Sofia Nikolaievna still more.

About this period an event happened in Ufa which completely absorbed the attention of all the inhabitants, and in which the young Bagrovs took an especial interest, as the hero of the adventure was one of their intimate friends, and indeed, if I make no mistake, a distant relative of Alexei Stepanovitsch. Sofia Nikolaievna, by reason of her imaginative temperament, was especially enchanted by the romantic occurrence which I will proceed to relate. A young man, a member of one of the richest and most aristocratic families of the Province of Ufa or Orenburg, R. I. Timaschev, fell in love with a beautiful Tartar girl, the daughter of the wealthy chief, Tevkelev. Like the Alkins, this family had adopted an external European culture and spoke good Russian, but retained the strictest Mahommedan faith. The fair Salmé did not fail to return the passion of the young Russian, who, at that time, was a captain in a regiment stationed in Ufa. It was quite hopeless to dream of ever gaining the consent of the father and the elder brothers to the marriage, as Salmé, in order to marry a Christian, would be compelled to embrace the Christian Faith. The girl fought against her love, which burns with a fiercer flame in the hearts of Asiatics than in the breasts of our colder European women. At length, however, as was to be expected, Mahomet was conquered, and Salmé resolved to fly with her beloved captain, to receive baptism and to be married to him. The commander of the regiment, the charming and universally beloved Major General Mansurov, who was later to distinguish himself under Suvorov in the Alps at the passage of the Devil's Bridge, and who himself had married for love a short time previously, was made a party to the captain's adventure and promised his protection. On a dark and stormy night Salmé quitted her father's house : in the forest close at hand Timaschev was awaiting her with horses : it was necessary to cover the hundred versts to Ufa with the utmost speed. Salmé was a superb horsewoman ; at distances of ten to fifteen versts fresh horses were stationed, in the charge of soldiers who were devoted to the service of their captain, and away flew the fugitives " on the wings of love " as any poet of the day would inevitably have remarked. The attachment existing between Salmé and Timaschev had long been suspected in the Tevkelev family and a strict watch had been kept on the girl, whose absence was very soon noted. It only took a few moments to summon a large troop of fully-armed Tartars, who, infuriated with rage and led by the injured father,[1] pursued the lovers with howls of wrath. It was easy to guess in which direction the pair had fled. Most assuredly they would never have escaped ; or, at the least, a bloody combat would have been fought between the numerous

---

[1] Another account of the affair states that it was the girl's *mother*, who, escorted by her sons, rode in pursuit of her eloping daughter.

soldiers and officers who were stationed along the route (all of whom took the warmest interest in the affair) and the pursuing horde . . . . had not someone had the presence of mind to destroy the bridge over a deep and dangerous mountain stream after the passage of the fugitives. The pursuers had to swim across the torrent at the risk of their lives, which involved the loss of two hours' time. Even with this delay, the barque, which was conveying Timaschev and his Salmé across the Bielaia to Ufa, had barely reached the middle of the stream, when old Tevkelev with his sons and the half of his faithful retainers (the other half had ridden their horses to death), appeared on the river bank. But by some extraordinary accident, every available boat, raft, or shallop was filled by parties of soldiers who were anxious to reach the city. The disappointed father, gnashing his teeth with rage, shrieked curses after his daughter, and turning his horse, rode away from the river. Half-dead with fright and fatigue, Salmé was assisted into a carriage on landing and taken to the house of Timaschev's mother. The matter assumed a strictly legal and formal aspect : a Mahommedan had renounced her faith and, of free will, desired to receive Christian Baptism. Accordingly, she was placed under the protection of the city magistracy, while all the circumstances of the case were placed before the resident *Mufti* in Ufa (whom the Russians called the Tartar bishop) who was then requested to prohibit the Tevkelev family—as well as any other Mahommedan whatsoever—from making any attempt to hinder the maiden Salmé from " voluntarily " embracing the Christian religion. In a very few days the clergy had prepared the neophyte for receiving Holy Baptism and Sacred Unction. These ceremonies were performed with the utmost pomp in the Cathedral, Salmé received the Christian name of Serafima, with the addition of Ivanovna (after that of her godfather) and she and Timaschev were married before quitting the Church. The whole city took a great and sympathetic interest in the extraordinary event. Of course the young men—and every man in the place for the matter of that—were great partisans of the beautiful bride ; but the ladies, many of whom had had their own secret hopes sadly dashed by the occurrence, blamed and criticised Salmé's conduct. However there remained a fair number who extended the hand of friendship to the convert, who by her marriage had gained the right of entry to the most aristocratic circles of Ufa society. To this latter party belonged Sofia Nikolaievna and her husband, who made the most friendly advances to the newly-married pair. With the assistance of the young and amiable wife of the general, Madame A. N. Mansurova, the friends of the young folks were able to place them on a secure and honoured footing. The ladies took the utmost pains to impart the culture lacking to the captain's young wife, who shewed herself such an apt pupil that she very soon took her place as a most graceful and interesting woman of the highest fashion, causing no little sensation and envy, to which her uncommon beauty and unusual situation contributed in a great measure. Sofia Nikolaievna remained a firm friend of Serafima Ivanovna until the latter's death, which, unhappily, occurred very shortly. Three years after her marriage she died of consumption, leaving two baby sons and an inconsolable husband to mourn her loss. Timaschev nearly went mad with grief, quitted the army, lived only for his children, and never married again. It was said at the time, and I repeat it for what it is worth, that the young wife wasted away with longing for her forsaken family and with remorse for denying her former religion.

Meanwhile time jogged steadily along, quite undeterred by all these remarkable happenings. Already Sofia Nikolaievna had ceased to visit her friends ; even her daily drives were forbidden. On fine days she walked for half-an-hour in her garden ; when it rained she walked backwards and forwards in a room where the windows stood open. Really, all this fuss and formality and strict rule was quite unnecessary, and likely to cause as much harm as good ; all the same Sofia Nikolaievna continued in most excellent health. Alexei Stepanovitsch was compelled to defer to all the strict instructions of the medical men, as his father was continually writing letters telling him to cherish his wife as the very apple of his eye. All the family friends, the Tschitschagovs and the Mertvagos—to say nothing of the doctors who were so devoted to their patient—watched and tended Sofia Nikolaievna with such care and solicitude that she could not

walk a step or eat a mouthful or even drink a drop of water
without their special permission. Avenarius had been called
away from Ufa on business, so Klauss, who at that time was
settled in Ufa as an accoucheur, took over all responsibility
for Sofia Nikolaievna's health. Klauss was a worthy, skilful,
highly-educated, but very absurd-looking German. Although
by no means an old man, he invariably wore a bright yellow
wig. It was a mystery where he had discovered a peruke of such
an uncommon hue. His eyebrows and the pupils of his little
eyes were equally of a yellow tinge, whereas his face was of a
permanent glowing scarlet.[1]   Many peculiarities marked his
intercourse with his friends : for instance, he was very zealous
in kissing the ladies' hands, but had the utmost objection to
being kissed on the cheek in return, vowing that it was very
impolite on the part of a man to permit this salute. He was
exceedingly fond of small children ; his way of shewing his
affection to them was quaint. He would take a child in his
lap, and holding its little fingers in his left hand, would caress
it for hours with his right.   But the word " savage " expressed
the very fullness of his love. Sofia Nikolaievna, whom he
adored, was always his " savage." As an intimate friend of
the Bagrovs, Klauss had heard a great deal about Stepan
Michailovitsch, and could well realise the old man's passionate
desire and burning impatience to have a grandson. Klauss
could write very good Russian, and wrote a letter to the
expectant grandfather in legible script, in which he calculated
Sofia Nikolaievna would most certainly bear a son between
the 13th and 22nd September. This prophecy was forwarded
to Stepan Michailovitsch, who remarked : " The German is a
liar ! " while secretly believing every word of the letter. After
this, a carefully-restrained but joyous expectation lurked in
every word and action. About this time it happened that
our old acquaintance Afrosinia Andreievna—from whom he
had never tried to conceal his apprehension lest Sofia Nikolaievna should again produce a daughter—related the following
history to him : While staying in Moscow, she had once visited

---

[1] The same year, (1791), Andrei Michailovitsch Klauss migrated to
Moscow, where he was installed as Professor of Midwifery at the Found-
ling Hospital. For a period of thirty years he remained stedfastly
at his post, dying in 1821. The yellow wig remained his invariable
head-covering. He was a keen and learned numismatist.

the Troizko Convent to pray to the blessed St. Sergei, and there had encountered an aristocratic lady, who for many years had only had daughters. This lady had vowed that, in the event of her bearing a son, he should receive the name of Sergei. It came to pass that the following year this lady had a son who was duly baptised Sergei in fulfilment of her vow . . . . Stepan Michailovitsch listened to the tale in silence. But by the first post he wrote himself to his son and daughter-in-law, telling them to have a mass said in honour of the blessed St. Sergei, the Worker of Miracles ; and they must both vow that if a son should be born, his name should be Sergei. In order to attribute some motive or other to the command, he added that, so far, there had never been a Sergei in the Bagrov family. The request was strictly carried out. Sofia Nikolaievna was feverishly active providing all that a thoughtful mother deems necessary for the welfare and comfort of her expected child. The most important item of all, namely an excellent foster-mother, had been most fortunately secured. She was a peasant from the Subins' village of Kasi-movka, who fulfilled all the necessary conditions which are most to be desired on these occasions ; who was only too overjoyed to accept her mistress's charge, and who had already arrived in Ufa with her young baby.

The great moment drew near. Sofia Nikolaievna was now forbidden to leave her bed. Katerina Borisovna Tschitschagova was ill and unable to go out, and less intimate friends were not received. Katerina Alexeievna Tscheprunova was continually beside her beloved cousin and only left her at rare intervals to attend to her darling Andryscha. Klauss came to breakfast every morning, returning at six o'clock in the evening, when he would drink his tea and rum and play a hand at cards with his friends ; and as the stakes were of trifling value, the frugal German used to bring worn-out cards with him. It was a mystery to all where he bought them. Frequently card-playing was varied by reading aloud, which Klauss enjoyed equally. The reader was always Alexei Stepanovitsch, who through constant practice read exceedingly well. Now and again the doctor brought a German book with him which he read aloud and translated into Russian at the same time. The young pair enjoyed this very much, especially

Sofia Nikolaievna, who was very anxious to become acquainted with German literature.

Ever since she had experienced that boundless mother's love, to which no other love can ever be compared, Sofia Nikolaievna had contemplated her condition with feelings of the most earnest awe. She held it a sacred duty to keep her mind in serenity and composure, so as to ensure the welfare and safety of her babe and to attain her object . . . . this object on which all her hopes, her whole future, her very life itself . . . . were centred. We already know enough of Sofia Nikolaievna not to feel any astonishment at beholding her so utterly abandoned to and overwhelmed by the love of an as yet unborn child. The preservation of this child by her own self-sacrifice was her sole care, day and night. She fixed her whole mind on this one object with the most earnest attention, caring for nothing else, and even appeared perfectly satisfied with Alexei Stepanovitsch, although the latter gave her plenty of grounds for annoyance. The more Alexei Stepanovitsch learnt about his wife's character, the less comprehensible she appeared to him. The very least matter of which he was capable was the comprehension of enthusiasm—with the exception perhaps of joining in it himself. This enthusiastic maternal instinct of Sofia Nikolaievna caused him quite as much perplexity and alarm as his father's fits of passion. Enthusiasm is invariably objectionable to calm, gentle, phlegmatic dispositions ; they find such moods unnatural, and they look upon enthusiasts as people of disordered mind and subject to fits of eccentricity. They have no faith in anyone's balance, if it can be upset at any moment by a sudden shock, and are afraid of such people. There is no sentiment in life so fatal to love, even love for father or mother, as that of fear. And so it happened that instead of any progress being made in the strengthening of their relations or in harmony of feeling between the husband and wife, as might well have been hoped, they were growing still farther apart. This may sound strange ; it happens, however, far too frequently in this world.

Just at this time Klauss received his Moscow appointment. He had already taken leave of his superiors, said good-bye to all his friends, and was only awaiting Sofia Nikolaievna's accouchement, in the event of his advice and assistance being needed. Firmly convinced that the confinement would take place on the fifteenth, or on one or other of the two following days, he had bespoken his post-horses. He was unable to travel by the diligence, as he had arranged to quit the main road and travel to the remotely-situated estate of a German friend of his whom he was going to visit. The fifteenth of September came, but passed without any of the expected symptoms occurring. Sofia Nikolaievna was surprisingly well and cheerful, and only the doctor's silly orders prevented her getting up. The sixteenth, seventeenth, and eighteenth of September all passed in like manner ; and, for all his attachment to Sofia Nikolaievna, the doctor began to be very seriously annoyed, because he was obliged to pay the driver a rouble a day while waiting, which in those days was a considerable sum. But in spite of his impatience, the worthy Klauss was as fond as ever of his young friends, and came every evening as usual to play cards, or listen to Alexei Stepanovitsch's reading. When the German won some sixty copecks he was delighted, and declared that the driver had not cost him quite so much that day. And so passed the nineteenth of September. Early on the morning of the twentieth, Klauss came to see Sofia Nikolaievna and was received very politely by her as he entered the door. The German was very cross indeed : " How long are you going to take advantage of me like this, you little savage ? " he asked, kissing her hands as usual. " Yes, Alexei Stepanovitsch," he went on, turning to her husband, " your wife has made up her mind to ruin me. She ought to have had this baby on the fifteenth, and here she is on the twentieth making curtseys ! " " Oh, let it rest ! " replied Alexei Stepanovitsch clapping him on the shoulder, " come along to-night and win some money from us ; the cards are getting quite worn out." Klauss promised to come and bring some new cards. He then had breakfast and remained with the Bagrovs until two o'clock . . . . Punctually at six o'clock the honest German was standing at the door of the well-known little house in Golubinaya Street : as he found no one in the ante-room, dining or drawing rooms, he betook himself to the bedroom, whose door he found closed. He knocked, and Katerina Alexeievna opened the door. Andrei Michailovitsch walked in, and then paused in amazement : a rich carpet was spread on the floor, the window was hung with green silk curtains, and at the head of the wide bed was a beautiful tester of the same stuff. In a corner of the room a light was burning behind a screen. Lying upon the bed, supported by pillows covered with beautifully-embroidered slips, and clad in a charming dressing gown, was Sofia Nikolaievna : her face was fresh and rosy, and her eyes sparkled with joy. " Congratulate me, best of friends ! " said she in an earnest, thrilling voice ; " I am once more a mother, and have a son ! " The doctor, observing Sofia Nikolaievna's rosy cheeks and hearing her clear voice, thought the whole thing was a joke : " Don't try to make fun of me, Barbarian, I am an old slyboots and not so easily deceived," he replied, smiling. " Get up. I have brought some new cards." And as he approached the bed and she remained lying on the pillows, he added : " This is my present for baby ! " " Dear friend," replied Sofia Nikolaievna, " before Heaven, this is not a joke. Here is my son ! " And in fact there lay the new-born babe on a large pillow, covered with a counterpane of pink satin, a sound, healthy, strong boy ; while near the bed stood the midwife, Aliona Maximovna. In an access of comical rage Klauss bounced backwards as if he had been burnt. " What ? " he roared, wrathfully, " without my assistance ? Here I have been waiting a whole week and paying away my money, and you never even sent word to me ! " His red face grew positively purple, his yellow wig was all awry, and his whole fat, little figure was so droll that the young mother could not help laughing. " Little father Andrei Michailovitsch," pleaded the midwife, " it happened so quickly that we lost our heads in the excitement. When we remembered you, Sofia Nikolaievna said it was no use sending as you would be here almost directly." But this faithful friend of the Bagrovs had recovered his temper. His fit of irritation had passed and tears of joy glittered in his eyes. With a practised hand he lifted the little boy from the bed, examined him by the light of the taper, pinched him in every limb until the child screamed again, put his finger in the little mouth, and, as the baby began to suck with the greatest vigour, shouted delightedly : " Oh, the young savage ! How strong and sound he is ! " Sofia

Nikolaievna was terrified at the way in which Klauss was pulling her heart's delight about, while the midwife feared lest the German should bewitch the little one by the Evil Eye,[1] and wished to take the child away from him. But Klauss was not going to give him up; he sprang about the room, holding the child in his arms, then asked for a basin, sponge, soap, warm water, and a swaddling band; stripped the poor baby again, tied an apron round his own waist, threw the wig into a corner of the room, and set to work to wash the child himself, while he chattered away : " Aha, you little savage, you don't scream now ! You like this warm water ! " At last Alexei Stepanovitsch arrived in a state of joy bordering on lunacy : he had just sent an express messenger to Bagrovo with a letter which he himself had written to his parents, as well as one to Aksinia Stepanovna begging her to come as quickly as she could and stand sponsor for the child. Alexei Stepanovitsch nearly suffocated the still damp doctor with his embraces : he had already kissed everyone in the house nearly to death, and shed tears of joy with everyone. Sofia Nikolaievna . . . . but I dare not attempt to portray what she felt. This was bliss and rapture such as she was to experience but rarely on earth, and then for how short a time !

The birth of the son roused such an extraordinary outburst of joy and excitement in the house that even the neighbours joined in it. The whole of the Bagrov servants, at first overcome by joy (and later by brandy) sang and danced in the courtyard. Even those who were ordinarily sober on this great occasion had drunk too deeply of the wine cup. Among these last must be included Yefrem Yevseyitsch, who could hardly be kept under control. He wanted to force his way into the mistress's room to have a look at the child. At length his wife, assisted by the handy Parascha, tied him down on a hard bench. But even on this uneasy couch he continued to wave his legs about as if dancing, and snap his fingers, as with a stammering tongue he tried to sing " Eia popeia ! "

Andrei Michailovitsch Klauss, fairly worn out by his own joyous excitement and by his zealous attentions upon the

[1] The Russians hold the belief that people who possess the Evil Eye injure children by their praise and admiration of them. [Tr. S.R.]

little one, had at last thrown himself into an armchair and sat sipping his tea with great enjoyment. This evening the soothing beverage was laced with such a mighty charge of rum that he became somewhat dizzy after his third cup. He forbade the child being suckled before morning, ordered him a little dose of rhubarb syrup, took leave of his happy friends, kissing the diminutive hand of the new-comer, and betook himself to his own house to rest himself, after promising to call early the next morning for a farewell visit to his patient. As he crossed the courtyard, he saw the servants dancing merrily, and heard the songs which resounded from the windows of kitchen and hall. He paused, and while he regretted being compelled to check the rejoicings of the good souls, he advised them to put a stop to the revels, as the noise was likely to prevent their mistress getting any sleep. To his astonishment, he was instantly obeyed, the merry company became silent, and dispersed. As he stepped out of the gate, the German murmured to himself : " A fortunate child ! How they all rejoice over him ! "

Ah, yes, this little boy was indeed born under the happiest of circumstances ! His mother, who had suffered every moment throughout her first pregnancy, had enjoyed the best of health while he was yet unborn ; no domestic differences had disturbed her peace of mind during this period ; she had found a foster-mother, who proved herself capable of more self-sacrifice and true affection than many a mother. Much desired, longed-for, and besought from Heaven, this child came into the world, filling not only the hearts of his parents— but the hearts of all around him—with supremest joy : even that autumnal day was as warm as midsummer !

And what happened at Bagrovo, when the joyful news arrived that God had given a son and heir to Alexei Stepanovitsch ? Now this had been the plan at Bagrovo : ever since the fifteenth of September Stepan Michailovitsch had counted the days and hours while awaiting the arrival of the messenger from Ufa, who had orders to be ready, day and night, with post horses. Such expense was an unheard-of thing in those days, and at any other time Stepan Michailovitsch would have considered it a waste of money and would have preferred employing his own horses. But now the importance and significance of the occasion quite overcame his economical scruples, and an exception was made. He had not long to wait. On the twenty-second of September, while he was taking his after-dinner nap, the messenger arrived with the glad tidings. Scarcely had the old man awakened from a deep sleep, and turned over with a yawn, than Masan burst into the room, and stammering with excitement, shouted : " I wish you joy of your grandson, little father Stepan Michail-ovitsch ! " Stepan Michailovitsch's first act was to cross himself. Then he jumped nimbly out of bed, hurried with his bare feet to the old press, pulled out the familiar family tree, and seized a pen. From the circle which contained the name of Alexei he drew a perpendicular line, at the end of which he made another circle, and wrote within it :

SERGEI

DATE DUE

HIGHSMITH 45-102   PRINTED IN U.S.A.